Our Primary Expertise

Our Primary Expertise

A Future for the Study of Religion

RUSSELL T. MCCUTCHEON

Rutgers University Press
New Brunswick, Camden, and Newark, New Jersey
London and Oxford

Rutgers University Press is a department of Rutgers, The State University of New Jersey, one of the leading public research universities in the nation. By publishing worldwide, it furthers the University's mission of dedication to excellence in teaching, scholarship, research, and clinical care.

Library of Congress Cataloging-in-Publication Data

Names: McCutcheon, Russell T., 1961–author.
Title: Our primary expertise: a future for the study of religion / Russell T. McCutcheon.
Description: New Brunswick: Rutgers University Press, [2025] |
Includes bibliographical references and index.
Identifiers: LCCN 2025000855 (print) | LCCN 2025000856 (ebook) |
ISBN 9781978843929 (paperback) | ISBN 9781978843936 (hardcover) | ISBN 9781978843943 (epub)
Subjects: LCSH: Religion—Study and teaching.
Classification: LCC BL41 .M357 2025 (print) | LCC BL41 (ebook) |
DDC 200.71—dc23/eng/20250117
LC record available at https://lccn.loc.gov/2025000855
LC ebook record available at https://lccn.loc.gov/2025000856

A British Cataloging-in-Publication record for this book is available from the British Library.

∞ The paper used in this publication meets the requirements of the American National Standard for Information Sciences—Permanence of Paper for Printed Library Materials, ANSI Z39.48-1992.

rutgersuniversitypress.org

This volume is dedicated to the many staff members with whom I've had the pleasure to have worked throughout my career; your efforts, though sometimes unseen by others, have animated our entire enterprise. I am in your debt.

But I hate the word "unique," obviously . . .

—Jonathan Z. Smith, *Reading J. Z. Smith: Interviews and Essay*, 41

Contents

Preface

Given all of their talk of agency and meaning-making, it strikes me as perplexing that so many humanists in the study of religion—those who see religion to be a deeply personal experience, indicative of this originary "thing" that they often call the human condition, which, or so they say, is only secondarily expressed in public and thereby put into action—seem to be waiting for someone else to swoop in and save them from the market forces that have taken over higher education. It is therefore ironic that those of us who emphasize structure in our work (the nonagential, impersonal factors, from economies to grammars and even dining etiquette, that determine the environments in which our actions take place and our meanings are expressed, as they phrase it) seem to be the ones who are trying to inspire colleagues to organize and act in a way that might help them to save their own academic field (and, along with it, their own jobs). Often, when I make the case in person that I put forward in the following chapters, both the critique of the traditional approach to the field and the alternative that I think holds some hope for us, I am met with assertions about "the life of the mind" (Latin: *vita mentis*; an early nineteenth-century idealist phrase, once opposed to "the life of the body," that you'd think would have been put to bed by now but no, it certainly has not) along with claims that any focus on the practical, so-called transferable skills that our students might use to help support themselves after they graduate is all a sign that we have succumbed to the dehumanizing, instrumentalist logic of neoliberalism, thereby turning the supposed calling of an academic into mere vocational training. To say that I find such a stark representation of the issues explored in this volume unhelpful (because they are profoundly elitist) would be a terrible understatement. More accurately, I would say that such claims are inspired by (perhaps nostalgic for) a level of privilege that our students can no longer afford, let alone those of our colleagues who work in schools where administrators have already decided that the humanities in general, and the study of religion in particular, are no longer needed. (Undoubtedly, more will have gone that way by the time this book gets into print.) That some who espouse such rhetorics often are themselves at risk because they work in these very settings makes this all the more curious to me—prompting me to think that there's still plenty of room in our field for the study ideology, defined in a rather traditional sense.

Over the years many readers have dismissed the various critiques that have long anchored this analysis, one that I again support in the following chapters; I offer them again because I think the truisms that tend to ground how our field is usually organized and practiced continue to be worth reconsidering, notably, the manner in which (per chapters 2 through 7) many scholars of religion (i) explicitly play favorites in their work; (ii) simplify rather than complicate the items that they study; (iii) often fall short of scrutinizing the wider structures in which social actors work (including those of their own academic institutions); (iv) fail to practice self-reflexivity; and (v) often are reluctant to redescribe the claims that the people they study make (going so far as to represent such disclosures as transparently conveying supposedly interior and self-evident states commonly called belief, faith, or meaning). My past experiences leading a religious studies department at a large public university for almost twenty years, one desperately in need of reinvention when I was first hired to lead it back in 2001 (as I've documented elsewhere, it was already slated to lose the major and minor and probably to be closed), tells me that it is indeed possible to carry out the field in a rather different way, one that makes a deep dive into thick research skills, as applied to a wide variety of items from human history that fascinate us, a worthwhile endeavor—even when the measure of this worth has something to do with how a student later operationalizes, in diverse settings, what they once learned in our classes. The challenge today is that our typical model for such a student has changed; apart from the broad array of students whom faculty in the United States would teach in so-called general education introductory classes, for many years that student was assumed to be someone who would apprentice in our specialty, and, eventually, the best of them would follow us into the career of being a professor. Transferable skills was not something we talked about back then, since the ideal student was not assumed to be going anywhere outside the field. Rather, they were intending to take our place at the front of the lecture hall. But no more; national education policies along with both local and international economic trends, not to mention the always blowing political winds, have ensured that tenured or tenure-track humanities professors across a variety of fields are becoming an increasingly rare bird these days, though—*and this is the message of this book*—that doesn't mean that our field is not worth teaching and practicing. For our current situation doesn't mean that thick research skills focused on specific artifacts, practices, or groups are not worth acquiring and using. Sure, our new circumstances will require faculty to make some shifts and learn a new thing or two; sure, our degree programs will have to be reimagined as training more than just faculty-members-in-waiting; sure, it will require us to design classes that are cognizant of payoffs other than just research papers; sure, it will invite us to think explicitly about the sorts of skills that we're teaching to our students and the diverse sites where the ability to carry out the work exemplified in the main chapters of this volume (e.g., equitable treatment among alternatives, complication, structural analysis, self-reflexivity, redescription) can make a valued contribution; sure, it will prompt us to mull over the role of practical experience (i.e., internship courses) at all degree levels and to have some conversations with people well outside our field but who might nonetheless have a need of someone who knows how to describe some domain fairly and in detail, compare novelly within specific parameters, and analyze the results of that work so that we learn something that we didn't know before. The shift demanded by our times will require all of this and far more. But mainly, it will require current faculty to give up on a particular mythology (and to quit passing it on to a new generation of their students) that, more than likely, was pretty important to many of them in their own career development, let alone their own current sense of self as a scholar: they'll have to leave "the life of the mind" rhetoric behind them and take seriously the institutional and structural settings in which that life has *always* taken place—a move you'd think uncontroversial, what with the many scholars of religion who now seem intent on material and embodied studies. But, as I've argued on other occasions, there's a recurring sense of idealism and privilege in much of that work—after all, precisely what do such scholars think is being put into the body in all of those embodiment studies and what ethereal thing is supposedly materialized or expressed in all those material religion studies?—suggesting that claims about the life of the mind, along with the perks that come with it when everyone buys into it, dies hard. But if you look around at what is happening to the humanities on many campuses, that's just what's happening: it's dying—not just hard but also fast. It's long been time to change lanes and see if we can revive the field by providing it with a new rationale and maybe a new future.

One final prefatory word: this volume is written in solidarity with a younger generation of those in our field who had these painful truths demonstrated for them early on in their training and careers, those who more than understood the need to reinvent themselves upon graduation. Sadly, there's a very good chance that this was done on their own time, and not as part of their program of study. Training our students—whether undergraduate or graduate, whether they are studying religion because of a fascination with some ancient text or some modern group—means preparing them for the wider application of what we've been doing with them in their classrooms. Our field therefore has a very real stake in their futures, and we (the rest of the field) had better recognize it. The volume is also in allegiance with a number of faculty in departments who already do recognize all of this, that is, those who are now doing the hard work of turning their local ships around—work that is often invisible to others and which is therefore difficult to track and report (and reward!) in the way that faculty accomplishments are usually recorded so as to benefit our careers as scholars. Proposing a new course, such as an internship class, is not terribly onerous, of course, but to be successful it must be thought through in ways that benefit the degree as a whole along with the student enrolling in such a nontraditional class, not to mention that it must be promoted well and assigned to a faculty member who not just understands the importance of such classes but also can reach out to offices across campus as well as to local businesses or nonprofits in the local community to find creative venues where their students can apply their skills (seemingly implicit skills that have been explicitly brought to their attention in all of their previous classes). Doing all of this is work, to be sure, but in a career where one's next book and the status of the press that publishes it carry significant weight, such work can understandably be rather low on some faculty members' priority lists. So, for those who are tackling such innovations nonetheless—I think of a department chair in Canada who messaged me recently, discussing the newsletter, student common room, events, symposia, even writing tutors that his unit has developed *in just the past year* (in part inspired by a couple of faculty from our campus who visited his department not too long ago)—this volume is not meant to persuade you about anything, since you clearly get it and your sleeves are already rolled up. Instead, I hope that such readers consider the book a tip of the hat in their direction, from someone who sees the (often behind the scenes and therefore uncredited) work that they're doing and who would also like to be of some assistance. For they understand the world in which our field now exists, the world in which we all work and into which our students will move upon graduation. While no set of initiatives can guarantee the results for which we each aim, the energy invested in such actions can produce results in surprising ways, from nurturing or cementing collective bonds among the faculty who pitch in (collaborations that will animate all kinds of other things in their careers and the unit as a whole) to sending a message to those in other offices on a campus concerning your focus on your students. None of this ensures anything, indeed, but we all know what inaction produces.

For whom is this book then written? All throughout my career I've mainly aimed at a far younger generation, trying to model for them an alternative way in which the field could be practiced, one in which religion, even "religion" as a term, was a mundane aspect of culture but an interesting one, nonetheless. As I wrote I would often imagine myself, at a much earlier stage in my own studies, and write to inspire that person, one who was dissatisfied with how the field worked but who did not yet know how else it could be done. Whether such a reader agreed with me or not, at least they would see that things could be otherwise, as I've often phrased it over the years. For even early in my career it was clear to me that I probably was not going to persuade my peers, let alone those ahead of me; they were already well entrenched in their views that religion was special, that the scholar of religion was special, and suggesting to them that we studied what others scholars did—people doing things and what they left behind after they were done with their doings—was virtually sacrilegious, akin to the emotions that my work apparently roused in some of them when finding me to use the word "data" to talk about human actions. But now, the stakes are far higher than I ever thought they were before, the attacks on the humanities are far more organized, the academic job market is far worse, and I am twice as old as that unknown, marginal scholar who, in the early 1990s, wrote what became his first (and somewhat controversial) book. So, this book is instead aimed directly at those near to or in my scholarly generation, those in positions of leadership within departments or the profession as a whole. You may not have invited these responsibilities but, for a variety of reasons (many of which are related to past generations' taken-for-granted privileges and then their unfortunate inaction), they have landed directly in your laps; if the field is to have a future, as part of whatever the university will then look like, it will be because of things that you do now—not in a year or two, but *now*. My hope is that the following inspires that action and provides an idea or two—come up with your own, for sure, but realize that you don't have to reinvent the wheel, since others are also thinking about these topics and they're already making the sorts of changes that might benefit you in your setting. That I've been involved in successfully doing this—not just writing about it but hosting the movie nights and the pizza parties, developing an array of policies and procedures within the unit, hiring faculty and staff and seeing their careers develop, devising the internship programs, helping to plan and implement new degree programs, and coming up with a logo and the mugs for our unit, creating the websites, writing the blog posts, and posting a number of cool pics of our building on social media more often than I can count—hopefully sends the message that it can be done. I'd be naive to think that your setting is the same as the one where we did all of this, but I bet there are overlaps where we can swap ideas.

Author's Note on Sources

While I retain the right to use the following pieces in collections of my own, I nonetheless wish to acknowledge the publications where earlier versions of each first appeared in print—and, along with that, to thank, once again, the various editors, peer reviewers, and publishers for all of their past efforts on my behalf. Although the ideas may be our own—along with an array of friends and colleagues who, whether we recognize it or not, have influenced our thinking—the means whereby those ideas get not only into print but also into the hands of people around the world are, as a political economist of some note told us long ago, owned and controlled by others.

Chapter 1: "Religious Studies: Wither and Why?" *Religious Studies Review* 50, no. 1 (2024): 17–24.

Chapter 2: "'It's a Lie. There's No Truth in It! It's a Sin!': On the Limits of the Humanistic Study of Religion and the Costs of Saving Others from Themselves." *Journal of the American Academy of Religion* 74, no. 3 (2006): 720–750.

Chapter 3: "And That's Why No One Takes the Humanities Seriously." In *A Modest Proposal on Method: Essaying the Study of Religion*, 165–192. Leiden: Brill, 2015.

Chapter 4: "The Gatekeeping Rhetoric of Collegiality in the Study of Religion." Co-authored with Aaron W. Hughes. In *Constructing "Data" in Religious Studies: Examining the Architecture of the Academy*, edited by Leslie Dorrough Smith. Sheffield: Equinox, 2019.

Chapter 5: "Scholars Are People Too: The (Sometimes) Difficult Shift to the Discourse of Crisis." In *Discourses of Crisis and the Study of Religion*, edited by Lauren Horn Griffin. Sheffield: Equinox, 2025.

Chapter 6: "'I'm Spiritual but Not Religious.'" Co-authored with Andie R. Alexander. In *Stereotyping Religion: Critiquing Clichés*, edited by Craig Martin and Brad Stoddard. London: Bloomsbury, 2017.

Chapter 7: "Redescribing Our Primary Expertise or, In Praise of Promiscuous Curiosities." *Method & Theory in the Study of Religion* 35, no. 5 (2023): 478–494.

Our Primary Expertise

"And He Was Gone"

An Introduction

"Precious, precious, precious!" Gollum cried. "My Precious! O my Precious!"
And with that, even as his eyes were lifted up to gloat on his prize,
he stepped too far, toppled, wavered for a moment on the brink, and then with a
shriek he fell. Out of the depths came his last wail Precious, and he was gone.
—J.R.R. Tolkien, *The Return of the King* (1955, 224)

Sometime in the summer or early fall of 2023, while I was finishing the previous version of the essay that has become the opening chapter, and thus the rationale, for this new collection of my writings, a certain image of the field that I have called home for all of my career and, along with it, a certain image of some of its practitioners, coalesced in my mind. It is one that I have not been able to shake in the months that followed, as more bad news about programs and units, both large public and small private, has made its way to me (word of another small program closing, resulting in a tenured, midcareer person losing their job, reached me just last week). If anything, it has continually been reinforced, such as the recent Zoom meeting with faculty from another department elsewhere in the United States, whose members were concerned about the future of one of their degree programs, when someone there (younger than I, mind you, so this was hardly an old, out-of-touch faculty member) lamented how "the life of the mind" is being undermined on campuses today, with our field being one of, as I recall it being phrased, its last bastions in the university. The certain image that I have in mind, which I can't help but think of at moments like that Zoom meeting, is captured in the above, opening quotation, one that I read for the first time during the summer after grade twelve, when, as a lifeguard, I had broken both bones in my lower left leg and, in a full cast for the entire summer, discovered for the first time the joy of reading.

But why *this* image?

Well, for quite a while a real frustration with colleagues, and the scholarly field that they created but then also took for granted as the only way to do it, has been evident in my scholarly work; anyone following my writing career even casually will more than likely know this—in fact it might be all that they know about my work. I am, after all, the person who was labeled, pretty much from the start of my career, as the one who was trying to kill the study of religion. (The late Gary Lease once carried this honor, what with his role in the demise of religious studies at UC Santa Cruz—a story rather more complex than the caricatures that followed him afterward [Lease 1995].) In fact, when hired, back in 2001, to lead the reinvention of a struggling unit at the University of Alabama (one due to lose the major and more than likely close, as a cost-cutting measure, with the state budget once again falling on hard times back then and not nearly enough students majoring in the study of religion [for more details on this, see chapter 8 in McCutcheon 2021]), some of my new colleagues returned from our annual national conference in November of 2022 and reported to me how friends had peppered them with questions about what it was like working with someone intent on putting an end to the field. But, as I've written before, anyone paying just a little more attention to what I was writing and doing might be aware that this couldn't have been further from what I've been up to all this time. (And yes, looking back from twenty-five years later, our reinvention at Alabama was far more successful than we could have ever imagined—due to a host of factors, no doubt, some accidents and others well beyond our control, surely, while others were carefully planned and rolled out.) But the model of the field for which I've advocated all along—one based on naturalistic explanation early on but then, later on, one that emphasized social theory and identity formation, rather than the usual description, comparison, and interpretation that dominate our classes and our scholarship—has certainly struck many throughout the field as being so alien, perhaps so challenging and even threatening to their own assumptions about how special religion is (and thus how carefully, even delicately scholars ought to approach it in their research and teaching), that, at least to them, I might as well have been trying to blow it all up, I guess. For I think that they quite well understood the implications for their own work if my vision of the field held sway, since my critiques were always accompanied by a series of often detailed practical suggestions for an alternative, something that has characterized pretty much all of my work in the field—done pointedly sometimes, to be sure, but even playfully at other times, written for colleagues often but just as frequently written for novice readers and students. And those scholars likely saw little room for their studies of how precious religion was—at least to them. I've remarked elsewhere of how tired that caricature of me has become, as one who is always "deconstructing," as these critics often put it, and never building up or offering a positive way forward; in fact, from my first published pieces there has always been an alternative on offer—as I said, it's just not one that many have ever wanted to entertain. Accordingly, I guess it was easier to just dismiss it all than to consider it seriously or maybe give it a test drive for themselves; instead, make light of it—like some politicians do with their opponents' views, so as to avoid the issue at hand. But, as I've reasoned all along, if the plan worked at a public university in Alabama, then maybe it would work elsewhere—such as all those programs that I'm regularly hearing from where they're losing the major and, sometimes, losing the department and jobs. I zoomed with a faculty member from another of them just two weeks ago.

But not until recently—say, the past decade or so—have my longstanding frustrations with the field been directly connected to the future viability of the institutions that we, as scholars, all inhabit. For during that time my alternative suggestions for the field (what I've written on under the banner of the examples approach [with a nod to J. Z. Smith's work]) have increasingly been more clearly linked to the moment in higher education that we were, that we still are, occupying. To put it simply, although the academic job market in the humanities has been declining for decades (I have my own tales of career woe from thirty years ago), post-2008 cuts to higher education (linked to the worldwide financial collapse) and then the ongoing economic impact of COVID-era cuts, linked to the increasing professionalization of what some term the neoliberal university (i.e., a shift away from the humanities and toward so-called STEM disciplines as well as prioritizing such professional schools as business, engineering, and nursing), have created conditions in which the future for the study of religion is, at least at the time of writing this, entirely up in the air. Returning to the timeframe mentioned at the outset, all throughout the summer and fall of 2023 news of a variety of religious studies programs' being cut, losing their undergraduate major, or even being closed outright was being shared online almost weekly. I kept track, until there were too many to remember. I emailed with department leadership on those campuses most times when I heard the news—commiserated with them, offering whatever assistance that I might, sometimes privately writing on their behalf to their campus's senior administration (what good that does, who knows). At the same time I devised a monthly webinar, in my capacity then as the chair of the American Academy of Religion's academic relations committee, that featured a number of those colleagues who were in the trenches of our field's, shall we say, uninvited reinvention (a webinar series that aimed to achieve, if nothing else, a connection between people facing related challenges, to help prevent them from feeling like they were each reinventing a rather well-worn wheel.) Although sometimes it was a cut focused on the field directly, or maybe along with a handful of other vulnerable liberal arts programs, at other times it was part of a much larger, campus-wide reorganization that reprioritized resources, often focused instead on disciplines said to be more practical and applied—those that students, parents, administrators, and politicians alike thought would lead directly to a career. As I elaborated in a multiauthored book that I was completing at the time, titled *Religious Studies beyond the Discipline: On Earning and Awarding a Humanities Ph.D.* (McCutcheon 2024b—a book that I hope readers will find for themselves and not expect to be repeated here, though, yes, this volume might be seen as a companion volume, to some extent), declining public support for U.S. higher ed over recent decades (long before the more recent political attacks we've seen mounted from some states) has meant a far greater share of the costs of the operation has fallen in the laps of students (and, of course, their families) via always increasing tuitions and fees, resulting in student loan debt ballooning in the United States to now be greater than all credit card debt combined (with only mortgage debt outpacing student loan debt); it does not take a rocket scientist to conclude that such circumstances provide a very real incentive for students and their families to look toward well-paying careers after they graduate, where their degree credentials them for immediate employment. While the various professional schools that, over past decades, have steadily taken over much of campus easily sell themselves as meeting such a need (though, yes, their graduates often experience challenges finding work), the study of religion, along with a few other fields, is usually not among those that first, or maybe ever, come to mind for many people—at least at a time when a university degree is seen as but one more form of job training.

But now, long-standing concerns that I had about the field, once animated mainly by a sense of what it meant for any subject to be part of a modern university, became explicitly linked to the practical (i.e., political, economic) conditions that make any scholarly field possible today. After all, we have long known that the field's prehistory in the mid- and later nineteenth century was directly linked to the zenith of European imperialism, and the immense descriptive information from the so-called colonies that was by then back in the hands of puzzled intellectuals from across Europe, ensconced in their proverbial armchairs while poring over data that were screaming out to them for analysis, what with how shockingly exotic yet hauntingly familiar it all was to what they were doing back in such places as

England, France, the Netherlands, and Germany. But for some decades many of us have also known how closely associated the mid-twentieth-century rise of the field in North America was to the Cold War, what with the United States' growing focus on the mysterious East and the dangers of "godless Communists"; many of our recent predecessors, earning doctoral degrees just a few academic generations ago, strategically benefited from funding meant to enhance foreign language instruction, so crucial during the Cold War for gathering and interpreting information on peoples from around the globe. (The degree to which such scholars from that era listed grants and fellowships linked to the U.S. National Defense Act on their résumés can be rather shocking to anyone who persists in thinking that the Ivory Tower is somehow apolitical [see McCutcheon 2004].) If these two examples were taken seriously, then it would make sense that in an early twenty-first-century university, one that was increasingly focused on practical job training for the abovementioned practical reasons, ramifications would again sweep across a field such as ours—but this time not spurring or animating it, as in the two instances just mentioned, but, for all we know, conspiring to end it. For what good is a degree in the study of religion—let alone American studies, gender studies, not to mention anthropology, English, and history—if that good is measured in ways favored mainly by the natural sciences, let alone a College of Engineering or a School of Business? For the once privileged justification of the subjects that have long constituted the humanities, as being the keys to living the so-called good life, or even the more recent rationale of these subjects as helping to create informed citizens who were supposedly prepared to participate fully in our shared democratic experiment, no longer hold water for many of our peers, including some of the students who are paying the fees, the university administrators charged with deciding on what those funds will be spent, and the politicians deciding to what extent those funds will be supplemented with tax dollars that could just as easily be spent elsewhere (or maybe returned to taxpayers; after all, voters are always partial to campaign promises involving tax cuts). Accordingly, and as already noted, the so-called life of the mind that some people so enjoy turns out to be a privilege that many no longer wish to subsidize—which, I gather, rather frustrates those who expect a university to insulate them from the pressures of the so-called real world. But what else is to be expected when the onetime public good of a postsecondary education has successfully been rebranded, at least here in the United States, as a private luxury, and so, why should taxes derived from "my" hard-earned income be used to subsidize "their" choices—or so the issue is now routinely framed in public discourse (as evidence, consult the backlash against recent attempts in the United States to provide federally funded student debt relief). The question is how we, as scholars in the humanities in general and in the study of religion in particular, respond to this shift in the conditions of the field's own possibility. Complaining about the demise of the life of the mind and continuing to act as if the material that we each study is unique and therefore inherently compelling strike me as the least inventive or effective among the various options. If anything, they both more than likely make our situation even worse.

But academic fields move slowly—likely a functional thing, at least in some circumstances, what with the linkage between the ability to create and sanction knowledge, on the one hand, and its impact on the social order, on the other. Given that, we probably should not have an information and possibly a political revolution every few years; but the conservative approach to change that seems to be baked into academia—evident everywhere from the institution of peer review and the time it takes something to get into print to the structure of graduate training and the timing of the tenure-track process itself—seems to have proved incapable of handling the pace of political, social, and economic change that has overtaken the university in recent decades. While many faculty in various humanities disciplines, and at various career stages, seem still to long for the Renaissance—somewhat akin to various characters in Woody Allen's masterful *Midnight in Paris* (2011), with members of its cast nostalgic for some idyllic golden age just before their own time—the increasingly cost-conscious university has changed out from under them, what with its ever-growing emphasis on contingent faculty and its current explorations in farming out aspects of faculty jobs to the continually refined abilities of artificial intelligence. Lacking nimbleness, which once might have been an honorable trait—oh, for the solemn customs of the Ivy League, and the manicured quads of Oxbridge . . . —we seem to have been caught with our pants down, as they used to say, with administrators increasingly over the past decades making decisions that surprised but also confounded many faculty members. Not fill a line vacant due to a retirement? Sunset our major? Cut our program? Fire tenured faculty members? "But don't you know how important our work is?!" is pretty much all that many could say in reply to such announcements, coming from administrations that made the idea of shared governance on a campus sound like a quaint relic from some distant past. (The strategy of a college declaring financial exigency—a situation often created, I would argue, by poor management in the past, we should add—usually kicks into gear a host of policies that effectively sidestep any number of conventions and policies on a campus, often making shared governance an irrelevant item.) Some in our field, those who are a little more nimble and rather more practically minded than some of their peers, came back with religious literacy—the North American version of what many European democracies have long called religious education in their public school systems; they argued, in a fashion already familiar to many in our field, that our classes could make students better (and by better they usually mean more liberal, i.e., free, and tolerant) global citizens—or, to get a little more specific, better at, for example, conducting global business, since this literacy usually is not represented as a good in and of itself. But today this gambit could fail as often as it might work, what with the significant divergence of opinion, at least in parts of the United States today, concerning such once favored social values as diversity and inclusion. In fact, depending on the state in which one works, efforts to advance religious literacy, if they are described or implemented a little too carelessly, could now be caricatured as "woke" or even judged to be illegal (i.e., supposedly coercing students to take a certain stand on so-called divisive issues, at least according to laws passed in some state legislatures), at least when promoted by using public state funds. In fact, as teachers in many U.S. public elementary and high schools learned long ago, even just describing how other people do things can sometimes be represented as advocating for such people and their practices; with regard to our field in the United States, although it is entirely legal to teach classes on the study of religion in public schools akin to what we do in colleges, it has long seemed to be far easier for school boards, principals, and teachers just to leave it entirely alone, thereby avoiding a host of potential controversies (not dissimilar to how science classes in American public schools have sometimes steered well clear of the theory of evolution). As for those scholars who have long been critical of what has been labeled the world religions paradigm (as named by Owen 2011), opting for enhanced religious literacy as the field's new rationale amounts to entrenching the already troublesome world religions discourse even further, by seeing our new raison d'être as ensuring that our students learn how to use this still surviving colonial-era discourse better than ever—hardly a desirable goal, at least for those critically minded scholars among us.

So where does all of this leave us? Largely, I would argue, with a number of ill-equipped colleagues who, in response to the changing conditions of their work, often have little choice but to double down on assertions of their work's deep meaning and enduring importance—whether in making tolerant citizens or in helping students to appreciate (what often goes by the name of interpreting and understanding) what many before them had claimed to be the universal but always disguised nature of the Sacred. (We may not read Mircea Eliade all that much anymore, but the popularity of the approach best represented by his work still shows no signs of diminishing—consider Bryan Rennie [2024] offering yet another defense of Eliade's life and work, in the light of Bruce Lincoln's thoroughgoing critique [2024].) But even if such claims ever really worked (such as when successfully arguing all across the United States, back in the 1960s, for the need to establish autonomous departments of religious studies in public universities, where people studied unique instances of the sacred throughout history), their day now seems to be well passed; writing a critical letter to either a dean or a provost today, when cuts are announced, asking them to keep a religious studies major or to fill an open position in Asian religions because of how important it is to study some group of people or certain things that they do now seems, at best, quaint and, at worst, rather oblivious to the moment in which we find ourselves. It is right up there with faculty expecting a sabbatical so they can read and "recharge their batteries"—as necessary or desirable as that may be, we have been in the day of practical, measurable outcomes for about two decades now, and so a sabbatical to reboot is no longer seen as a legitimate use of time and resources. Like it or not, this is the setting in which most faculty in the humanities now work (thankfully, we've yet to be impacted fully by the culture of external grants, as have much of the social sciences and all of the natural sciences—but we'd be naïve to think it was not coming, or in some ways already here).

But, returning to my opening, what has all of this got to do with that fictional character who found, lost, and then eventually regained that cursed ring?

The image that I earlier said came to my mind late last summer or early in the fall—long before the current dire (not the wrong word, I think) situation in which at least U.S. universities now find themselves in early 2025, when pondering the worsening conditions of higher education, coupled with what I still take to be the weird silence from much of the field; sure, individual faculty on campuses that are hit by cuts sound the alarm when they feel the sting, but as yet there has been no concerted, field-wide response or organization, let alone an appreciation for how long it takes to marshal and then implement an effective plan (indicating that, much like climate change, by the time the problem is apparent it may be long past the moment when any intervention can actually be made)—was that of Gollum, the notorious character from J.R.R. Tolkien's *The Hobbit* as well as *The Lord of the Rings* trilogy. Specifically, it was this creature at his very end (spoilers . . .), initially as I pictured him in the 2003 movie, *The Lord of the Rings: The Return of the King*. Having fought Frodo on the cliff's edge and now, finally in possession of his treasure once again, he is seen in that film from above, as he teeters and then plummets into the glowing river of lava below, contentedly clutching his Precious as he meets his molten end. That, I decided, very sadly but just as aptly captured this moment in our field—when many faculty members feel overworked, overwhelmed, unappreciated, and more than likely powerless to effect any change.

Certainly, there are those who would say that I'm being either somewhat or maybe grossly uncharitable in conceiving of it in those terms, what with it seeming to blame the victim and all; but, in my defense, there have been several decades of inaction in our field as all of higher education was steadily reinvented right out from under us. We've resisted campuses' professionalization, out of what I agree to be the legitimate fear of turning our degrees into mere job training, but we did so while more and more of our doctoral graduates were unsuccessful finding work for themselves as faculty in the university, having no choice other than reinventing themselves—mostly on their own time, given that their doctoral programs pretty much completely lacked any creative thinking about how their own alums might use the skills they'd gained during their several-year-long deep dive into this ritual, that text, or some group of people. All that time many of us remained content with undergraduate programs with only a handful of majors, suggestive to me of faculty failing to see how those student numbers directly impact their own livelihoods. (You'd be amazed the number of times over the years that I've talked with faculty elsewhere who, sooner or later, disclosed that their program only had a handful of majors, if even that; a very real problem, what with numbers of graduates, i.e., majors, often amounting to the coin of the modern university's realm. You might also be just as amazed—or maybe not—by how frequently faculty understand service in their departments to infringe on their real jobs, reading and writing—service often aimed at recruiting and retaining students in their own departments, mind you—the measure that often keeps them employed, they often fail to see.) All throughout, faculty have continued to study, write, and publish on a host of topics near and dear to each of them (topics that often are far too nuanced or specialized to directly impact their classes), and they've continued attending conferences devoted to these specialties, and thus operating as if it was business as usual—pursuing the life of the mind wherever it may take them; rarely, if ever, would a publication appear on the practical conditions of the field itself, let alone something written by a senior person aiming to help professionalize those coming along after them; let's be honest, such work likely wouldn't help their authors to secure an offer from a better school, one "back east" or on the coast, one with a lighter undergraduate teaching load and access to doctoral students—for *these* are the incentives and rewards of the career, at least for many of us (i.e., those of us who are lucky enough to still be part of the tenure system). And thus, a concern about the practical conditions of the field itself were, somewhat ironically, all too often seen as far too specialized a focus, what with the main concern for most everyone being this or that discrete manifestation of the Sacred, in this text, that action, these institutions, or those material artifacts. Case in point: my first book, *Manufacturing Religion*, was not reviewed in the North American field's main journal, the *Journal of the American Academy for the Study of Religion*, because it was judged as being too specialized (or so I was told by the then editor); a book on the recent history of the field as a whole was too specialized?! A later editor of the same journal rejected out-of-hand a piece on collegiality in our field that I co-wrote with Aaron Hughes (included as a chapter in this collection) because, as detailed in the introduction to that chapter, it was not devoted to some aspect of one of the world's religions (supposedly the defining trait of all that the journal published—or so we were told). And an even more recent editor of that same journal rejected just as quickly a co-written manifesto (of which I was one of five co-authors, three of whom have had to make careers for themselves outside academia after earning their doctoral degrees) that focused on the pressing need to revise graduate education to suit the world that doctoral students now enter upon graduation, judging that essay's scholarly references to be insufficient (see Aghapour et al. 2023; the last episode is recounted in the introduction to McCutcheon 2024a). These are just three anecdotes, of course, but the message is clear: the practical conditions of our own work have generally been of little importance to us.

And so, all throughout the steady (though now significantly quickening) decline of the field's conditions what remained constant was each journal's, each scholar's, each book's, each class's, and each dissertation's riveted attention on their special datum, their uniquely meaningful object of study—in a word, their precious. It has been a focus that, or so I argue in what follows, has left many of them ill-equipped to do much other than reassert its deep, timeless value when practically minded and cost-cutting administrators, armed with such things as faculty-to-student ratios and stats concerning instructional costs per student credit hour, came knocking on their office doors. I therefore couldn't help but think that such people were content with, or maybe just resigned to, going down with the ship, as it were, while clutching their pearls, whatever it was that they happened to study, probably lamenting to anyone who would listen how no one else understood its importance or how they were never trained to grapple with reinventing themselves. And so, while I would never want to insinuate that they were as possessed or as conniving as that unfortunate little fictional creature once known by the name of Sméagol, the image of his later self being enveloped by an approaching doom while happily in possession of a much valued, dare I say sacred, item couldn't help but stick when I thought of so many colleagues throughout the field. So, visiting an old book on my shelves at home, wondering how Tolkien himself had phrased an end that the director, Peter Jackson, much later visualized in his film, I again found the words that open this introduction: "Out of the depths came his last wail *Precious*, and he was gone."

Don't believe me? Think my account is unfair? While I could cite a variety of old-timers or even a younger generation now in positions of influence in the current field but who all look at the current academic job market and unhelpfully reply "It was tough in my day too"—thereby entirely missing the manner in which a mounting change in degree and extent presents us today with a brand new kind of problem—or identify those in leadership positions in various of our field's professional settings who, when confronted with "Our house is on fire, what can we do?" seemed rather more concerned with a variety of other issues, instead, consider but one example, from the current literature, of the precious that we are unwilling to relinquish.

From the introduction to the co-edited volume *Teaching Critical Religious Studies: Pedagogy and Critique in the Classroom* (2024), we learn the following: "As sociologist William Barylo argues, 'Using terms and concepts rooted in Latin and Greek language to describe spiritual systems which are not native to them, holding to Eurocentric concepts and visions and performing a binary segregation between what is "religious" and what is not, puts research at risk of major simplification'" (Gray-Hildenbrand et al. 2024, 4; citing Barylo 2018, 13). I can think of few better current examples of the failure of our field, prompted by an uncritical gaze on the presumed self-evidency of the sacred. Their argument is straightforward enough: the imposition of an alien system may prompt scholars to miss something in the local that's under study—that thing missed is apparently part of other people's "spiritual systems." Yet in recognizing the Latin and Greek basis to our "terms and concepts," something "spiritual" seemingly predates that imposed vocabulary, since *our* inevitably limited words seem to overlook or distort *their* worlds. Yet, as I think most everyone in our field knows, this word "spiritual" itself comes from the Latin *spiritus*, for breath, and later coming to signify some presumed animating force to the human. Nonetheless, it is clear in this quotation that this word and the concept that it signifies for us is hardly one that receives the same sort of critical attention as do our other terms and concepts. For Barylo here imagines—and that's the key word, *imagines*—just some item in the worlds under study to elude specificity, situation, and thus history, thereby defying a scholar's vocabulary and attempts at translation, and therefore something that curiously resists what he offers at the start of that quotation, back when he was recognizing the inevitably local nature of our scholarly terms and concepts. That this whole quotation is in English, not just a colonial inheritance—it is no accident that I, coming from Canada, and a good friend with whom I once worked, coming from India, could seamlessly converse with each other at a southern American university, now was it?—but also one that is as deeply as any immersed in a variety of prior language systems (and not just Latin and Greek) is also lost on us at times like these, assuming that just some of our words, "spiritual," for example, somehow escape time and signify, in some unmediated fashion, universal features that transcend our sadly limited dialects and perspectives. Somehow this author knows all of this—knows things that predate language—as if floating outside of history and situation.

The message, then, is that only parts of our discourse need to be historicized, since other parts—the deeply meaningful parts, apparently, the ones dealing with all those big ideas that animate the life of the mind, I guess—are somehow in lockstep with reality itself, making them immediately and intuitively accessible to us regardless of our setting. The result is a picture of the world in which only some portions, the portions that just *we* imagine, are eternal, self-evidently set apart, and deeply significant, thereby evading all attempts at theorization, while other parts—the mundane parts, I gather, which means the ones *other* people imagine—are local, historical, and of rather limited use. How curiously that the much-criticized binary logic reasserts itself, a rather more critically minded commentator might say at this point, suggesting that a more modest approach would be wise to be rather suspicious of those who claim to be able to discern which parts of life rise above history and language.

The editors of the above-cited volume—one that is purportedly devoted to being *critical* in our teaching, whatever that may mean to them—fail to notice any of this, and so conclude by merely repeating the rather problematic, half-theorized claim in the source that they cited, by writing as follows: "The very use of language, like Greek and Latin, to describe religious phenomena among communities who do not speak those languages automatically curtails a complete understanding of those phenomena." (The editors conclude this passage by citing, for what precise reason it is not at all clear, all of an over 100-page-long article on medieval Muslim discourses on the Arabic term *dīn*, most often translated into English as "religion" [Abbasi 2021].) Here the introduction reproduces the typically uncritical position that religion—or, more properly, *religious phenomena*, a term of not inconsequential use in the history of our field—somehow predates and thereby eludes language and thus history (a sensible enough position for its authors, I should add, what with their, at least to me, somewhat odd or at least dated presumption that comparative religion developed mainly from, and thereby reproduces, comparative theology). This, as I've just argued, is rather unlike the case of our many other words, which all seem to be locked in their own historical setting; yet, although they seem to miss it, this is no less the case for the Latin roots of "religion" than that of "spirit"; and not just these words, for we have medieval Latin to thank for "community" taking on its role as a synonym to "society," and Old Latin is our source for linking the notion of being born to our idea of being "native" to a place (with one either being native or not, itself but one more supposedly alien binary system). But these words are used in the preceding quotations as somehow immune from such historicist critique. This is all not limited just to language, of course, for our ability to think and act such supposedly discrete zones of the social into existence is no less a contingent, historical exercise, a form of thinking/acting/organizing that's probably alien to those groups that such scholars so casually study by means of these terms. What's more, in making the critique as they do, these authors perpetuate the fantasy that some sort of "complete understanding" (eerily akin to what Joachim Wach, Mircea Eliade, and others famously called the total hermeneutic, no? [see Alles 1988]) is possible, if only scholars studied religion the *proper way*—presumably as an inherently meaningful signifier that transcends time and place.

This is a position that I once dubbed as "religion before 'religion'" (e.g., see McCutcheon 2010), one that I think results from reading, or at least remembering, only part of the now common critique of the category "religion," in what appears to be an effort to privilege just part of what that discourse enables us to say about the world and ourselves. (Another quick example: concerning the sacred/secular binary pair, such scholars often assume that only the latter was invented and then inappropriately applied to curtail or privatize the eternal former, completely failing to understand that the two terms, and thus the opposed social spheres that they allow us to imagine and act within, are, by definition, mutually defining and thus always coterminous.) But the full critique instead argues that the supposedly privileged part (the precious that such scholars seem loathe to relinquish) is no less a product of history, situation, and language, of course—in fact, the apparent privilege of the items "set apart and forbidden" is just as much a product of, as Émile Durkheim told us generations ago, *our own efforts* as anything else—something evident to those among us who take seriously that "spiritual," as both word and concept, is no less alien to many of the groups that we might study, a word and an idea that comes to certain of us today from Latin and then French (for more on this term's history, see Hughes and McCutcheon 2022b, 245–250). But it is a term that helps some people to do something practical and advantageous when they use it—and, yes, the "I'm spiritual but not religious" people are certainly among them no less than scholars intent on studying so-called spirituality as something other than the product of discourses on spirituality; what's being accomplished by means of this discourse on deep meanings and universal sentiments is so useful or important to them that, per the quotation discussed just above, they give their use of such terms a pass when critical intelligence comes calling. For, as I have argued at length throughout my career, such words (and the social worlds that they help to make possible) as "spiritual" and "religious" are hardly neutral, descriptive terms and so they do not innocently trace the outlines of obviously existing things in the world (for a succinct discussion on the historicity of "religion," see Hughes and McCutcheon 2022a, 247–254). In fact, just the other day, I was watching a documentary in which Jean-Denis Vigne, the noted French archeologist, described an ancient practice in Cyprus involving the remains of cat as a sacrifice but then claimed that the reason why it was done was open to interpretation—thereby failing to see that the very designation of "sacrifice" as already deeply embedded in interpretations of long past acts and thus hardly an innocently descriptive term. Instead, such terms are socially formative tools, rhetorics that help to make things happen in the world (whether the past, present, or anticipated future). And so, despite some scholars' focus on such now-trendy issues as power and colonialism, upon closer inspection so-called critical work in the field, per the introduction cited above, often turns out to be surprisingly conservative in its approach—not unlike those lamenting the loss of the life of the mind—inasmuch as it assumes that, for example, once we deal with biases we might get on with the business of actually understanding religion itself—and so we see precisely how sui generis religion reappears where it had seemed to have been banished. Instead, I have argued at a variety of past sites that inasmuch as scholars, let alone anyone else, designate some aspect of the world *as* uniquely religious, they have simultaneously engaged in an act of both cognitive and social control (i.e., governmentality, itself an imperial strategy; for more, see McCutcheon 2003); for such a designation constitutes a moment when a certain sort of social world seems possible and maybe even legitimate, one comprised of socially free and authentically experiencing individuals of seeming self-evident place and value but who, nonetheless, can somehow intuit the experiences of others. *Et voila*: the good old apolitical, universal self is born—making possible a classically humanistic field intent on, in the words of the editors of the volume just cited, "exploring and expanding the human experience" (Gray-Hildenbrand et al. 2024, 13). And so we see the linkage between the critique of a classically humanistic field, on the one hand, and our inability to be nimble in our current moment.

But I think we could be far better scholars than this—better than the seemingly critical historiographical stand that, even today, criticizes scholars for "distorting the past," as if there was some Archimedean spot outside time and from which to view history in all its original and thus proper glory, providing a bird's eye view that illuminates a standard by which to identify the supposed shortcomings of others' discourses on it. I also think that it could be otherwise for our field—that, as dim as its prospects may look at the moment, it might still have a future. For although Frodo had to lose a finger to give up the ring, his uncle Bilbo—for those who recall the story—had previously released it of his own accord (though assisted by some stern words from an old friend). If my words above seem overly harsh, then consider me to be in some way akin to that well-meaning old friend, one who, despite the caricatures, has spent over two decades successfully leading a department's reinvention, pretty much from the ground up, to the benefit of its faculty, staff, and students. And so, perhaps those words may inspire some to let go of a few cherished things that, though we may think they empower us with timelessness, are actually weighing us down, since no one else seems to understand their relevance in this modern world of ours. For starters, we might let go of the notion of experience as some pre-social internal authenticity that's somehow universally available if only we listen carefully and in the proper fashion to so-called human experience and, in its place, see that elusive thing that we think we're here to study as rhetorically constituted by us, in our efforts to study it. (I could have been talking about the Nones there, no?) But, as already mentioned, making this shift means that we cease playing favorites by exempting just some of our terms and just some of our methods (let alone some of the groups that we study) from critical scrutiny. It also means thinking about how our students might pay their bills after they're done studying with us—a concern that does not automatically reduce us to "mere" job training.

So, my hope in revising and then collecting together the following pieces and writing new introductions to each along with providing a few practical examples in the appendix—all of which outline ways of moving beyond the dominant model of uniqueness in our field and the links between our approach and our institutional situation in higher ed today—is that it may not be too late to turn this ship around. After all, if not an optimist, what else is a critic? For, as I say whenever given the chance these days, critics tend to think and act as if things could be otherwise. I therefore offer this collection, one that reinforces my frank diagnosis of ongoing problems with the classically humanistic model on offer in the study of religion (and on this, see also the first chapter to McCutcheon 2024a) but which, while identifying many of its shortcomings, also endorses an alternative model—one on which I also elaborate in detail in my previous collection, *On Making a Shift in the Study of Religion and Other Essays* (2021), as well as in the introduction and appendices that I wrote, as editor, for the abovementioned volume on rethinking how we train doctoral students in the field. That few others in our field currently seem to be preoccupied with these issues—or at least preoccupied enough to be making them the focus of at least some of their research and writing—suggests that the problem may be more daunting than any of us realize. Again, like climate change, we may all just awake one morning and see a rising tide carrying a memo from the provost announcing that our programs are on the chopping block. To be sure, there are forces at work that we would be naive to think that any of us could ever control—but I'd be terribly shortsighted to throw up my hands and claim that we have no agency whatsoever and thus no way to adapt to or to act in support of what seems to be in our shared interests.

Recognizing how disengaged many of us have been with this all along, due I maintain to our field's long-entrenched assumption of being set apart from everything around us, is a first step to getting our house in order, I think. As I've also written elsewhere, the job market's challenges began decades ago, and so no one now working in our field can claim that they are unaware of this—as wonderfully as my career happened to turn out, it caused me to get a passport, change countries, and live apart from my wife for just a nine-month instructor's position, back when I was starting out, let alone included twelve years living in different parts of the United States trying to get jobs in the same city. But now I'm lucky enough to be among the old guard in the profession. So, whether it impacted them personally, affected onetime friends from their grad school days, or impacted the many students whom they've supervised over the years, even the old timers are all aware of how bad it has been and how much worse it has gotten. But collectively, we have pretty much done nothing substantive to address it; in the spirit of being frank, offering mock campus interviews and CV writing workshops are of little to no use to a generation of grad students lacking a sufficient number of academic jobs to which to apply. What all of this might make plain is that scholars, at least in my experience, are notorious for failing to apply the critical tools that help them to understand other people's worlds to analyze the workings of their own. We need to acknowledge all of this if we're going to try to do something about it—after all, isn't the first step always said to be identifying that you have a problem?

The second step, which resists turning the field into mere job training (whatever that actually means), is recognizing and then promoting the value and thus relevance of the skills that we've been teaching to students *all along*—careful attention to definition, description, comparison, and analysis (whether interpretive or explanatory). This step is possible only if we first understand that our work is connected to the work of those all around us, across disciplines—we all study people, and the stuff they made, after all. Only then will we be able to pay more attention to the varied uses of our tools, empowering our students to see their application and adaptability at an assortment of cross-cultural sites from throughout history that happen to catch their attention and their imaginations. But that means shifting our attention from the self-evident value of our precious, as interested in it as we may ourselves be, to the tools and techniques that we used to create and maintain that supposed value all along. So yes, remain interested in whatever ritual or text you may be studying, but also recognize the manner in which its seemingly compelling value is made and sustained over time and place, realizing that this latter focus may be what your students take away with them and apply in a surprising way far removed from that ritual or that text, domains unimagined in your classes with them.

The third interconnected step is being humble enough to recognize that our content—whatever specialized group, item, behavior, region, or historic period we may each study, on which we focus in our classes and in our research—is always best approached as an e.g. (and here, as already signaled, I'm explicitly channeling J. Z. Smith's work) of some wider, more general human issue that we can find in other places and at other times, at diverse sites that have nothing necessarily to do with religion *but which have everything to do with being human* (which includes, I should add, acts of designating humans as somehow distinct from so-called nonhuman things across the globe). Simply put, in resisting the very strong temptation to see the items that we study as special, unique, one-of-a-kind, and thus self-authenticating, we free the field to be relevant in far more ways than it ever was before—not because religion lurks everywhere in some camouflaged fashion (let's call this the old "religion of baseball" approach that sees religion's deep meaning everywhere in disguise), but because those things commonly designated *as* religion have been comprised of mundane human doings all along and their very designation as being religious was itself but one more of those curious, signifying acts. Putting it all together, we reinvent ourselves by proactively enabling students to apply the skills that have always been so important in the study of these objects or those institutions to yet other items, far removed from the scholar of religion's usual terrain, but in that far broader domain of anyone interested in the exercise of forming groups, contesting groups, and being members of groups. They come to know how systems of authority work, how systems of rank function, how identities are made and negotiated, and how prior structures and inventive agency intertwine and mutually inform one another. Understanding how such things work provides skills needed by government, by private business, by NGOs, by schools, and by a host of other institutions that comprise our daily lives. Why shouldn't our students be the ones bringing these skills to bear in such other venues? Why shouldn't we be thinking about this when we design a syllabus, revise a curriculum, grade their assignments, let alone when we admit them to our graduate programs? We want to see them all succeed, no? And given that our success is so closely linked to their own, we have a degree of self-interest to take all this rather seriously.

And so, I offer this collection, specifically for the moment in which we now find ourselves. It's not a self-help book for the humanities and does not provide a step-by-step plan for reorganizing a department. Instead, its chapters try to animate a reader to see how pervasive is the problem of thinking that our situation (i.e., our data, our methods, and our institutional locale) is distinct from all others. Changing this, I argue, is the first step to entertaining how connected to the rest of academia we have always been, let alone to figuring out some specific strategies to help keep the field afloat let alone the careers of its many members. The recommendations suggested may not work everywhere, of course; I'm mindful of the specific character of many local challenges. So, unlike Gollum, I hope not to step too far and lose my footing by making too many grandiose gestures. But, like anyone in the game long enough, I've a few hard-won lessons that, before I call it quits, I'd like to enter into the record, at most in hopes that they prompt a strategic player or two to come up with some inventive strategies of their own and, at the least, to signal to those who may come long after us, should our field find its way out of this mess, that some of their predecessors plainly saw what was coming and tried to do something about it.

References

Abbasi, Rushain. 2021. "Islam and the Invention of Religion: A Study of Medieval Muslim Discourses on Din." *Studia Islamica* 116 (1): 1–106.

Aghapour, Andrew Ali, Shannon Trosper Schorey, Thomas J. Whitley, Vaia Touna, and Russell T. McCutcheon. 2023. "Religious Studies beyond the Discipline: A

Manifesto on Earning and Awarding a Ph.D." *Bulletin for the Study of Religion* 51 (3–4): 83–92.

Alles, Gregory. 1988. "Wach, Eliade, and the Critique from Totality." *Numen* 35 (1): 108–138.

Barylo, William. 2018. *Young Muslim Change-Makers: Grassroots Charities Rethinking Modern Societies.* New York: Routledge.

Gray-Hildenbrand, Jenna, Beverly McGuire, and Hussein Rashid, eds. 2024. *Teaching Critical Religious Studies: Pedagogy and Critique in the Classroom.* London: Bloomsbury.

Hughes, Aaron W., and Russell T. McCutcheon. 2022a. *Religion in 50 Words.* New York: Routledge.

———. 2022b. *Religion in 50 More Words.* New York: Routledge.

Lease, Gary. 1995. "The Rise and Fall of Religious Studies at Santa Cruz: A Case Study in Pathology, or The Rest of the Story." *Method & Theory in the Study of Religion* 7 (4): 305–324.

Lincoln, Bruce. 2024. *Secrets, Lies, and Consequences: A Great Scholar's Hidden Past and His Protégé's Unsolved Murder.* New York: Oxford University Press.

McCutcheon, Russell T. 2003. "Religion and the Governable Self." In *The Discipline of Religion: Structure, Meaning, Rhetoric.* New York: Routledge.

———. 2004. "'Just Follow the Money': The Cold War, the Humanistic Study of Religion, and the Fallacy of Misplaced Cynicism." *Culture and Religion* 5 (1): 41–69.

———. 2010. "Religion before 'Religion'?" In *Chasing Down Religion: In the Sights of History and the Cognitive Sciences: Essay in Honour of Luther H. Martin*, edited by Donald Wiebe and Panayotis Pachis. Thessaloniki, Greece: Barbounakis Publications.

———. 2021. *On Making a Shift in the Study of Religion and Other Essays.* Berlin: Walter de Gruyter.

———. 2024a. "'Not Nearly Critical Enough': Studying Religion as Part of the Humanities." In *Critics Not Caretakers: Redescribing the Public Study of Religion*, 2nd ed. New York: Routledge.

———, ed. 2024b. *Religious Studies beyond the Discipline: On Earning and Awarding a Humanities Ph.D.* Sheffield: Equinox Publishing.

Owen, Suzanne. 2011. "The World Religions Paradigm Time for a Change." *Arts and Humanities in Higher Education* 10 (1): 253–268.

Rennie, Bryan. 2024. "Alternative Interpretations of Manifold Texts: The Case of Mircea Eliade's Political Writings." *Religion* 55 (1): 67–88.

Tolkien, J.R.R. 1955. *The Return of the King, Being the Third Part of The Lord of the Rings.* New York: Houghton Mifflin.

PART 1

Overview

1
Religious Studies
Wither and Why?

> There are a number of signs which suggest a growing concern among scholars of religion regarding the shape and future of the field of religious studies within higher education.
> —Linell E. Cady, "Religious Studies and the Public University" (1995, 393)

Although it may seem to be a typo-laden reference to the title assigned to me for the invited essay that served as the basis for this opening chapter—one that marked the fiftieth anniversary of *Religious Studies Review* (*RSR*), a journal that, from the very start of my career, I've often relied upon[1]—this chapter's title is instead an undisguised nod to what now might be a forgotten essay of Jonathan Z. Smith's, one that dates to almost thirty years ago. It ran as an afterword to yet another special issue, one that was edited by

[1] In fact, I was president of the Council of Societies for the Study of Religion (CSSR)—the umbrella organization that founded this periodical in 1975—when a decline in member societies left us no choice but to disband an organization that, over its forty years, had played a key role in the development of the North American field. (For more on the CSSR's history, see Remus 2014; it is worth noting that Remus wrote the postscript to the very first issue of *RSR* (1975: 63–64). As part of this, working closely with Andy Fort, the CSSR's final executive director, we negotiated the sale of *RSR* to Rice University (after Valparaiso in the 1990s being the CSSR's home and host, Rice's Department of Religion, under Jeff Kripal's leadership at the time, took over this role) and *The CSSR Bulletin*—once the widest-circulating periodical in the North American field—was sold to Equinox Publishers (now simply titled *The Bulletin for the Study of Religion*, whose editorial home, these past few years, has been my own department at the University of Alabama, with Merinda Simmons now as its editor). It is quite gratifying to see that both periodicals have continued their service to the field, with *RSR* marking its fiftieth anniversary in 2024 and *The Bulletin* its fifty-fourth year.

Gary Lease titled "Pathologies in the Academic Study of Religion: North American Institutional Case Studies." Appearing in *Method and Theory in the Study of Religion* (*MTSR*) in 1995 as the last issue of volume 7, the issue was conceived by Lease almost two years prior (this was all during the time when I was one of the co-editors of the journal) and was motivated by events then taking place on the campus of the University of Pennsylvania (in early fall of 1993), when a plan to restructure their School of Arts and Sciences was announced—one that initially involved closing three units, which included religious studies. It was therefore more than evident at that time that a number of departments of religious studies in both Canada and the United States were under threat or had already been either closed or collapsed into yet other, larger and cross-disciplinary units, suggesting to Lease that an issue reflecting on these case studies (what lessons could be learned?) would benefit the journal's readers. That the situation has changed little in the thirty years since then—if anything, it has worsened—should not go without notice. The degree to which anyone read those essays as cautionary tales for the fate of the field on their own campus is something worth mulling over, especially as we sit here today hearing news every few weeks about yet another program in our field closing.

That special issue included reports from the University of Alberta (written by Eva Neumair-Dargay—their unit is today part of the Department of History, Classics, and Religion); the University of Lethbridge (by Marilyn Nefsky—their small department remains today); and the University of Toronto (by Donald Wiebe—Toronto's once autonomous and cross-disciplinary graduate unit was collapsed into the undergraduate department which had close ties to the Toronto School of Theology), all in Canada, along with American cases from Arizona State (by Linell Cady—although included as an example of a success story, Arizona State's unit was eventually collapsed into what is called the School of Historical, Philosophical and Religious Studies, on a campus now very much focused on online education) and the University of Pennsylvania (by Ann Matter—the University of Pennsylvania's department remains today, small but also offering a Ph.D. degree). The case studies were joined by Lease's own blow-by-blow account of the challenges faced some years prior at his own campus, UC Santa Cruz, where the Department of Religious Studies had been "disestablished" back in the 1979–80 academic year, after a rather critical assessment from an outside team of reviewers, which included Ray Hart, Ninian Smart, and Christine Downing.[2]

[2] "Disestablishment was the *best* thing which could have ever happened to it," given UCSC's dysfunctionality as a unit, Lease concludes (1995b, 323).

(Subsequent to that, students in the History of Consciousness, itself a once noted cross-disciplinary program chaired by Lease, could fashion a doctoral program in the study of religion, as several successfully did [e.g., Tim Murphy, Karen DeVries, and Matt Waggoner, among others.])

And so it was to that collection of dispatches—well worth the read even today, I might add, or better put, especially today—that Smith was asked to respond by way of an afterword with a title whose less than optimistic parenthetical—"Whither (wither) and Why?" (Smith 1995)—was itself in reference to the subtitle of a much earlier essay by yet another famous Smith (more than likely inspiring the title for the special issue in *Religious Studies Review* for which an earlier version of this very essay was written), one in which W. C. famously offered what J. Z. later considered to be the "crazy idea" that "no statement about a religion is valid unless it can be acknowledged by that religion's believers" (W. C. Smith 1959, 42).[3]

Concerning the case studies on which J. Z. Smith was asked to comment, in his introduction to the issue, Lease writes that Smith "opined on first seeing the essays collected here [that] they read like an obituary" (Lease 1995a, 302). With reference to such a critical assessment of the field's institutional health three decades ago—a field that today is still nicely summed up by the gulf between the methods proposed by these two Smiths, with the earlier of the two, though writing over sixty years ago, aptly representing what I see as the still dominant strain in the field—I aim to identify here some of the reasons why I now tend to think that, without a serious intervention and then recalibration, departments of religious studies may soon wilt away from the ranks of units populating at least the public university's humanities programs (if they even remain, what with what's now happening to the field all over), perhaps leaving behind (at least for the time being) a few scholars of religion housed in, say, history departments as well as a handful of privileged private colleges where one or another form of theological work has often passed for the academic study of religion. Although, as the preface and introduction should have already made evident, I think that the time is not

[3] In a 2008 interview, J. Z. Smith had the following (sensibly, I think) to say about W. C. Smith's methodological rule—it is worth quoting in full: "I said, Wilfred, the difference between you and me is that I'm at Chicago and you're at Harvard. You're rich, I'm poor. Who are you calling up? My God, what a phone bill! I mean, you're calling up the entire Muslim world, and asking what they think of your sentence? Because if not, I want to know how you picked out the person you asked. And I suspect you picked him out because he talks just like you! And then you're asking a mirror, How do I look today? I mean, it's a crazy idea. Call up the whole world and ask them, What do you think about what I was about to say? Every sentence? I mean good lord, what a bill. I think even with the cell phones, I see all the ads say 'unlimited'—I don't think they had that in mind" (Braun and McCutcheon 2018, 12).

too late to address some of these issues, to try to ensure a far more secure future for our field, given larger institutional trends in higher education over the past decades and even just the last year or two, not to mention a variety of growing national and international pressures, I admit that I would not be surprised to learn that some readers may have concluded that the ship has already sailed and that, much as with some people's assessment of climate change, the time for effective intervention may have already passed us by. Given that I'm an optimist at heart—for, as I wrote in the introduction, what else motivates even the most ardent critic but a hope for things to change for what they consider to be the better?—I refuse to relinquish the idea that we each have some tactical agency that might impact our situation, despite the admittedly daunting structural moment in which much of higher education now finds itself.

And so, returning to Smith's afterword: among the challenges facing the field at that time, or so he concluded, was a lack of professionalism and thus disciplinary unity; or, to put it differently, despite some common issues, the story that he took away from the six separate case studies was that local challenges and opportunities on each campus drove idiosyncratic curriculums and presented to each department problems of their own. Despite Lease's hope for that set of papers, shared solutions—let alone beneficial takeaways from others' experiences—were hard to come by. As Smith goes on, in a rather undisguised criticism of the American Academy of Religion's and the Society of Biblical Literature's longtime "Let a thousand flowers bloom" approach to the field: "Our professional associations appear to have chosen (this may be too deliberate a term) to foster localisms of every stripe, thus undercutting the very function that requires their existence" (1995, 408). That the vagaries of this word "religion" were linked to all of this, as was the manner in which our field, at least in North America, usually grew out of no less local campus ministries fifty to sixty years ago, was not lost on Smith, of course. (Notably, Lethbridge's program did not share that common-origins tale.) That today we continue to lack any field-wide rationale and thus agreement on what it is that we're all doing when we say that we study religion should be more than evident to anyone even giving the study of religion just a cursory glance. (The significant distance between Johannes Wolfart's persuasive critique of the so-called religious literacy approach [2022], on the one hand, and on the other, those whose units' futures are now firmly wedded to such an initiative [some of whom replied to his paper in the issue where it appeared] provides suitable evidence.) Those wanting more than just anecdotal evidence can instead consult the diversity of uses of "religion" among the seventeen leading scholars included in the volume that Aaron Hughes and I recently co-edited (2021) or, perhaps, consider Richard Miller's criticism of J. Z. Smith for his failure to make a pronouncement on whether certain religions are, to put it as bluntly as does Miller, either good or bad for people (Miller 2021, 65—see chapter 7 for my own assessment of his proposals).[4] Much like the gap between the two Smiths, the distance between such contemporary approaches is sobering—informing my choice of the term "gulf" just above; given this disconnect, how could one imagine ever coming up with solutions to shared institutional challenges, let alone even agreeing on what constitutes a challenge, let alone a crisis (on the latter, see chapter 5 of this volume) in the first place? In fact, that more faculty today seem not to have entertained that Cady's admittedly dated comment from 1995, per the epigraph to this opening chapter, remains as relevant as ever is evidence of this lack of shared vision throughout the history of the field; I have no doubt, however, that the relevance of Cady's observation is not lost on the many faculty who, over just the past few years, have also had their departments either closed or merged out from under them.[5]

Lacking such agreement—and now going beyond that old *MTSR* issue—means that the field as a whole is ill-prepared for the sort of structural changes that have been taking place in higher education all across the country (and beyond) over the past few decades. To rephrase: each department, and in those cases where departments lack strong leadership, sometimes each individual faculty member, are largely on their own, continually forced to reinvent a wheel that, unbeknownst to them, may be functioning rather well elsewhere.[6] Now, despite a degree of localism still informing colleges and

[4] For a detailed, critical assessment of Miller's proposal for an unapologetically normative and methodologically uniform field, see Stausberg et al. (2023).

[5] Having learned in early August 2023 that Missouri State's longtime Department of Religious Studies (where I once worked for five years—a unit with a BA and MA program) had just been collapsed into a Languages, Cultures, and Religions unit (along with what was once known there as Modern and Classical Languages—part of a series of mergers there that even involved entire colleges), I queried others on social media, only to learn how many more units in the United States and elsewhere are either soon anticipated to be collapsed into such interdisciplinary units or already have been, making that seemingly old *MTSR* issue (sadly, perhaps) as relevant as ever. However, there appears to be no field-wide initiative even just to track these closures and mergers, let alone evidence of any sort of centralized response, since Missouri State's news was but one of many to hit social media in the past months. The American Academy of Religion's academic relations committee, which I happen to chair at the time of writing this, is now doing what it can (hosting monthly webinars on a variety of professional topics, devising a "toolbox" website with resources for those in leadership positions within departments, and starting to track challenges to departments), but one volunteer committee comprised of a handful of people is hardly the site at which to expect the field to save itself.

[6] Over the years I've invested energy in, for example, hosting or being involved in assorted department chair workshops in our field, which are useful for those able to attend but, generally

universities as a whole,[7] the extent to which they now have little choice but to be tightly woven into national, not to mention international economic, social, and political, issues means that each seemingly isolated and to a large degree distinctive department of religious studies or department of religion (the names once made a difference but now likely do not, for the most part) is being presented with a rather uniform set of pressures. From decades of government funding cuts at the state and federal level,[8] leading to continually rising tuition costs which, in turn, prompt students and their families, many of whom are accumulating truly staggering student loans,[9] to increasingly consider their financial investment in a college education as needing to bear immediate practical fruits, that is, a career and an income. This has all led, sensibly enough, to a strong preference for the many so-called professional majors that, over the past several decades, have increasingly populated campuses—majors that, in response to market demand, colleges have been investing in heavily and promoting in recent years (e.g., engineering, business, nursing, social work, etc., including STEM, of course).[10] Add to

speaking, they seem not to be a high priority for many who might benefit from them. My sense is that not just such events but, for many, the role of chair itself is seen as an inconvenience or, at best, an onerous obligation that interrupts their own scholarly output. I would strongly argue *against* seeing such a crucial role as a dagger on which only the brave or foolhardy fall.

[7] Case in point: for a variety of reasons, my own campus (a large southern U.S. flagship state school) came rather late to the game of wagering on the beneficial impact to the campus's bottom line of online distance education courses, at least as judged by my previous university (itself a second-tier or regional Midwest state school) where the move toward more technologically innovative online education was already well underway by the mid-1990s. Thus, it stood out to me that when I arrived on my new campus in 2001, we were still mailing booklets and textbooks to our distance learners. Not long after that, this began to change, of course, and by now our campus is fully invested in online distance education as well as the use of learning management systems in on-campus lecture courses.

[8] This is a pressure from which private institutions, whether small liberal arts or Ivy League, are exempt by and large—though they come with their own challenges, of course, especially the declining enrollments seen at some small liberal arts colleges today.

[9] As of March 2023, $1.775 trillion is owed on student loans in the United States, according to the National Reserve's July 10, 2023, report—which is about 10 percent of all consumer debt. This number "includes student loans originated under the Federal Family Education Loan Program and the Direct Loan Program; Perkins loans; and private student loans without government guarantees." See "Consumer Credit—G.19," Board of Governors of the Federal Reserve System, accessed July 11, 2023, https://www.federalreserve.gov/releases/g19/current/default.htm. Aside: student loan debt in the United States is second only to mortgage debt, having already dwarfed consumer credit card debt.

[10] There was a time in North American postsecondary education, of course, when students seeking such credentials attended separate business colleges, for example; I think of my own two older sisters in Canada (born in 1946 and 1947), neither of whom went to university but who,

this that the very governments cutting university funding while subsidizing yet other sectors of the economy then cite the decline in the humanities that results, along with their disciplines' inability to achieve certain short-term, practical outcomes that their administrations prioritize, to justify further cuts to this portion of their curriculums, and you arrive at what might be described unironically as the imperfect storm that has been circling for decades around the humanities. (England's recently announced plan to limit enrollment in so-called low-value subjects is but the latest of such measures.)[11] And bearing in mind the worldwide economic collapse of 2008 (which rocked many college operating budgets and thus hiring plans, from which some have yet to recover) followed just over a decade later by the (sometimes dramatic) cuts (on my campus these were strategically called "taxes" by the administration) necessitated by the 2020 pandemic-induced economic decline, then we arrive at a situation where likening the present predicament to past hiring slumps or seeing it all as being akin to, say, ongoing challenges in recruiting new religious studies majors seems ill-considered at best, due to the manner in which such claims of continuity and similarity appear to minimize the heightened peculiarities of our current situation. A dramatic change in degree understandably makes it seem like a change in kind, especially to those now leaving doctoral programs and going on the academic job market. They, more than anyone else, know that *our house is on fire.*

Speaking as someone who, in the summer of 2023, stepped down after completing eighteen years as a department chair in a large southern U.S. public university, I can attest to the energy and inventiveness needed among a faculty to try to help their department (thereby helping themselves, to be sure) to succeed in times like these. (This, of course, assumes that there is already a shared agreement among them as to the sad state of affairs; if not, then even more energy will be needed to persuade them that their insulated, tenured positions—what some, as I've already noted, still refer to as "the life of the mind"—may be shielding them from what's actually going on out

---

instead, attended nursing college and teachers college, respectively—an indication of the recent professionalization of universities, to be sure, but also evidence of the highly restricted careers outside the home that were available to women of their generation. See Labaree (2008) for an institutional history of teacher training in the United States. On nursing education in the United States, the Nursing Training Act of 1964 played a key role in moving this training into bachelor's programs within universities (see Lynaugh 2008).

[11] See the July 14, 2023, report: Richard Adams and Aubrey Allegretti, "Sunak to Force English Universities to Cap Numbers of Students on 'Low-Value' Degrees," *The Guardian*, July 14, 2023, https://www.theguardian.com/education/2023/jul/14/rishi-sunak-force-english-universities-cap-low-value-degrees.

there.) But the well-known outside, structural pressures itemized already are not the whole story, for there are also what we might characterize as internal and internalized pressures that hamper a department trying to remain not just relevant but also institutionally viable (for the sake of their students, staff, and faculty). And here is where I return to Smith's much earlier thoughts on what I'll just call the field's self-imposed limitations.

In the past I've argued that the largely successful efforts to create an autonomous field in North America, using arguments about an utterly unique datum and the unique methods and institutional location required for its satisfactory study, actually ended up marginalizing the field in the very act of establishing it (for, to this day, few of our disciplinary neighbors seem to understand what we do, with contemporary colleagues in anthropology, history, political science, etc., often thinking we're theologians—even on public university campuses). But now I think that the problem goes deeper. For, not unlike many other scholarly fields, legitimacy in the study of religion is linked to specificity: while undergraduates most often start with sweeping surveys of the world's religions, they soon are offered courses that begin to zero in on just one tradition, and then just one text or region or time period or subgroup within the tradition, moving on, perhaps, to graduate work on an increasingly focused aspect of that one text, place, time, or group, eventually producing a dissertation on such a narrow specialty that, in most cases, only a handful of other equally specialized experts will ever read let alone cite their work. While this model is not indictable in and of itself—after all, basic science research is needed in all academic fields and specialized focus is part of what such work requires—I would argue that this long-standing mode of scholarly work further sabotages the field, especially *at a moment such as this*. For in a field where the vast majority of our students will never take more than one course with us (at least in the United States, where religious studies programs more than likely depend almost completely on serving the needs of other disciplines and their majors via what is variously known as the core curriculum or general education), the presumption that such a standardized approach to specialized scholarship and education suits our institutional needs is, I would argue, rather mistaken.

But if you add to this that, due to those larger structural factors itemized earlier, few of the current doctoral students training for careers in the faculty ranks will likely have success, at least in the foreseeable future, in obtaining a secure tenure-track position, then there's more reason than ever to reconsider undergraduate *and* graduate education completely and, along with it, the rationale for students even entering our field, much less earning a

Ph.D.[12] For—and this is where the "why" connects to the "wither" of this chapter's title—if we are not able to address the contradiction between data specialization, on the one hand, and the lack of career opportunities for our graduate students (not to mention our undergraduates, who lack the sort of religious education option available to many of their European peers and who, in many cases, add the study of religion as a second major while depending on their first major for their futures), then I find it difficult to imagine autonomous departments of religious studies continuing to exist in the near future. After all, as just mentioned, the majority of our undergraduate classes have long been so-called service courses (providing those earning professional degrees with a degree of breadth) while many of our field's open faculty lines are no longer regularly being filled with tenure-track faculty (if we do get a hire, there's a rather good chance it will be a contract "teaching professor" or an instructor). Sure, some units will remain, given their varying degrees of insulation from at least some of these forces, but the service role that most departments across the United States have long played, despite having a small number of their own majors and thus a small number of more specialized upper-level undergraduate seminars (something faculty often immersed in survey courses surely find rewarding to teach), will more than likely completely envelop the majority of programs, possibly leading to their demise since many other units on campus—some rather better established and staffed than religious studies—are also eagerly vying for those same, limited number of humanities credit hours as part of their own core or gen ed offerings.[13]

[12] Aside: I rarely see just tenure-track appointments reported by doctoral schools for their graduate placement rates (itself a marketing technique to recruit new students); instead, these numbers now tend to be inflated by an assortment of contingent positions being included. While some in the latter sort of positions may indeed move to the former, the number who will remain in such nonpermanent positions, let alone the number of people who will eventually leave them (more than likely disillusioned with academia) to seek work outside the university, cannot go unnoticed. Truth in advertising mandates that placement rates must be broken down in this fashion.

[13] Not unlike other campuses in the United States, my own college developed a new core curriculum over the past several years, to be implemented in the fall of 2025, in which the overall number of required hours has been significantly reduced, with a variety of new requirements introduced (e.g., engaged learning courses, etc.) along with the ability of the professional schools across campus to begin offering some such courses for the first time. Such changes therefore come at the expense of such things as the number of humanities or foreign language hours necessary to gain any undergraduate degree. And, by possibly dropping the previous requirement for history classes, the new core curriculum may be adding the Department of History to the mix of units competing for students to help justify their existence.

And so, thinking back once again to that *MTSR* issue, I believe that we are in part to blame for our present situation—to blame, at least, for creating and perpetuating a field in which we have succumbed to our own rhetoric of being set apart and special, resulting in one that is not nimble and able to effectively respond, to whatever degree that we are able, to changing conditions. For the long-standing assumption that still drives much work in the field—that religion is different, special, set apart, or maybe even mysteriously unique and thus deeply meaningful—also drives the specialization model described above. As a one-year instructor once said to me long ago, at a time when the department had requested a replacement line to study and teach on religion in Asia, "It's Asia—of course you'll get that position"; I responded by noting the many departments on our campus that were currently missing one or more positions, those whose area and expertise they each took as self-evidently important to their teaching and research mission. This suggested, I then went on, that the administration would likely settle the issue of distributing limited resources by appealing to factors other than a discipline's own sense of its subject matter's importance, relying instead on such other metrics as faculty-to-student ratios (i.e., class sizes), the cost of instruction (after all, it's far cheaper to have an instructor teach a class than a full professor), student credit hour (and thus tuition) production, number of majors, retention rates, graduation rates, job placement rates, external funding success among the faculty, etc. And so, whether there ever was a time when an open line studying, let's say, religion in Asia was just naturally or inevitably filled (and despite the nostalgia for some higher education golden age just a few academic generations ago, I'm not convinced there really ever was such a time), that moment is probably long past at the sorts of institutions in which most of us work.

Yet, as I'm arguing, our model for how faculty carry out their work (i.e., do research, produce scholarship, teach students, and supervise graduate education) has, for the most part, not kept pace with these structural changes, with some scholars (often subsidized by teams of contingent faculty and graduate teaching assistants) still following a script that goes back several hundred years, to a time when our institution had certain privileges and protections that are no longer in force in quite the same way. In fact, Smith himself made an argument against traditional specialization in what I still see as his important and underutilized Society of Biblical Literature presidential address (presented in Boston on the evening of November 22, 2008), where he strongly advocated for Hebrew bible and New Testament scholars to be doing cross-cultural comparative work, *by training to be versed in multiple canons*; as such, their work ought to include "comparisons between canons, comparative processes of canon formation and supplementation, but also to undertake comparative investigations of strategies for the interpretation of canonical collections, as well as comparative inquiries into their several ritual settings and employments" (Smith 2009, 22). In this way, scholars would treat each dataset as an e.g., as he would have phrased it, but not of religion in general but, instead, of some wider, common, and even seemingly mundane human process that we also see elsewhere in history or in contemporary culture—for instance, the dynamics of canon formation, for one, let alone the various uses of texts in social formation and contests over such things as prestige, place, and authority. Such work would therefore explicitly be aimed at producing conclusions with general application well beyond any one exemplary instance, that is, any one tradition, scripture, region, or group, not to mention honing skills applicable to the study of a variety of other items well outside our field, both of which are significant steps beyond the current model that assumes that each site where scholars of religion invest their energy is unique and self-evidently important. After all, it's no accident that Smith, although having written a dissertation on Frazer's *The Golden Bough* and then becoming a scholar of a variety of ancient texts, myths, and rituals, also possessed sufficient skills to tackle how U.S. Supreme Court justices reasoned themselves into various conclusions, a suitable instance of the breadth and applicability of our skills (Smith 2004).

If this was how both our undergrad and, importantly, graduate curriculums worked—emphasizing novel comparative work and thus the categories (e.g., canon, scripture, myth, ritual, etc.)[14] along with the scholarly curiosities and interests that drive such work—then, as J. Z. Smith approvingly cites an earlier essay of W. C. Smith's which made much the same argument, we might reasonably ask: Where can we find people with doctoral training that equips them to do such work? (see J. Z. Smith 2009, 22, quoting W. C. Smith 1971).[15] If I'm permitted to rephrase this question, remembering what has brought us to this point in the chapter, let's go

[14] While there may be a variety of examples of how such terms as "myth" or "ritual" (or "mythmaking" and "ritualization") are often used profitably beyond scholarship on religion, Newton (2020) provides a very helpful example of how the term "scripture" (or better put, "scripturalization") can be redescribed and then used far wider in cultural analysis than a traditional scholar of religion might employ the term. See also Wimbush (2021) for another example of the more general use of this refashioned technical term. On improving our use of such technical categories, see the two volumes written by Aaron Hughes and myself (2022a and 2022b).

[15] Sadly (or predictably perhaps), I'm unaware of a doctoral program that has yet to take Smith up on his challenge from fifteen years ago.

well beyond that question and instead ask: Where might someone equipped with such training find a rewarding career? For it is increasingly unlikely that many of us will continue to be able to train doctoral students in the usual fashion and in our own likeness, aiming to have them walk into future positions vacated upon our departure or created as our departments grow. After all, in many of our departments' cases, treading water or marking time—pick your imagery—is the most reasonable hope for the near future. But, bearing in mind the sort of shift that Smith recommended, it may now be apparent that in studying religion *we are not really studying religion at all*, whatever that may or may not even be defined as being; instead, all along, many of us have been using this one domain of human action and organization, delimited for the sake of our work by *our* definitions and *our* choices, as an entry point for examining in detail far broader cross-cultural social trends or human capacities, work that has more general implications than just for the focused datasets on which we happen to have based our research and teaching; in fact, that general application might turn out to be the whole point of doing the specialized and comparative work in the first place (a point I argue in greater detail in the last chapter to this collection).

What I'm suggesting, then, is something more radical than what is now sometimes designated as engaged religious studies[16]—a term that I could get behind far more if it did not so often seem to name applying expertise on the specialized data of religion (conceptualized usually as a beneficial cultural good) but as it apparently also appears in adjacent domains (i.e., in the so-called helping professions, nonprofit work, and interreligious dialogue or as part of the practical impact on civic life of so-called religious literacy).[17] Instead, if we relativize and thereby historicize and even humanize this term "religion" by no longer seeing it as obviously or rightly naming a distinct, pre-social and therefore special part of so-called human experience and, instead, see it as tactically designating discursive objects that are created by

[16] I think here of the work being done by Georgia State's Department of Religious Studies, specifically in its graduate program; it describes itself as "tak[ing] an applied approach to studying religions. That means we work with a variety of community partners to incorporate learning opportunities into our courses to prepare our students for careers and advanced graduate study" (see "A Practical Approach," Georgia State University, accessed July 13, 2023, https://religiousstudies.gsu.edu/).

[17] See *MTSR* 34 (5) (2022) for the previously mentioned set of papers in response to Wolfart's rather critical assessment of the roots and applications of the now many religious literacy initiatives in our field (including his reply)—an assessment that agrees with my own (see McCutcheon 2021, 21 ff.).

situated social actors for always practical purposes,[18] then the skills needed to go about such work—e.g., description, comparison, and analysis (whether interpretive or explanatory)—will have extremely wide application, and the question might now become "Who wouldn't want just such a person on their team?" Accordingly, our students (and yes, their families too), once they are made aware of the practical benefits of this shift in approach, will be empowered to answer the inevitable "And you have a degree in . . . , religious studies . . . ?" comment at their future job interviews by making apparent how studying whatever it was that fascinated them while a student in our field actually set the table for a manner of detailed, nuanced, and critical analysis that they will bring to all sorts of other datasets and duties—assuming we're willing to relinquish the pretense that our object of study is utterly unique. I'm reminded here of the risk analyst in the 2011 film *Margin Call*, set during the days going into the 2008 mortgage crisis, who, as it turns out, holds a Ph.D. in engineering, studying propulsion (i.e., he's a rocket scientist, as one of his surprised supervisors puts it) but who now works for a financial investor since, as the character says at a meeting when the impending crisis is first becoming apparent, "it's all just numbers, really, changing what you're adding up." Also, he adds that the money was considerably better at the investment firm. At times like these in higher ed, such empowered nimbleness, created by means of an explicit focus on practical, adaptable skills, is an extremely useful thing for humanities students.

Failing to adapt our field and its curriculums and graduate student supervision in this way will, I'm convinced, hasten the already begun withering of the field that many campuses have already more than experienced, resulting in a field whose best days may have been a couple decades behind us, back when all those debates over reductionism continually populated scholarly periodicals (which amounted to growing-pain debates over the nature and limits of the field itself). As an optimistic critic (again, a redundant phrasing, I'd argue) who happens not to want to finish his career in a field whose best years are well behind it—we're all here to leave things in better shape than we found them, after all—I therefore feel some animation toward offering the foregoing frank assessment of our current predicament. That includes offering an unvarnished look at the inadequacies of current graduate training (for example, see Aghapour et al. 2023, a paper that is also the basis for a

[18] This might be painfully evident to anyone studying how the term is used in some U.S. courts to, as most recently evident in Supreme Court decisions, skirt around a variety of recent federal laws, thereby paving the way to turn onetime discrimination cases into efforts to protect so-called free expression of (potentially unpopular) sincerely held beliefs and commitments.

multiauthored volume that I've edited on rethinking doctoral training in our field) at a time when the severely deflated academic job market means that a program offering, let's say, mock-interviews and CV-writing workshops, instead of internships for course credit, a reimagined dissertation, thick digital humanities skills, and incremental class projects other than essay writing (whose results can be collected into a portfolio of accomplishments), constitutes one that's peddling solutions to the last decade's problems. But my hope is that in the midst of some honest talk about where we now stand there are also some empowering suggestions for at least one port where we can find some shelter during the current storm, hoping that our action now can have impact even if the winds have long been howling.

But exercising this agency means faculty trained in their academic silos and who are rather used to flying solo will need to be far more daring, collaborative, and willing to retool by venturing outside their comfort zone once they realize that there's likely no one out there who is going to come to their rescue. (In my experience, larger units on a university campus, such as colleges or schools, are more than likely not focused on managing the items that we see to be threatening our programs; in fact, a pragmatic approach to all of this must entertain that the conditions that threaten us may actually be benefiting other units on campus or even the university as a whole.) It means recognizing that those who trained us were unable to predict the world into which their students would move and have their careers—I can't list the number of times, over the years, when I've thought to myself, "This is *not* what I thought I'd end up doing when I got my Ph.D."—a sentiment many of us share, I know. But now we're in the position of trying to empower *our* students, the next generation, and it will require us to be bold and inventive. And so, thinking back to the surprise that greeted us when, not so long ago, a few of us from Alabama mentioned to some colleagues elsewhere about the résumé workshop (significantly not a CV, mind you) that our graduate director annually offers for our MA students—students who largely seek careers in a wide variety of areas upon graduation, while a small number have aimed for admission to doctoral programs—and recalling those colleagues' earnest questions about who trained us to do this (answer: no one; we figured it out on our own, doing it because we believe that it is important for our students' eventual success after graduation) . . . , well, this cautious approach where faculty stay in their own specialized lane is going to have to change. Sure, there's a number of expectations that they're already juggling, but the one that we're discussing here is the future of their majors, their graduate programs, their departments, their discipline, and, yes, their own jobs. And so, transgressing the boundaries of specialization, or, better phrased, putting that specialized expertise to use in addressing general topics that can be of wide application and relevance, may be just the ticket to becoming a lot more relevant—for our own careers' sakes, perhaps, but mainly for the sake of our students. And who knows? If it works, then one of those very students might someday be celebrating *RSR*'s centenary by doing something other than rehashing the genre of pessimistic "retrospect and prospect" essays from the past.

References

Aghapour, Andrew Ali, Shannon Trosper Schorey, Thomas J. Whitley, Vaia Touna, and Russell T. McCutcheon. 2023. "Religious Studies beyond the Discipline: A Manifesto on Earning and Awarding a Ph.D." *Bulletin for the Study of Religion* 51 (3–4): 83–92.

Braun, Willi, and Russell T. McCutcheon, eds. 2018. *Reading J. Z. Smith: Interviews and Essay.* New York: Oxford University Press.

Cady, Linell E. 1995. "Religious Studies and the Public University: A Case Study at Arizona State University." *Method & Theory in the Study of Religion* 7 (4): 393–406.

Hughes, Aaron W., and Russell T. McCutcheon, eds. 2021. *What Is Religion? Debating the Academic Study of Religion.* New York: Oxford University Press.

Hughes, Aaron W., and Russell T. McCutcheon. 2022a. *Religion in 50 Words: A Critical Vocabulary.* New York: Routledge.

———. 2022b. *Religion in 50 More Words: A Redescriptive Vocabulary.* New York: Routledge.

Labaree, David F. 2008. "An Uneasy Relationship: The History of Teacher Education in the University." In *Handbook of Research on Teacher Education: Enduring Questions in Changing Contexts*, 3rd ed., edited by Marilyn Cochran-Smith et al. New York: Routledge.

Lease, Gary. 1995a. "Foreword: Pathologies in the Academic Study of Religion." *Method & Theory in the Study of Religion* 7 (4): 299–303.

———. 1995b. "The Rise and Fall of Religious Studies at Santa Cruz: A Case in Pathology, or the Rest of the Story." *Method & Theory in the Study of Religion* 7 (4): 305–324.

Lynaugh, Joan E. 2008. "Nursing the Great Society: The Impact of the Nurse Training Act of 1964." *Nursing History Review* 16 (1): 13–28.

McCutcheon, Russell T. 2021. *On Making a Shift in the Study of Religion and Other Essays.* Berlin: Walter de Gruyter.

Miller, Richard B. 2021. *Why Study Religion?* New York: Oxford University Press.

Newton, Richard W. 2020. *Identifying Roots: Alex Haley and the Anthropology of Scriptures.* Sheffield: Equinox Publishing.

Remus, Harold. 1975. "Postscript." *Religious Studies Review* 1 (1): 63–64.

———. 2014. "For Such a Time as This: The Council of Societies for the Study of Religion, 1969–2009." In *Reinventing Religious Studies Key Writings in the History of a Discipline*, edited by Scott S. Elliott. New York: Routledge.

Smith, Jonathan Z. 1995. "Religious Studies: Whither (wither) and Why?" *Method & Theory in the Study of Religion* 7 (4): 407–414.

———. 2004. "God Save This Honourable Court: Religion and Civic Discourse." In Jonathan Z. Smith, *Relating Religion: Essays in the Study of Religion*. Chicago: University of Chicago Press.

———. 2009. "Religion and Bible." *Journal of Biblical Literature* 128 (1): 5–27.

Smith, Wilfred Cantwell. 1959. "Comparative Religion: Whither—and Why?" In *The History of Religions: Essays in Methodology*, edited by Mircea Eliade and Joseph M. Kitagawa. Chicago: University of Chicago Press.

———. 1971. "The Study of Religion and the Study of the Bible." *Journal of the American Academy of Religion* 39 (1): 131–140.

Stausberg, Michael, Ingvild Sælid Gilhus, Christian Hervik Bull, and Alexander van der Haven. 2023. "A Normative Turn in the Study of Religions? Reflections on Richard Miller's *Why Study Religion?*" *Method & Theory in the Study of Religion* 36 (1): 43–57.

Wimbush, Vincent L. 2021. "Scripturalization as Management of Difference: A Reply to Kurtis R. Schaeffer." In *What Is Religion? Debating the Academic Study of Religion*, edited by Aaron W. Hughes and Russell T. McCutcheon. New York: Oxford University Press.

Wolfart, Johannes. 2022. "'Religious Literacy': Some Considerations and Reservations." *Method & Theory in the Study of Religion* 34 (5): 407–434.

PART 2

Contributions

2
Introduction
Not Playing Favorites

Earlier and much shorter versions of the following chapter were presented as public lectures in the fall of 2005 and spring of 2006 at the University of Copenhagen, the University of Southern Denmark (my thanks to Tim Jensen for arranging that wonderful visit to Denmark), the University of Virginia (my thanks to Kurtis Schaeffer for arranging the visit), the Institute for the Advanced Study of Religion at Trinity College, Toronto (my thanks to Donald Wiebe for the invitation to speak there), Universität Berne (thanks to Jens Schlieter for making the arrangements), and Universität Zürich (my thanks to Dorothea Lüddeckens for arranging that talk). The version that was eventually published in the *Journal of the American Academy of Religion* (appearing in 2006 in issue 74 [3], 720–750) therefore benefited from the feedback of those in attendance at each of these talks, notably Jeppe Sinding Jensen, of Aarhus University, Denmark, who offered a formal reply to my presentation in Toronto. It also benefited from the comments of Glenn Yocum, *JAAR*'s longtime editor when the paper was first submitted and then reviewed, as well as the journal's two anonymous reviewers. As described in the chapter itself, it resulted from reading Robert Orsi's rather critical review of my 2003 collection of essays, *The Discipline of Religion*, part of a review symposium that was commissioned by Craig Prentiss, then the editor of the *Bulletin for the Council of Societies for the Study of Religion* (a society disbanded in 2009, with that periodical now published by Equinox and known simply as *The Bulletin for the Study of Religion*). Although I had a chance to reply briefly in the issue where that set of reviews appeared (33 [3&4] [2004]), that rather short text aimed to comment on the reviews of all participants, which, apart from Orsi, also included Henry Goldschmidt, Carol Wayne White, and Joanne Punzo Waghorne. Replying in detail to

Orsi was certainly not an option there, though I did focus a portion of that short response on his accusation that the method that I employed in my work was chilling because it was dehumanizing. Given the nature of this critique, his words stuck with me; over the course of the coming year, while also working on the essays that were to become my little book, *Religion and the Domestication of Dissent* (on whose second edition I now also happen to be working), the earlier version of the following chapter was written and, eventually, submitted and accepted by the journal and then published. I am unsure whether Orsi was invited to respond to that essay, as Paul Courtright in fact did (2006, leading to my own brief reply to him [2006]); back then, soliciting such responses to papers directly tackling the work of a specific scholar was a routine practice of that journal, like many others (I would argue that this was always a healthy exercise for the field), though lately this practice has ended at *JAAR* as far as I can tell. Whatever the case, no direct response from him was ever published, as far as I know.

Apart from agreeing to its reproduction in a volume edited by Monica Miller and which involved the original members of the once active research initiative Culture on the Edge (see McCutcheon 2015—along with Miller those founding members were Craig Martin, Steven Ramey, Merinda Simmons, Leslie Dorrough Smith, Vaia Touna, and myself), I've never included this essay in any of my own collections. But now seemed to be the right occasion to do so, what with the challenges now facing the field (broadly understood). For the shortcomings of the classic humanistic approach that, long ago, was so widely adopted in our field—an adoption probably fueled by many of our colleagues' assumptions that if they handle it correctly, whatever it is that they designate as religion will provide them with a special case of deeply meaningful insight into the enduring human spirit—are exemplified rather sharply in this piece. It is therefore a chapter that, to put it bluntly, demonstrates the self-serving nature of the approach that has long been used in much of the field (see McCutcheon 2024, 3–18 for a more general critique of the humanistic approach to the study of religion). While the troubles that it documents in detail are certainly not entirely responsible for the situation in which we now find ourselves—much of that responsibility surely should be laid at the feet of a professional managerial class that now runs universities as if they were private corporations catering to customers—I would argue that the manner in which the field has never really lived up to the demands of scholarship carried out from within the human sciences has nonetheless played a role in marginalizing us within the university and, perhaps, making us sitting ducks for some of the cuts that have now come our way. For even to this day, after more than twenty years of collective, focused investments and reinventions in our department—its teaching, its scholarly productions, and its reputation within and well beyond the campus—a number of people in other departments continue to assume that, despite being a unit at a public university, we're more akin to theology than to anthropology or sociology. As I have argued on a variety of past occasions, I maintain that this is a direct result of the strategy adopted in the 1960s when the field was (re)established all across public, North American higher education: an utterly unique phenomenon requires special methods housed in distinct disciplinary settings (or so it was then, and still, claimed). While this approach was indeed successful in the short term, helping to create autonomous departments of religious studies (as they're all mostly known in public universities on this side of the Atlantic), in the long term the specialness that we claimed for ourselves eventually served to isolate and ostracize us, setting us apart from possible allies in other units where yet other discrete aspects of human claims, behaviors, institutions, and artifacts were also studied. Being unique cuts both ways, after all. And so, to better understand the moment in which we find ourselves, let alone the current against which those trying to reinvent their units are probably swimming, understanding the extent to which a liberal humanistic model yet informs the field is necessary. And so, it made sense to open this section of a book contesting all of this with the following essay.

Rereading the following chapter, although it is now twenty years old, as I considered the contents of this new book convinced me that its argument is as relevant today as when it was first written, given that the presumption that what we study is somehow set apart from everything else, thereby requiring more delicate treatment than any other aspect of the human, remains as entrenched as ever. A result of this is that scholars, much like the media and politicians, not to mention many people going about their daily lives, regularly use this category "religion" in a variety of socially formative ways—it's good not just to think with but to act and organize with as well. Most often it is paired with its opposite and then used to sort the world into either this or that, usually related to each other in a ranked order (as is the case with many other binary pairs). I don't mean the sacred versus the secular here, though this pairing has rightly attracted much attention in recent decades and continues to deserve our time; rather, I mean religion versus that which is not religion *but looks an awful lot like it.* Or, better put, we could discuss authentic religion as opposed to its opposite, variously known, along a sliding scale, as everything from implicit religion, invented religions, and magic to superstition, political religion, cults, and even extremism or terrorism (it should be apparent that it's a sliding scale of otherness). In this way, most scholars of religion know which people to treat as truly special (and thus the method on which many of us continue to rely) and which to treat as (i.e., contest as) illegitimate and possibly dangerous. To put it another way, the history of our field has always been characterized by scholars playing favorites (and I think it is often rather more purposeful than my generous colleague Steven Ramey once argued [2015]), something they do by designating *this* group as orthodox and *that* group as heterodox (usually uncritically reproducing the classification employed by the dominant groups of the people under study); after all, every side in a war seems to call on its gods in their support. Sooner or later, someone is going to win the battle and designate *their* claims as heresy and *ours* as victorious orthodoxy; often, that rhetoric is just adopted uncritically by scholars who later come along to study it all, thereby authorizing propaganda as descriptive fact. That this process by which classificatory systems reproduce and entrench social affinities deserves to be studied should go without saying; it is likely at the heart of understanding how any group works over time and place—the old imperial chestnut "Divide and conquer" (Latin: *divide et impera*) can productively be redescribed as "Classify and conquer," as David Chidester once correctly observed, citing none other than F. Max Müller (Chidester 2003). But the fact that scholars of religion so easily fall into reproducing all of this themselves—and thereby protecting just some of the people whom we study and exposing yet others as frauds—is what I find to be indictable. To put it succinctly, a scholar designating some group of people as "mainline Protestant" is using something other than an innocently descriptive term; instead, when used by a scholar of religion as if it is a statement of fact, it is a full-throated affirmation of a group's own rhetorical efforts to authorize just one way of doing things—*its* way—in a competitive marketplace of actors and groups vying to take the representative lead.

The way to document this shortcoming in much scholarship on religion, at least as it is evidenced in the following chapter, is to look for which groups scholars protect by claiming that we must guard against "explaining away" their members' self-understandings and self-representations—explanatory work, that is, using frameworks other than those either provided by or sympathetic to the people under study, has long been ruled out of bounds by many of our colleagues. The other side of this coin, of course, is to find those groups for whom limiting scholarship on them just to description and interpretation would be seen by those same scholars as highly problematic. Case in point: find a group designated as a cult or extremists, and it will quickly become apparent that the role of the scholar in these cases is to figure out *why* anyone would even join such a group or do such a thing, an approach that calls for rigorous explanatory analysis, often of the psychological variety, and thus one that in no way conserves or authorizes the participants' own self-understandings. In fact, in such cases we're trying to figure out why anyone would even represent the world in this fashion or be attracted to such groups. Yet, for dominant groups, those with which many scholars may be familiar—from whose ranks many scholars themselves may have actually originated or with which they continue to be associated—our aim is rarely to *explain* them but, instead, to *interpret* what many claim to be their deeply abiding meanings. Few studies today aim to account for why someone would ever become or remain a Catholic or a Presbyterian, after all, yet such explanatory analysis abounds for groups with which most scholars share little affinity. I'd wager that looking up "Christian nationalism" in the literature today will yield few if any works aiming merely to understand, so as to better appreciate, how members of groups so designated see the world around them; instead, scholars are usually intent on accounting for the attractions of a movement uniformly represented in scholarship as an aberrant form of Christianity (i.e., one that fails to play nicely by the rules of liberalism).

Picking favorites and then adjusting one's methods and tools to suit those preexistent affinities and allegiances strikes me as evidence that, generally speaking, our field has never really adjusted to being a member of the university and a participant in that division some of us refer to as the human sciences. Instead, the onetime seminary model remains, if not in the curriculum (sure, church history and systematic theology courses were, for the most part, removed from our curriculums decades ago) then surely in the attitudes and assumptions that guide many scholars' choices and approaches. So, if we're going to do something different, to try to preserve the field in a higher ed setting sometimes not all that favorable to the traditional humanities, we need to address how our work often pits good guys against bad guys, all of whom are of our own making, rather than just getting on with the always difficult but also relevant work of studying how groups—any groups—work, even those of which we ourselves happen to be members.

The following chapter—which is long, I realize, but being told that your work dehumanizes people struck me as a pretty serious claim that needed to be met in detail—therefore explores all of this by juxtaposing a scholar who claims that our role is to respect and conserve the Other's agency with one who was once caught in a difficult situation where the Other spoke back, sometimes violently. This comparison seemed to me to be a particularly good place to think through some of the problems that I then found to be associated with the still dominant view in the field (and still do)—one that privileges and thereby protects just some of the people whom we study. For if we're to reinvent this field and provide a decent future for it, then developing an equal opportunity method, as we can call it, that treats all those whom we study the same by avoiding playing favorites by stacking the deck surely must be high on our "to do" list. Rethinking all of this will not come easy, of course, given the well-placed and therefore influential vested interests that have so far won the day in our field. Perhaps that's why the following chapter, when it first appeared, seemed to strike some readers as rather controversial; more than likely it is because of such controversy that it still is pretty much the only thing someone saw fit to write about when creating that small Wikipedia page that bears my name. What I hope is clear is that nothing here is meant personally; I don't think I've ever really interacted with Orsi in person, other than a question that I recall him asking of me from the audience after a presentation that I made long ago at the American Academy of Religion's annual conference. So, it's not about him and never was; after all, we invited him to join a project that Aaron Hughes and I co-edited not too long ago (Hughes and McCutcheon 2021), though, even after coaxing, he declined the invitation. So, I don't actually know Orsi and I bet his friends really like him; instead, it's about his work, which has become very important to a number of scholars today who continue to assume that religion is somehow a special case. This makes the way that he goes about his own scholarship, what with the very serious claims that he made about my own, a rather useful place to demonstrate what I see to be one of our field's nagging problems that need to be addressed if we're to move forward.

"It's a Lie. There's No Truth in It! It's a Sin!"

On the Limits of the Humanistic Study of Religion and the Costs of Saving Others from Themselves

How many things have to happen to you before
something occurs to you?
—attributed to Robert Frost

If, as Jonathan Z. Smith so often told us, gains in knowledge come about by means of unexpected, even provocative juxtapositions—quoting a teacher of his own, Smith once referred to this method as "an exaggeration in the direction of truth" (2024, 154)[1]—then I'd like to place alongside each other two scholarly texts concerned with methodology. For, when first reading them, they both prompted me to consider some of the costs to be paid when scholars of religion attempt to negotiate and thereby resolve issues of difference.

First, there was an essay written by Robert Orsi, devoted to reviewing my own 2003 collection of essays, *The Discipline of Religion*. Commenting on the manner in which the beliefs, behaviors, and institutions of human subjects are described in my book by means of that four-lettered word, "data,"[2] Orsi evaluated the book's method as "chilling," noting how

Epigraph: Quoted by the U.S. poet Edward Hirsch (as previously conveyed to him by William Meredith); see the conclusion of Hirsch's full National Public Radio interview, "For Hirsch, Reading Poetry Is Fundamental," April 8, 2006, https://www.npr.org/2006/04/08/5331955/for-hirsch-reading-poetry-is-fundamental. See the Spring 1985 issue of *The Paris Review* (vol. 95, 39) for Hirsch's interview with Meredith where this Frost quotation is discussed.

[1] Elsewhere, Smith phrased it as "the cognitive power of distortion" (1996, 19).

[2] See Smith (1997) or Lincoln (1999 and 2003) for examples of two other scholars of religion content with naming the human artifacts, actions, and institutions under study as data (in the

dehumanizing it is to study people in ways that they themselves have not authorized. When it comes to the scholar who thinks it necessary to subject human behaviors to such theoretical analysis, he asks: "From what authoritative and normative vantage point (or political or intellectual imperatives) is this need identified? . . . Nowhere—absolutely nowhere—in this volume is any reference made to the moral requirement of obtaining the consent of those upon whom this theoretical action is to be performed. . . . Rather, the assumption appears to be that the scholar of religion by virtue of his or her normative epistemology, theoretical acuity, and political knowingness, has the authority and the right to make the lives of others the objects of his or her scrutiny. He or she theorizes them" (Orsi 2004, 88). To drive home his critique, Orsi draws on a few hypothetical examples:

> a devout working-class man who kneels to pray at his wife's grave, suddenly uncertain and afraid at the end of his own life of what lies ahead, has attained the status of data; he has become a fit candidate for theorization. A suburban Pentecostal woman speaking in tongues, an Orthodox family preparing for high holy days, a Mexican migrant imploring Guadalupe for a healing, a pilgrim to the shrine of the imprint of Krishna's foot: these are our specimens, their words [according to McCutcheon] "*heuristically useful, everyday rhetorical fictions.*" Do the theorized have any voice to speak back to the italicizing theorizer? Can they challenge the assertion that they are in need of theorization or this construal of their lives? Can they protest being made into a theoretician's "fair game"? If they do, McCutcheon never says so, which is a serious omission: the data remain silent, as one might expect of data. A book that sets out to call attention to the dynamics of power/knowledge in the study of religion winds up proposing the most egregious exercise of power as the disciplines' fundamental work. And once again, religious studies can't look its subject in the eyes.

It strikes me that Orsi, in (what shall we call it?) villainizing my work, is here presenting a version of the late Wilfred Cantwell Smith's well-known methodological rule of thumb which presumed that, insomuch as they share a common human nature and thus dignity, both scholar and religious participant are involved in a consensual conversation. As famously stated in Smith's now classic essay, "Comparative Religion: Whither—and

former case, theologians are considered the data for the scholar of religion). That, as far as I am aware, no one has yet criticized either of these scholars for using this term strikes me as curious, given Orsi's rather strong reaction to my use of the term.

Why?" it goes as follows: "No statement about a religion is valid unless it can be acknowledged by that religion's believers" (1959, 42).[3] It would seem that for Orsi, much as it was for Smith, scholars risk presenting a false and thereby potentially harmful image of their research subjects if those subjects have not first signed off on these scholarly representations (what I take him to mean by "the moral requirement of obtaining the consent" of those whom we study). As already suggested, implicit here is the assumption that scholarship is a type of Habermasian conversation, comprised of a series of good-will negotiations between partners, in which the goal is to arrive at some sort of mutual understanding that either addresses (if not resolves) the differences between potentially competing systems of representation or at the least has the partners agree to disagree. Anything short of these and scholars can legitimately be judged as being immoral or—judging from their inability, at least in Orsi's estimation, to look their subject straight in the eye—perhaps even cowardly. For Orsi, then, it appears that scholars play the role of disciples and prophets, speaking only insomuch as they are authorized by an Other.

Curiously, in the hypothetical situations quoted above, Orsi fails to take into consideration those occasions when the Others whom scholars study do indeed speak up (or, better put, act up), but in ways other than some idealized, collegial conversation. And so, I turn to the second text that I would like to consider alongside Orsi's review essay: a brief article by Paul Courtright which, though first published in Emory's in-house periodical, *Academic Exchange*, was later republished in the American Academy of Religion's onetime hardcopy periodical, *Religious Studies News* (Courtright 2004). Titled "Studying Religion in an Age of Terror," Courtright makes use of what was at the time the well-known rhetoric of terror to reflect on the wider issues involved in the furor created by some people within the U.S.-based south Asian community when his award-winning book, *Ganeśa: Lord of Obstacles, Lord of Beginnings*, was reprinted in India in 2001.[4] With a cover depicting a small statue of a nude infant Ganesha (the elephant-headed

[3] Or, as my former colleague, the late Tim Murphy, reminded me long ago, this position is also nicely represented by the Dutch phenomenologist W. Brede Kristensen, who phrased it as follows (in the words of Eric Sharpe's English translation of Kristensen's 1954 work, *Religionshistorisk studium*): "If our opinion about another religion differs from the opinion and evaluation of the believers, then we are no longer talking about their religion" (Sharpe 1986, 228).

[4] The disputes ranged from an online petition posted by the Hindu Students' Council of the University of Louisiana, that attracted several thousand signatures, to anger expressed to Emory University's president by some well-placed members of Atlanta's local south Asian population, as well as actual threats against Courtright himself.

Hindu god), and a small portion of the text offering a Freudian analysis of Shiva and Ganesha's complex and, at times, violent father/son relationship (e.g., 2001, 114 ff.), the controversy prompted by this reprint calls to mind the similarly angry reactions to, among others, Jeffrey Kripal's 1995 book, *Kālī's Child: The Mystical and the Erotic in the Life and Teachings of Ramakrishna*, and James Laine's little 2003 book, *Shivaji: Hindu King in Islamic India*, along with such incidents as the egg reportedly flung at Wendy Doniger during her November 2003 public lecture at the London School of Oriental and African Studies.[5]

Although one could draw on a number of incidents and articles (many of which are available on the web) that exemplify what greeted Courtright's reprinted volume, consider this one-star review that can still be found at Amazon.com's website for the book. Dated August 17, 2004, the review reads as follows:

> A reading of this book revealed to me how Courtright, a professor of religion, who teaches Hinduism in a Christian university in the South, is so absurdly prejudiced—anti-Hindu. He has written utter profanities of a gross sexual nature, totally a fabrication originating from his filthy mind, like a pornographic novel, with no basis in any Hindu literature or source document. This is the most stupid book I have read on the subject. It is astounding how such bigotted [*sic*] professors are allowed to teach the religion they despise. He should be let go of the university so he can follow his true calling as an evangelical missionary in some remote corner of the world where he can fool some illeterate [*sic*] people to convert them to christianity [*sic*]—rather than practicing his craft in a university that I am

[5] As an aside, I should say that, when the earlier form of this chapter was first submitted to *JAAR*, one anonymous reviewer drew attention to the fact that, in some of the cases here cited, people other than those about whom the scholarly work was written took offense, implying that this essay's analysis is insufficient since the cited cases are all rather different from one another. To me, highlighting this point in an attempt to ungroup the cases here placed alongside each other (i.e., in an attempt to correct this paper's "simplistic" approach as it was described) is rather dubious, for it implies that scholars are in the position to decide who can legitimately be offended by their work. This, in turn, presupposes that one can rather easily settle issues of authenticity among the groups we study. However, this issue of authenticity (explored in greater detail in McCutcheon 2003, 167–188 and 2005b) can itself be understood as but one strategy to minimize and thereby manage a broad range of dissent, for it enables one to ignore those voices determined (by whom and using what criteria?) as coming from a so-called illegitimate fringe. Case in point: noting that Courtright's detractors were not from the group which he studied, making those protests somehow less legitimate, normalizes one set of standards for who gets to be counted as members of an offended group—a set of standards that certainly favor one way of portraying the issue by deauthorizing those U.S.-based South Asians who seem to have felt so offended.

> sure receives government funding in some way—that is: my taxes are going to support this hate mongering university professor. What a travesty of noble concepts like democracy, separation of church and state and academic freedom. This guy has trashed all these noble concepts in pursuit of his perverse agenda.[6]

Or consider a more recent, far briefer, one star review on the bookseller's site, this one from February 6, 2023: "Complete opinion with absolutely no merit. Courtright seems to be another disciple of the anti-hindu RISA cult [presumably referring to the AAR's Religion in South Asia section]. Maybe he might have better luck psychoanalyzing Mohammed or Joseph." Or, again, there's this one-star review from June 9, 2019: "False interpretation! Very misinformed! Naked propaganda to disgrace Hindu spiritual ideas and beliefs to weaken the backbone of robust Indic civilization. Dr Cartwright [*sic*] has been successful in promoting false interpretation of Lord Ganesha, who is the most venerable figure amongst the hindu gods. It offends hindu feelings because it's completely wrong and has been only published to strengthen and propel anti-hindu sentiments. Do not buy this book if looking to understand hindu culture. Wanted to give 0 stars but guess Amazon doesn't allow it!"[7] Reflecting on the affair of which such reviews are but a brief illustration, Courtright's 2004 article describes how "well-financed and organized groups on the political and religious right want to control the memory of India's past in ways that suit their own ideological agendas. Consequently, scholars within or outside India who challenge those constructions becomes targets of attack." Because, as he puts it, "to write is to resist the sloth of familiar forms of knowing and being in the world," Courtright understands scholarship long to have been "suspect by orthodoxies of one sort or another in many cultures." His brush with angry readers—though one never knows who, among his critics, has actually read his book—therefore provides evidence that, as he phrases it, "service to the pursuit of knowledge and understanding" can be dangerous business. Indeed.

Echoing Courtright's assessment of this controversy over what we often call "the insider/outsider problem,"[8] Wendy Doniger (who wrote the

[6] At the time of revising this chapter this review had received eleven responses claiming that it was helpful.

[7] Of importance to note is that all three of these negative reviews, according to the Amazon site, were posted from with the United States; in fact, all reviews, negative and positive, posted on the book's Amazon site are from U.S. customers.

[8] The very fact that differing viewpoints are considered a "problem" is itself the issue that requires attention; on this, see McCutcheon (2005b, 16–32).

foreword to both Courtright's and Kripal's books) has observed that, in the case of so-called Hindu nationalists at least, it is asserted that "no one who is not a Hindu has the right to speak about Hinduism at all" (Vedantam 2004; see also Braverman 2004). For William Dalrymple, writing in the *New York Review of Books* (2005), this amounts to nothing less than a war over India's history, a war that has profound contemporary political implications, none more central than the topic of concern here: the scholar's role when it comes to differing systems of representation.

Elaborating on what he sees this role to be, Courtright's brief article continues: "as a scholar and interpreter, my intent is not to demean, dismantle, or offend. Rather, it is to explore, probe, and imagine, using whatever approaches the content of the religious tradition and the tradition of critical inquiry call upon—even drawing on forms of interpretation that may not be indigenous to that tradition itself but may be illuminating and novel." Unlike Orsi's use of the language of *morality* to sanction one set of representations—those said to be in accord with, or at least sanctioned by the consent of, the subject's own self-representations[9]—Courtright speaks the language of *integrity* to legitimize yet another set of representations—those of the scholar, who potentially is writing contrary to participant self-understandings. He therefore concludes that: "The integrity of what we do must be protected" from the "self-appointed guardians of sentiment." And what scholars *do*, Courtright notes, is engage in "the pursuit of knowledge," otherwise described as "critical inquiry"—the sort of work that results in what one commentator has described as the "accessible, well-written, and balanced histories of India" (Dalrymple 2005, 65) that are, in this one reviewer's estimation, so badly needed in contemporary Indian schools.[10] To abandon the effort to produce

[9] As an aside, let me say that I recognize that Orsi does not say that participants must agree with our representations, but I have difficulty imagining many of our research subjects consenting to be—at least in their opinion—misrepresented, misquoted, and used for ends with which they disagree (e.g., submitting to naturalistic studies of their religion). The issue of *consent*, therefore, implicitly raises the issue of, to whatever degree, *assent*, implying the possible end to work that is seen as critical.

[10] Not to give away the punch line to this chapter so early, but (as intimated in an earlier note) who gets to determine this *need*, how do we decide what counts as well-written, and, most importantly perhaps, what constitutes *balance* (interestingly, this is the same argument Creationists once used, and which Intelligent Design proponents now use, to try to include their views in high school biology curriculums)—these are *the* questions that are unaddressed when we presume an *authentic* Other to exist in contradistinction to *illegitimate* Others. Such questions are generally left unaddressed, though, because scrutinizing the apparently self-evident criteria that commentators, such as Dalrymple, use to determine the elements that constitute this fairness would betray that *all* sides in these controversies are comprised of political actors (including scholars) working to normalize sets of local interests that are not

scholarship when our conclusions offend against the so-called self-appointed, local guardians of sentiment is—Courtright concludes, drawing once again on a vocabulary well known to anyone who was watching the evening news early on in the post–September 11 world—"to give victory to the vigilantes. To remain silent is to abandon our students and surrender ourselves to those who seek, through terror, *to erase us*" (italics added).

These two texts—Orsi's and Courtright's—are both meditations on a basic and well-known methodological problem; though basic, the issues involved endure (suggesting why these two dated texts remain relevant) and no single chapter can hope to juxtapose them in any adequate manner. Nonetheless, I wish to have readers consider why these two scholars' positions differ so much despite both having originated from within what I would characterize as the same liberal humanistic tradition in the study of religion. By this I mean one that understands religion's significance—as well as the significance of the study of religion practiced as a form of conversation, interpretation, and understanding—to have something to do with its being both deeply human *and* humane. Although I would not be so flippant as to say that what we have here are simply modern day instances of Mircea Eliade's well-known notion of a new humanism—in which the scholar is thought vicariously to re-experience the supposedly deep existential situations contained in the remnants and artifacts of other people's lives (e.g., see Eliade [1969] 1984)—I *would* argue that both Orsi's work and at least Courtright's early work are premised on the classic liberal humanist assumption, found all throughout the field, that scholars share a foundational commonality with their research subjects—call it "the human condition" or "human experience," if you will—making them all participants in a common dialogue that addresses and, ideally, overcomes the particularities that might otherwise situate and divide them. This is a view aptly summed up by Arvind Sharma, when, in an article on these very sorts of controversies, he is quoted as saying something akin to the old religious pluralist's parable of the blind men and the elephant: "both the insider and the outsider see the truth . . . but genuine understanding may be said to arise at the point of their intersection" (quoted in Braverman 2004). Although not accessible to any single one

necessarily shared universally. Simply put, there are very real interests at stake *on all sides* concerning, at least in the case at hand, what India's current sociopolitical and economic structure, and its citizens' sense of their past, ought to look like—an "ought" that's more than likely based on contemporary geopolitic interests rather than on the passive recognition of stable, factual self-evidencies. Sadly, it goes well beyond this already excessively long chapter to explore the geo-political aspect of the issues here being used as examples.

of us, there apparently *is* a big picture and collaborative representations are our best hope for getting at a "balanced" picture of it.[11]

I place Orsi's work into this tradition of seeking a supposedly balanced, genuine understanding not only because of his strong commitment to the moral requirement to obtain the consent of our research subjects[12] but also because of his interest, as expressed in the closing chapter to one of his books, in entering a mutual conversation with the Other "in order to discover something about human life and culture, about religion, and about ourselves" (2005, 178). This theme of using the study of religion to bridge the gap between Self and Other is found all throughout the humanistic study of religion, what with it being premised on the assumption of a common human condition that transcends or undergirds the particularities of historical existence; for example, recall Wendy Doniger's once well-known claim that what drives the study of other people's stories is the realization that "their myths have always been our myths, though we may not have known it. We recognize ourselves in those myths more vividly than we have ever recognized ourselves in the myths of our own culture" (O'Flaherty 1986, 224). Or think of José Cabezón's *JAAR* essay which, in a fashion supported by a variety of scholars today (notably some of those working with indigenous communities), redefines "theory" in order to pave the way toward a specific sort of pluralism, one that would allow elite religious participants to contribute what he terms their "indigenous theory" to our collective, scholarly conversation—an inclusion whose intended effect is the "weakening of the structures that under gird a facile Self/Other dichotomy" (2006, 25).[13]

[11] At the level of logic, it is unclear how those who hold this viewpoint arrive at it in the first place for, if we grant their premise (that local perspectives prevent one from seeing the whole—one already addressed in the introduction to this volume), then how can any local actor even know that there is a whole worth seeing? Simply put, the sort of "god's eye" perspective that this view says we do not have must be assumed from the outset for this position even to make sense to those who hold it. For additional comments on the parable of the blind men and the elephant, see McCutcheon (1997, 109–111) as well as McCutcheon (2018).

[12] Let me say at this point that I am not sure how this moral requirement can be applied to the artifacts we study which have been left by either recently or long departed human actors. Presumably, one would have to invoke a hermeneutical principle—such as authorial intention?—capable of portraying one reading of an artifact as the authentic, normative, or correct understanding, which could then be used by the modern actor to judge the accuracy, and thus adequacy, of scholarly readings. The problems involved in this speculative move should be more than apparent to a critical scholar.

[13] Unlike the technical understanding of "theory" as a systematically related set of propositions with predictive capability (which necessitates that they are empirically testable), Cabezón defines theory merely as critical, self-reflexive awareness (unfortunately, his essay does not offer a basis for distinguishing what constitutes critique). Curiously, such a redefinition of the category of theory has also been the preferred strategy of those aiming to have either

With this socially formative goal of collapsing the gap between Self and Other in mind, I turn to what I see as the unenviable position in which Paul Courtright found himself, when an Other vehemently disagreed with his representations and threatened to do something violent about it. What strikes me as curious in all this is that in Courtright's earlier work I think that we find the same liberal humanist viewpoint motivating his research as apparently does Orsi's. For instance, consider the preface to the Indian reprint of his book on the elephant-headed god. To pick but one simple yet telling example, in thinking back on his earlier fieldwork in India, somewhat like Sharma and Cabezón, Courtright acknowledges a plurality of "ways of knowing" by saying that "my categories of knowing and seeing do not exhaust all possible ways of knowing and seeing." This recognition prompts him to wish that, as a scholar, he could "find ways for people to represent themselves and be subject to less interpretation from me" (2001, xii, x). Because Courtright's earlier book came to my attention only after first reading his later article on methodology, I was perplexed to learn that the goal which he had once shared with many of his scholarly peers (of working toward ways of allowing the Other to represent him or herself, unimpeded by scholarly intermediaries) seems to have been dropped from his post-controversy article, in which Courtright warns readers not about the dangers of silencing the Other, as some others might phrase it, but, rather, of the very different danger of the scholar's own possible erasure!

So, to sum up: unlike Orsi's—and perhaps we should also add Courtright's pre-controversy—idea of the scholar, those whose legitimacy is linked to the degree to which they enter into what is characterized as a mutually beneficial dialogue with a consenting Other, Courtright's post-controversy idea of the scholar is legitimized by their autonomy, insomuch as they do *not* measure the adequacy of their academic work in terms of any one set of participant self-interests; for, given the variety of people we as scholars study, it is easy to imagine such interests actually threatening our

Creationism or Intelligent Design included in the high school biology curriculum. This approach was *not* persuasive in the recent case of Kitzmiller et al. v. Dover Area School District et al.; Judge John E. Jones's December 20, 2005, decision against teaching creation science in science classrooms—a decision premised on its utter inability to be empirically testable and, thus, it is not being a theory—is available at Kitzmiller v. Dover Area School Dist., 400 F. Supp. 2d 707 (M.D. Pa. 2005), Justia.com, accessed June 9, 2024, https://law.justia.com/cases/federal/district-courts/FSupp2/400/707/2414073/. On the effort to change the long-standing technical understanding of "theory" in our field, so as to undermine traditional distinctions between scholars and that which they study, so-called insider and outsider, and the possibly surprising similarities of this strategy to those adopted by Intelligent Design representatives, see McCutcheon (2024, 150–155).

academic institutions and the people who work within them. Instead, scholars are free, as Courtright phrases it in that short, post-controversy essay, to employ "forms of interpretation that may not be indigenous to that tradition." His idea of the scholar now treats the self-representations of living or past subjects (such things as texts, verbal reports, behaviors, architecture, etc.) as primary source materials that comprise the basis for subsequent scholarly acts of historicization and theorization (what I take him to have meant by his term "interpretation")[14] all of which follows the established conventions of the academy—conventions that can exist in sharp contradistinction to those of the groups under study. Yet these are the very conventions (the authoritative and normative vantage point, as Orsi names it) that scholars such as Orsi and Cabezón—and, ironically perhaps, those nationalists so angered by Courtright's, Kripal's, and Laine's books[15]—understand as imperialist strategies that dehumanize the participants by ignoring their agency and own right to self-interpretation.[16]

So, it was with Orsi's and Courtright's scholarly texts in front of me that I was struck by just how much they differed from one another, despite both being written from within the same scholarly tradition and both being deeply concerned with the practical ramifications of scholarship on the Other. For while Orsi occupies the *moral* high ground and chastises scholars who silence the Other, the post-controversy Courtright claims the *intellectual* high ground and laments when Others—or, to be more accurate, when a specific subgroup

[14] A further issue that could be raised involves teasing out the possible significance of assuming that the scholar is free to interpret *meanings* in human artifacts that subjects themselves have not understood or maybe even intended, on the one hand, and, on the other, a scholar's freedom to offer causal *explanations* for participant self-perceptions and actions. That is to say, although it is significant that he argues for scholarly autonomy here, the apparent assumption that our task is essentially interpretive may signal Courtright's continued position within a liberal humanist tradition that draws the line at offering causal accounts for *why* people may do as they do.
[15] To read an article that argues that, "whereas elite colleges in the West teach great respect for Greek and other Western Classics as being the bedrock of their civilization, it has become fashionable for elitist (i.e., Westernized) Indians to denigrate their own Indian Classics," which amounts to a postcolonialist attempt to "reclaim" representations of India from scholars, see the once well-known and, to many scholars, controversial article by the New Jersey–based businessman, Rajiv Malhotra, "Wendy's Child Syndrome," archived at "RISA Lila—1: Wendy's Child Syndrome," Thalua Club, Wordpress.com, accessed June 12, 2024, https://thethaluaclub.wordpress.com/2015/05/20/risa-lila-1-wendys-child-syndrome/. The site at which this is essay was originally posted, named "Sulekha," was established in 1998 and was an online community for what could be called members of the worldwide, professional Indian diaspora.
[16] To avoid these outcomes we need, according to Cabezón (2006), to encourage a dialogue intended to arrive at what he terms "theory parity" (31); if not, he asserts that such negative consequences as denigration and manipulation will result (29, 30), both of which amount to scholarship that dismisses the Other (30n25).

that Martin Marty, in an article on this very topic, identifies as "militants" (2004)—look us squarely in the eye and speak (and act) for themselves. For Orsi, the people whom we study are our conversation partners, perhaps even our collaborators, while for the post-controversy Courtright—though I do not believe he uses this particular four-lettered word—our research subjects comprise our data and there is no moral requirement whatsoever for us to converse with them so as to reach any mutually beneficial understandings. Rather, or so Courtright argues, as scholars we have an intellectual and institutional imperative to, at times, study people *precisely* in ways unwelcomed by them. For we, as scholars, do not study other people's myths because they embody our own hopes and dreams or because studying the "theories" that are implicit in their tales helps us "to challenge our theoretical parochialism" (Cabezón 2006, 30); instead, scholars study the artifacts of other people's worlds—regardless of who created them or who claims to own their meanings—because they are the curious site at which such scholars can use analytic methods of their own devising, to answer questions that are theirs, and not necessarily anyone else's.[17]

So, I think it fair to ask: What *is* the scholar's role when it comes to difference and disagreement—either between their research subjects (e.g., a question given much momentum after the attacks of September 11, 2001, i.e., whose version of Islam counts as authentic Islam?) or between their research subject and themselves? When are we, as academics, in a conversation with the Other and when do we suspend the Other's right to his or her first-person interpretive authority (on this once well-known term, see Godlove 1994)? As already suggested, to answer such questions we must first determine *which* Others we're talking about and this seems to necessitate determining which differences are just a little *too* different—and just what criteria do we use to make *this* judgment? For, judging from the lack of controversy that Courtright's 2004 *Religious Studies News* article's strong advocacy of scholarly autonomy generated among North American scholars who might otherwise argue that our role is to enter a collaborative and collegial dialogue with our

[17] There is a fascinating triumphalism to those who see scholarship's goal to be overcoming parochialism; instead, as will become apparent below, I am suggesting quite the opposite: all human systems of knowing and acting are best understood as parochial, through and through, and that scholars would be wise to consider their own interests as hardly coterminous with the interests of those whom they study. To presume otherwise—to presume that one's interests set the parameters of the so-called level playing field, thereby providing the terms in which all representations can be assessed—strikes me as the height of imperialism. That scholars compare across cultures is beyond dispute; the question is: Are such comparisons and generalizations a product of their own curiosities and the theories that they develop to pursue them or are their comparisons getting at deeply essential traits and objective realities? I advise opting for the former.

research subjects, it appears that there are indeed consensually recognized times when scholars are allowed (perhaps even encouraged?) to suspend Orsi's rules of order, without risking that our methods, and those who use them, are classified by our peers as inhuman or cowardly.[18] Simply put, how did Courtright escape the criticisms directed around the same time at my own work and my own character?

To begin to investigate the issue of consent and the limits of difference, we need to look a little more closely at the specific Others studied by our two representative scholars. Although Courtright's subjects—or better put, the interests of these research subjects and those who identified with them—are quite obviously removed from many North American scholars, in the case of Orsi, much of his work remains rather close to home—specifically, close to his own often disclosed social identity as a contemporary U.S. Roman Catholic. On a variety of occasions his work has contained admittedly endearing, semi-autobiographical elements and is explicitly concerned with the relationships between himself and people who, "always and already" (as Louis Althusser might have phrased it), understand themselves to share deep social affinities. They are those to whom, in the Acknowledgments to his earlier and still much read *The Madonna of 115th Street: Faith and Community in Italian Harlem*, he says he owes "a very special debt of gratitude" for their "gracious cooperation," for it was they who, as he puts it, "sat me down at kitchen tables, in empty churches, . . . in living rooms and offices, candy stores and restaurants, and told me the stories of their lives" (1988, x).[19] As

[18] In fact, instead of seeing as immoral his efforts to study Others in ways that are highly unacceptable to the research subjects themselves, Courtright reports in his 2004 *RSN* article that "colleagues in my own association, the American Academy of Religion, have been extraordinarily supportive in both the administrative leadership of the organization and also in the scholarly conventions specific to my area of inquiry." A request made to the AAR for copies of "any and all letters written by the Executive of the AAR in support of colleagues—such as Paul Courtright, Jeffrey Kripal, and James Laine—whose work has come under fire by members of the public" did not produce any results since, as I was told by the AAR's head office, such correspondence, whether or not it exists, is not public. Given that I have been a member of this organization for thirty-five years, this was indeed a very curious policy, what with the organization existing to represent its membership.

[19] I am indebted to one anonymous reviewer of this chapter's earlier version for pointing out that, in the introduction to his earlier book's second edition (2002), Orsi points out that he too has had subjects contest his work. Specifically, he reports that "a woman named Antoinette" once sought him out each year when he attended the feast of the Madonna (that he once regularly attended). Orsi reports there that, given the fact that the event now thrives, she asks when he will take out of his book the conjecture that the festival was waning when he studied it in the early to mid-1980s. "She is very passionate about this," he concludes, before informing his reader that her "accusation has long troubled me" (2002, xxix). Pointing out this minor though no doubt interesting disagreement, as did this one anonymous reviewer, strikes me as begging

anyone from an anthropologist doing fieldwork to a stand-up comedian can likely report, obtaining the consent of those whom one holds dear prior to making their disclosures public is undoubtedly a requirement, for to use their stories—or to tell your own stories about them—in any public venue risks betraying what might otherwise be seen as a shared confidence, possibly damaging a social relationship beyond the point of repair. With just such social affinities in mind it is undoubtedly significant that, in another of his books, Orsi felt the need to report that his Uncle Sal, who is the subject for the first chapter (2005, 19–47), read the article shortly before his death "and liked it" (2005, 3).

Although I do not wish to appear to minimize the no doubt important sentiment behind this disclosure (after all, who among us has not thought about dedicating a book to a family member?), I still feel compelled to ask, what are readers to do with this information? What does this seal of approval signal and why do we need to know about it? What does having one's research subjects approve of one's work have to do with assessing whether its analysis is persuasive or produces new knowledge?

While Courtright's thoughts on methodology came in the context of a no less social situation than Orsi's, its context was characterized not by affinity but by severe estrangement—for his research subjects, or those who felt akin to them, had also read what he wrote but they didn't like it one bit. So, instead of being invited to swap tales while seated around a homey kitchen table,[20] Courtright became the object of verbal assaults and was threatened with physical violence. In such a circumstance it is difficult to imagine any scholar still wishing that he could, as Courtright had previously stated, "find ways for people to represent themselves and be subject to less interpretation from me." Instead, Courtright seems to have been (quite understandably, I would add) unable to overlook the differences between himself and the people

the issues raised in this paper, for despite her so-called passion, this disagreement has none of the passion of those in the other controversial cases cited in this essay. Moreover, the fact that Orsi takes the following few paragraphs in his Introduction to explain and qualify his earlier and, as it turns out, mistaken conjecture about the future of the event demonstrates his own affinity for these research subjects. Aside: here, he informs his readers that more Haitian immigrants now attend than do Catholics of Italian descent, which suggests that Orsi was indeed correct in his earlier conjecture, for the event he studied some decades ago has indeed waned and been reconstituted as a new event, complete with formerly unheard of Vodou elements. The point being that the supposed homogeneity of the various instantiations of the feast is obviously apparent to a participant such as Antoinette; however, one would hope that the specificity and historicity of each is more than apparent to the scholar.

[20] See McCutcheon (2005b, 16–17) for an illustration of how storytelling can make evident social limits that, formerly, might not have been apparent to members of a group.

about whom he was writing, for they had no trouble representing themselves—it just happened that their representations resisted efforts to collapse Self/Other as many scholars in our field might have liked; and this resistance is perceived by us as threatening the institutions in which our efforts are carried out. Quite understandably, then, all of this leaves the no doubt well-meaning scholar with little choice but to attempt to interpret or explain the motives of his or her *detractors* (note: they are no longer *interlocutors*) in ways that they themselves would likely not sanction.[21] But does it all come down simply to shared interests and sentiments of affinity and estrangement (categories that I again borrow from Bruce Lincoln 1989; see also McCutcheon 2005a)? Do our methods change, all depending on who it is we're studying and whether we like them or not? Are we only able to say nice things about those who have already said something nice about us? Or, as our parents might have taught us, if we can't say something nice about someone, should we just keep our scholarly mouths shut?

To start answering some of these questions, consider the selection that resulted in Orsi's list of hypotheticals, quoted near the outset of this chapter: the distraught widower, the suburban Pentecostal woman, the Orthodox family, the Mexican migrant, and the pious Hindu pilgrim. They all present what appears to be a rather uncontroversial face of the Other, thereby easily allowing us to collapse any perceived (inconsequential) difference between each of them (the means whereby such a collection is created in the first place), let alone between "them" as an apparently uniform group (i.e., each are an instance of what we might term "the faithful") and ourselves as their observers—differences that are overcome by means of our appeal to a presumably deeply shared sentiment that unites us all (either faith or human nature). Accordingly, each member of this list exemplifies what I shall term the "no cost Other"—those whose toleration requires little or no investment on our part. Case in point: who would not first seek these people's consent

[21] I am reminded of a session at the March 10–12, 2006, regional AAR meeting in Atlanta, during which we were told that studying Others in the world religions class requires empathy and a serious commitment to dialogue. Such qualities, though, apparently ended when, as part of a paper on teaching the world religions class, the presenter described his school's local setting, which prompted several members of the audience, along with the presenter, to laugh at his portrait of the traditional patriarchal and rural/hunting values of his regional university's surrounding community. Apparently, these people were (due to their supposedly unenlightened ways?) undeserving of being taken as seriously as those who are studied in our classes. Laughter at scholarly panels such as this sometimes functions as an important, though unintentional, indicator of taken-for-granted norms and transgressions. Because the presumed norm can just as easily be seen as odd, in the words of Jean-François Bayart, "we should not smirk too readily" ([1996] 2005, 199).

before sharing with others the stories they may have told to us over a cup of coffee in their homes? They are not so-called agitators, revolutionaries, militants, or vigilantes; instead, they are crying, in pain, and engaged in the ritual (as opposed to political?) behaviors that strike many of us as being of such obviously universal significance that the inevitable distance between some posited "us" and "them" is inconsequential.[22] Much like the case of a politician being in favor of an ill-defined "freedom," there is no cost in identifying with the grieving widower. But what if the hypothetical widower was kneeling at a grave somewhere in, let's just say for the sake of the argument, the Gaza Strip in the spring of 2024, grieving a wife killed by an Israeli bomb? Or maybe we imagine a rather different person, one in the immediate aftermath of the October 7, 2023, attacks on Israelis, grieving a spouse killed on a kibbutz by members of Hamas? Will our scholarly treatment of these two possible research subjects all depend on the affinity that we happen to feel toward them? What if we, as empathetic scholars, did not find any of this grief so easily universalizable and thus identifiable? To press my counterexamples further, what if a hypothetical grieving widower's uncertainty and fear were, instead, utter certainty and anger that was directed at the people whose tax dollars and political leaders made possible a series of events that, from his viewpoint, had taken his partner away from him, forever—let's say, for argument's sake, a man somewhere in Iraq in 2004 or 2005. . . . What then would the empathetic American scholar make of the grieving widower? Would this man even tolerate such a scholar's efforts to engage him in conversation, to come to understand him? And if he did not, if he refused our overtures or if his response to us was far worse than that, what would prevent us from labeling him a radical for his unwillingness to converse?

As should by now be apparent, the no cost Other with whom some in our field so easily presume themselves to share such deeply human affinities hardly exhausts the people whom we, as scholars, might study. For there are many other voices out there, those that cannot so easily be catalogued in the "easy listening" section, for these voices may strike our ears as strident and harsh; they are *too* Other for their own good, for their differences from us are rather difficult for scholars to overlook. Although there may be little cost incurred when many scholars pay attention to the stories of the Orthodox family members preparing for their ritual celebrations, being attentive to

[22] I say "inevitable" because, to cite but one quick example, documenting the lives of Mexican migrants seeking healing presupposes scholars who have access to material resources unavailable to the migrant him/herself (e.g., the affluent ability to travel, often on someone else's dime).

those *other* Others potentially carries considerable cost—just ask Courtright, Kripal, and Laine and all of those scholars who tackle topics far from their own taken-for-granted worlds.

So, switching to those with whom Courtright ended up interacting—not the people whom, early on, he wished that he could *let* represent themselves (and notice that it is *always* the scholar who is doing the "letting"—not an insignificant point)[23] but, instead, those whom his representations seem to have so deeply offended—we should ask why *they* are so ripe for the kind of theorization from which we must apparently refrain when studying the politically harmless? Or, to rephrase it, how would the work of such scholars as Courtright, Kripal, Laine, and Doniger fare in the hands of scholars who put Orsi's rules of order to use? Would such scholars condemn as "chilling" Courtright's assessment of his vocal critics? For, if we grant to those we often designate as Hindu nationalists the same sort of descriptive generosity that we are called upon to grant to the grieving widower—that is, one that suspends speculating on their sincerity, ulterior motives, or subconscious desires and, instead, takes them *seriously*, as anti-reductionists once told us we ought to do—then I seriously doubt whether they see themselves as a well-financed, right-wing, international cabal intent on controlling India's image to suit their own idiosyncratic, ideological (i.e., unbalanced) purposes. Although I'm willing to entertain that I'm being terribly naive here, being descriptively generous I would say that many who fall into this grouping more than likely see themselves as not being ideological but simply correct, righteous, and expressing a self-evidency about India, Hinduism, world affairs, or even reality as such. If I am indeed correct, then, apart from our significant estrangement from what a university administrator might call such people's "goals and strategies," what warrant do we, as scholars, have for instituting a different set of rules when it comes to their study? To rephrase: Why do scholars so easily suspend this particular group's right to describe themselves, never feeling the need to entertain that their views are but one more "indigenous theory" that sheds light on our own sad parochialism?

[23] My larger theoretical point, as will become apparent below, is that human beings do not usually engage in self-representation; instead, more than likely they are simply immersed in, and thereby performing and inhabiting, their complex sociosemantic worlds. Only as a result of the curious nonparticipant arriving on the scene, making novel claims and asking unanticipated questions, is the so-called authentic Other constituted so as to engage in acts of self-conscious self-representation. As many before me have argued (Althusser among them, to be sure), the creation of Self/Other is therefore a complexly intertwined process, but this fact does *not* necessarily mean that the two parties are involved in a collegial conversation—just as the person hailed by the police officer in Althusser's famous illustration of the process of interpellation.

For instance, what would a scholar in Orsi's camp think of Bruce Lincoln (2003, 93–98) for making data of the texts that were left behind by, and which purport to communicate the self-understandings of, the September 11 hijackers? Although his work indicates that these disclosures can be read as—regardless of how the hijackers themselves may have understood them or how their remaining allies might understand them—highly useful rhetorics that accomplished practical, emotive/sociopolitical ends, I cannot imagine such colleagues calling Lincoln's method "chilling" for the way that it avoids ever addressing the need to obtain such Others' consent for his use of their texts.[24] I find it equally difficult to imagine these colleagues criticizing a scholar such as, say, Mark Juergensmeyer ([2000] 2001), who, despite working very hard to take seriously the self-reports of actors who engage in what he terms religious violence, ends his once well-known book, *Terror in the Mind of God*, by concluding that "the nature of the religious imagination . . . always has had a propensity to absolutize and to project images of cosmic war. It also has much to do with social tensions of this moment of history that cry out for absolute solutions, and the sense of political humiliation experienced by men who long to restore an integrity they perceive as lost in the wake of virtually global social and political conflicts" (242). Despite how enlightening these words may have been to many of his readers, it seems clear to me that the people studied by Juergensmeyer were not themselves talking about "the nature of the religious imagination," neither were they talking about cosmic war being merely an "image," and they certainly were not self-diagnosing their actions as attempts to compensate for feelings of humiliation. As with Lincoln, so too in the case of Jurgensmeyer: these are both instances of higher order analysis and theorization, well removed from any possible self-representations, that takes as its starting point—as its data, if you will—the disclosures and behaviors of a specific group of human subjects—*regardless of how they represent them for themselves*. In fact, those self-representations *are* the data for such analysis! But our ability to do this sort of higher order theoretical work is threatened by Orsi's sense of morality; for the research subject's right to challenge what Orsi characterized as scholars' "assertions" means that we will have to entertain quite seriously that, in the case of those who engage in acts of religious violence (or what some of them might simply call righteous violence or divine retribution—and here

[24] Instead, some U.S. readers (such as Kurson [2003]) might have been angered by the fact that Lincoln found similarities in the rhetorical conventions used in speeches by Osama bin Laden and George W. Bush (e.g., Lincoln 2003, 19–32). Simply put, in this case we apparently need to retain distance from the Other, with identification and common understandings the last thing that our work aims at achieving.

you see the kernel of my point: classification matters once again!), they might report that they do it simply because this or that powerful, nonempirical being told them to. Period. Full stop. End of story. This is what it means to entertain allowing research subjects to represent themselves in competition with scholarly representations. It means the end of the human sciences as we know them, for it implies using different methods for different people, all depending on how closely they agree with—well, let's just be honest for a change—some posited "us."

Although I admit that I fear belaboring the point (something I realize I have already done, but, given his own prominent position in our field [i.e., an award-winning author, former president of the AAR, and much cited scholar in the now prominent lived religion movement], I believe that his charges must be taken very seriously), it is worth considering the issue from yet another angle. As my onetime colleague Kurtis Schaeffer, who himself studies the politics of medieval Tibetan Buddhism, phrased the issue to me long ago: because the collection of behaviors we have come to know since the nineteenth century as "Tantrism" is widely known by scholars to be regarded by its practitioners as based on secret teachings, is someone such as André Padoux (1987a, 1987b) to be criticized for letting some indigenous cat out of the bag by writing not one but two encyclopedia articles on it? I have a feeling that those who adopt Orsi's position would likely not bat an eye when it came to assessing the legitimacy of scholarship on Tantra for they likely do not feel bound to keep this particular secret (but why not?).[25]

[25] The question is, must "their" secret be "ours" as well? If so, what do we make of the tremendous body of scholarly, not to mention popular, literature (i.e., everything from self-help manuals to titillation) that today exists on this thing we all seem to know as Tantrism. Mircea Eliade's classic work *Yoga: Immortality and Freedom* ([1954] 1990) alone has eighty-four index entries on the topic, one of which is a seventy-three page chapter titled "Yoga and Tantrism" which informs readers that "Tantric texts are often composed in an 'intentional language' (*sandhā-bhāshā*), a secret, dark, ambiguous language . . . [that] seeks to conceal the doctrine from the noninitiate" (249–250). That examples such as this, drawn from the works of some of the most influential scholars in our field, could be reproduced virtually without end should be obvious; examples pertaining to recent literature on Tantra alone are numerous, for we could cite Kripal's *Kālī's Child*, in which it is argued that the text English readers know as *The Gospel of Sri Ramakrishna* is structured as it is "in order to conceal, however intentionally, a secret" (3), David White's examination of the "widely advertised secret practices prescribed and described in sacred and secular literature" in his *Kiss of the Yoginī* (2003, 126), as well as Hugh Urban's contributions to tantric studies (2001a, 2001b, 2003). Are these scholars also to be chided for failing to get the consent form signed before they spilled the beans? A useful discussion of the ethics of research on tantra is provided by Urban, who is not oblivious to this issue: "Either . . . we must leave these traditions alone . . . or we must risk doing violence to ancient esoteric traditions to which we have no right" (Urban 2001a, 19). Drawing on the work of Pierre Bourdieu and Michel Foucault, the solution Urban offers to what he describes as an insoluble is

And they probably would have no difficulty when, for instance, they read Jeffrey Kripal concluding, in the preface to the second edition of his book on Ramakrishna, that the vocal critics of his book's first edition are deeply conflicted, "*whether they know it or not*" (1998, xiii; emphasis added). Used in this case, the normative epistemology—at least as a scholar such as Orsi might phrase it—that some would say is signaled by such "whether they know it or not" statements would, at least to some of our peers, more than likely be unproblematic, and thus hardly imperialist.[26] Such a statement is likely unproblematic because it reflects a confidence, more than likely shared among many members of the academy today, that sexuality ought not to be considered to be a taboo, shameful, or embarrassing topic and, therefore, that it rightly ought to be but one more lens through which we, as scholars, are entitled to view the lives of other people—whether these other people like it or not.[27] So, despite the fact such Others no doubt take their own self-understandings as seriously as might Orsi's hypothetical widower, the people who angrily contested Courtright's psychological reading of Shiva and Ganesha's relationship, those who angrily contested Kripal's discussion of the possible homoerotic themes in the life and writings of Ramakrishna, or those who stormed the library in India where Laine worked on the history of "Islamic India," are easily judged by us to have mis-read and mis-performed their own traditions, leaving them wide open for experts to try to account for their puzzling distance from the so-called orthodoxy (as is done whenever we hear such categories as "Fundamentalism" and "political religion" let alone "radicalism," "Hindu nationalism," or "Christian nationalism" being invoked in contemporary geopolitical analysis). Much like the flawed human beings in the movie inspired by Isaac Asimov's first collection of short science fiction stories, *I, Robot*, all of these people apparently need to be saved

to study not the secrets themselves (i.e., content) but the strategies that create the phenomenon known as secrecy (i.e., form). With all this in mind, it is curious to ponder the implication Orsi's proposed methodological rule might have for how we view Eliade's entire corpus, given his oft-repeated attempt to disclose and then compare instances of what he termed the concealed and camouflaged sacred.

[26] Readers must be clear: I am *not* making this charge myself but trying to imagine how those scholars who wish to (re)authorize the participant in some scholarly work might react to statements that presuppose such a scholar's so-called privileged insight into other people's subconscious motives.

[27] That is to say, some scholars likely see their role not simply to be that of using a category such as sexuality as a legitimate scholarly lens through which to study other people's worlds (i.e., it is part of a scholarly toolbox) but, also, to be that of persuading the so-called inhibited or repressed occupants of these very worlds that they are wrong in seeing it to be out of bounds. My suspicion is that our research subjects detect this distinction and are justifiably angered by those who adopt the latter position.

from themselves. For the film's robots were up to the challenge and they set about systematically eliminating us; in the cases that I am discussing here, it is the liberal humanist scholar who is prepared to make the tough calls and distinguish between the toothless pious and the radical fanatics, authorizing the former while paving the way toward dispensing with the latter by defining them out of "the faithful"—which is nothing other than excommunication by other means, since it requires scholars to make decisions on what is and is not theologically orthodox.

It therefore appears to me that those who speak back *indecently* (i.e., those who are unwilling to put up with our presumed ability to speak and act as we wish) are no longer counted among the sincere and are therefore fair game for theorization—and just what are the limits of decency, how are they judged, established, and authorized, these are the questions that ought to attract our attention as social theorists! But my hunch is that those who adopt Orsi's methodological rule would likely not critique the abovementioned colleagues for their strong advocacy of a brand of theory-based redescriptive scholarship that unapologetically deviates from a participant's own self-representations and self-interests—so long as these research subjects failed to play by *our* rules, for in such a case we already know that their self-representations are insincere, inauthentic, duplicitous, fanatical, militant, and maybe even criminal.

To bring home my point, consider what a scholar in Orsi's methodological tradition would make of the privilege that Orsi himself exercises when, in the opening pages to one of his books, he has the following to say about his own colleagues: "Whether contemporary Americans working to understand particular religious phenomena *know it or not*, they bring to their inquiries local histories. . . . Built into the very tools of analysis are *hidden* normativities, *implicit* distinctions between 'good' and 'bad' religions, and these *need* to be unpacked" (Orsi 2005, 6; emphasis added). Have his research subjects consented to this much needed unpacking? If so, as a scholar of religion working in the United States—the research subjects about whom Orsi seems to be making the above claim—I admit that I do not recall signing the form (aside: exactly how does one seek the consent of national groupings that we might study?). Or, instead, is this need based on Orsi's own intellectual and political interests, regardless of what his or her subjects think is in their own best interest? Like a house guest coming to stay for the weekend, do we, as scholars, unpack our subjects' baggage only with their consent, or as seems to be the case here, are some bags so obviously messy that, as good hosts, we have every right to tidy them up, whether invited or not? Come to think of it, because we are told in the above quotation that this baggage is hidden to the people about whom he writes (echoing that earlier "whether they know it or not" statement), it makes little sense even to think of asking them about it—much less seeking their permission to neaten it up—for, by definition, they don't even know it's there, much less that it isn't neatly ordered.[28] If, as Orsi goes on to write, "religious practitioners usually do not like to hear" what he characterizes as his own "critical, analytic questions" (12), then given the moral requirement to seek subjects' consent, what warrant does he offer for subjecting the material of their lives to what he acknowledges to be his unwanted scrutiny? Moreover, what reason could he have to invoke the supreme privilege, as he does, of presuming that his research subjects have an active subconscious where the *latent* source of the issue lies, undetected by the very people whom he studies? How is this any less chilling than any other methodology that treats human disclosures as data in need of theorization?

To see how all this plays out in his own scholarship, consider this book's last chapter, which critiques an Alabama journalist, Dennis Covington (1995), for silencing the people about whom he wrote in what was once a widely read book on snake handling Pentecostal churches in the Appalachian region of the United States. In this chapter, Orsi describes Covington's explanation for why the people he met, who live in rural northeast Alabama's Sand Mountain region, take the last verses of the Gospel of Mark, concerning the various signs of a true believer, so seriously: "[Covington] came to see snake handling as a way for poor, displaced people in a ravaged land to contend with and to surmount, at least once in a while, with the snakes in their hands, the violence and danger that bore down on them in their everyday lives" (Orsi 2005, 180). Then, a few pages later, relying on Covington's own ethnographic narrative as his own primary source, Orsi describes how one of the leaders of a local church who befriended Covington—a man named Punkin' Brown—himself sees it all: "Brown believed that it was God present before him that caused him to pick up snakes at meetings; he embodied, in other words, the enduring power of sacred presence in the modern world and in modern persons' imaginations and memories, from which presence is disallowed" (182). Indeed, there is considerable distance between the journalist's loosely Marxist explanation, on the one hand, and, on the other, Orsi's redescription of Covington's own description of this one participant's reported

[28] We see here some indication of why the use of Freudian theory by some of those scholars in question may have sparked such controversy, for it necessarily presupposes that the scholar's object of study is unknown to participants themselves. When this assumption can, and cannot, be invoked is the interesting question that requires attention (as already begun by Godlove).

self-understanding concerning a powerful being who controls the universe ensuring that the following words be written in the Gospel of Mark—and taken by followers with deadly seriousness: "And these signs will accompany those who believe: in my name they will cast out demons; they will speak in new tongues; they will pick up serpents, and if they drink any deadly thing, it will not hurt them; they will lay their hands on the sick, and they will recover" (Mark 16: 17–18). But are these two accounts in competition (i.e., what, exactly, is the *problem* with the so-called insider/outsider problem)? If so, then there must exist some external vantage point, some fulcrum, from which their differences can be assessed, a point from which one could work toward having Dennis Covington and Punkin' Brown arrive at a balanced understanding and thereby mutual respect. Judging by his own book's account, and like many an ethnographer before him, this is the assumption that Covington employs in first making contact with his research subjects (i.e., he engages in participant-observation); he befriends his hosts and, eventually, handles snakes in a service and preaches a spontaneous sermon or two of his own. This strategy is of considerable utility to the journalist (providing him with the sort of access that made it possible to obtain his book's many engaging stories)—until, that is, its limit becomes painfully apparent to him. For, taking a little too seriously the impression of unity that was created by his participation in the group, Covington reports, toward the end of his book, how he blundered by making a series of impromptu, public statements during a worship service concerning his strong views on gender equality, statements that he may have taken as inspired and self-evident but which, once spoken as part of his sermon in that small rural church, provided the occasion for the local male leadership to cast him out of the group; for they ceased their echoes of his preaching with shouts of "You're in the Word" and "Amen" and, instead, replaced them with cold silence. "You're out of the Word," Covington was finally told, just before Punkin' Brown took the microphone from him and preached an impassioned sermon of his own on the false doctrine of women having authority over men (Covington 1995, 226 ff.). As Covington records it, Punkin' Brown's sermon ended with the preacher catching his eye, saying: "It's a lie, Dennis. . . . There's no truth in it! It's a sin!" (235).

As should be all too evident from this brief episode, there is a tremendous price to be paid when we try to overcome the significant gaps and see the study of the Other as an opportunity for nurturing solidarity. When the gap is too great to overlook—and what constitutes "significant" and "too great," now that's the question that social theorists need to study—then what do we do? Do we champion the right of participants to interpret and represent their own words and worlds, recognizing that our shared humanity requires scholars just to sit politely and—recalling that lesson our parents taught us so long ago—keep quiet? Being a scholar myself, I suspect that just listening respectfully is not actually an option. Instead, I bet that we all do precisely what Orsi does in the above quotation: we put *our* words into *their* mouths and, for whatever reason, fail to recognize the sound of our own voices. With this in mind, let me repeat Orsi's report of what he claims to be Punkin' Brown's own understanding of snake handling, and, this time, pay careful attention to the important shift signaled by the phrase, "in other words": "Brown believed that it was God present before him that caused him to pick up snakes at meetings; he embodied, *in other words*, the enduring power of sacred presence in the modern world and in modern persons' imaginations and memories, from which presence is disallowed" (emphasis added). This is a fascinating (and for most readers, undoubtedly undetected) rhetorical move, especially given the manner in which Covington, just earlier in Orsi's chapter, is criticized rather harshly for offering what Orsi describes as a "humiliating" representation of "Punkin' Brown"—a name that Orsi here places in quotation marks, presumably to distinguish Covington's mere representation from Punkin' Brown himself, thereby signaling to Orsi's reader the way that the preacher was inappropriately "constructed" and "rendered," as Orsi phrases it, into Covington's *version* of "Punkin' Brown" (2005, 182)—resulting in a stereotyped, exotic character that, as Orsi puts it, "makes the world safe again for Covington and his readers" (181).

But paying a little more attention to Orsi's own text demonstrates that he has made a classic error common to a number of liberal humanist scholars, what Wayne Proudfoot once called the confusion of descriptive reductionism, which scholars all agree must be avoided, with the explanatory reduction that inevitably characterizes every scholar's work (1985, 96 ff.). For immediately following his attempt to describe (i.e., to present) what a research subject might say about his own motives for handling snakes (i.e., he handles them because God told him to), Orsi signals a transition by means of "in other words" (i.e., to re-present), and then goes on to do just that: *he offers words other than those the research subject might himself offer, all in the guise of describing things from the indigenous subject's point of view*. Moreover, the *other words* Orsi offers are those of an Eliadean cross-cultural comparativist who understands local practices as a disguised instance of an otherwise uniform sacred presence, one that is manifested in the actions and artifacts of a diverse collection of others, *whether or not* these people themselves understand their behaviors to be but one relative node in a cross-cultural system of signification—at least I seriously doubt whether someone such as Punkin' Brown, what little I've read of the man, sees it this way. In fact, upon hearing Orsi's thoughts on how both the Appalachian snake handler and the Hindu pilgrim at the shrine of the imprint of Krisha's foot "embodied . . . the enduring power of sacred presence in the modern world," I can only imagine that someone such as Punkin' Brown would catch Orsi's eye and sternly reply: "It's a lie, Bob, There's no truth in it! It's a sin."

For, at least according to my ears, snake handlers say something remarkably different from a scholarly observer such as Orsi. For instance, consider the following quotation, transcribed from an explanation offered by Jimmy Williams—the main informant in "They Shall Take Up Serpents," a once well-known 1973 documentary on snake handling in east Tennessee. Speaking directly to the camera, beside the bed of a man who was "serpent bit" at that evening's service, he says:

> The reason that we take these serpents up is the Bible recommends to do it and all the apostles did it—everyone that believes. Jesus said these signs shall follow them that believe. He said, "In my name shall they cast out devils, they shall speak with new tongues, they shall take up serpents, and if they drink any deadly thing it shall not hurt them. They shall lay hands on the sick and they shall recover." Now, we believe that this interpretation of the scripture is for them that believe. In other words, them that believe, they shall take up serpents.[29]

What's his "indigenous theory," as Cabezón might name it, for his actions? The Bible says to do it, which means that Jesus said to do it. And all of the apostles did it. Therefore, we do it. Simple as that.[30]

[29] *They Shall Take Up Serpents*, produced by John E. Schrader and Thomas G. Burton (Eastern Tennessee State University, 1973). This documentary was filmed in early 1973 in Newport, Tennessee. Anyone familiar with this film—once widely used in our field—knows that, at its end, viewers are informed that Jimmy Williams died on April 8, 1973, while attending a service and ingesting strychnine. My thanks to my onetime student, Jennifer Goodman, for transcribing this segment of the film.

[30] That the ethnographer who has obviously posed some such question to him as, "Why do you handle snakes in your worship service" (to evoke this answer) is not seen in the film exemplifies the problems examined in this paper. Students once viewing the film would quite reasonably come away thinking that participants spontaneously and authentically engaged in acts of self-representation; if so, then our task, as scholars, is merely to listen carefully and faithfully record their words. However, taking into account the presence of the filmmakers/fieldworker (as a previous generation of anthropologists, e.g., James Clifford et al., told us so convincingly) makes it evident that the so-called participant is in fact *a creation of the curious observer.*

At least as I see it, then, Orsi's "other words" concerning the enduring power of sacred presence are therefore just that, entirely different words placed into a subject's mouth, *as if* they expressed sentiments lodged deep within a subject's subconscious and therefore known only to the careful (i.e., privileged) interpreter. Yet to my way of thinking, they are Othering words, *as is the case with all language and all representation*—and this is the point that many in the liberal humanist tradition, in their efforts to speak on behalf of humanity *an sich*, utterly fail to comprehend!—and not an innocent paraphrase of a universal subject's own self-perceptions. Instead, like all acts of signification, Orsi's "other words" are a translation of one set of claims into a language that is itself no closer than any other to some presumably authentic source of the Nile. To put it simply, *all* "Punkin' Brown"s ought to be written in quotation marks, not just Covington's but Orsi's and my own as well—for how could either mine or Orsi's representation be any closer to the authentic man, for both of our readings are based on Covington's text. Come to think of it, even the late Punkin' Brown's own sense(s) of himself deserve the same quotation marks—a point nicely made by Jorge Louis Borges in a little piece titled "Borges and I" in which, alienated from his own persona as famous author, he remarks: "I live, I allow myself to live, so that Borges can spin out his literature" ([1989] 1999, 324).

With this in mind, we can say that mistaking a representation for the real—and if Jean Baudrillard is to be trusted, then all we have are representations, each competing for the chance to stand in for a Real that never was present to begin with—was also a problem with Orsi's description of the "devout working class man who kneels to pray at his wife's grave, suddenly uncertain and afraid at the end of his own life of what lies ahead"? Like most readers, I too have experienced the deaths of loved ones, but how does one generalize from this to read this one man's mind? I suspect that there are any number of things going through this hypothetical widower's head, including the uncertainty and fear that Orsi qua privileged narrator somehow intuits, along with panic, desperation, loneliness, anger, even guilt—who knows what else. In fact, we may be in error in approaching our speculative thought experiment in the manner of Orsi, for I'm not even sure that, at the moment that this lone man catches the scholar's attention—becomes an item of discourse—anything much is actually going through his head. Not that he's oblivious to his surroundings or "overcome by emotion," as we sometimes say, but that, much of the time, human beings are completely immersed in their social worlds in rather unreflective ways, with nothing in particular in their heads, as it were, with no stories to tell let alone criteria to use in distinguishing a generic happening from an occurrence (recalling the words attributed to Robert Frost that appear as this chapter's epigraph). Case in point, I presume that, although many readers are by now wondering when I will signal that this chapter is drawing to a close—which will be soon, but not quite yet—few are now contemplating the significance of, say, their use of English grammar to make the symbols that appear on this page into units of meaning—though, now that the nonparticipant to their so-called immersive reading experience has made this apparent commonplace of their world curious to them, no doubt some readers are mulling it over and, if asked, could go on at some length about it. But scholars of signification will likely not measure the adequacy of their work in light of the participant's hindsight reflections on their reading experience (i.e., despite both being engaged in signification, at least to the scholar they are not necessarily working toward the same goal and are therefore *not* in competition with each other); instead, such scholars will set about describing and then analyzing a series of observable behaviors of which the participant may be completely unaware, seeing the participant's self-reflections on the process, if there are any, as but one more piece of data in need of analysis.

What I have in mind here is precisely what the mid-twentieth-century British novelist, Bryan Stanley Johnson, wrote about in his 1973 memoir: "Life does not tell stories. Life is chaotic, fluid, random; it leaves myriads of ends untied, untidily. Writers can extract a story from life only by strict, close selection, and this must mean falsification. Telling stories really is telling lies" (Johnson 1973, 14). If, as I'm suggesting, readers of this text are not necessarily spontaneously doing the choosing, highlighting, and ignoring that produces a narrative about the occurrence of their current subject-position as "readers"—but, instead, are immersed in a series of happenings and thereby acting out a subjectivity only apparent in hindsight—then scholarship is not a matter of an observer qua stenographer respectfully recording the widower's dictated reflections on his grief. Instead, it is more a matter of an observer, much like an ethnographic filmmaker, interrupting this man's world by posing unanticipated questions (i.e., by interpellating him) that prompt him to articulate something that wasn't necessarily in his head to begin with, prompting him to fabricate a story that, prior to being given its starting point—such as, "Why are you crying?"—wasn't a story at all, at least not to him. If this is the case, if the complexity of this thing that we call reality is only experienceable (i.e., as a series of connected occurrences rather than disjointed happenings) once a non-indigenous framework is brought to bear (i.e., made into an item of discourse), then Orsi's methodological rule, which on the surface appears to protect the meek, is nothing other than a cleverly disguised paternal strategy that enables scholars to portray themselves as being in solidarity with the Other while retaining the right not only to distinguish some Others from other Others, but also to inform both groups where their stories ought to start and end. For this methodological rule, like that of Smith, is a triumphalistic move that ensures such scholars' absolute monopoly over the means of representation, for they both speak and then report on their own words, all the while attributing the speech to their research subjects. It is somewhat akin to the manner in which government officials sometimes leak information to the press and then turn around and publicly quote the reported leak in support of the position that they are advocating; it strategically exercises a passive aggressive form of authority in which the supposedly authentic human subjects—to borrow some of Orsi's own words—remain silent despite the humanist's claims of listening carefully and empathetically. Much as in his critique of my own work, apparently Orsi's "other words" require no rationale or defense, for, to paraphrase him once again, the liberal humanist, by virtue of his or her normative epistemology, theoretical acuity, and political knowingness, apparently has the authority and the right to be a ventriloquist, for he or she speaks for those others who do not have the good sense or ability to recognize their misplaced emphasis on difference and particularity.[31]

But if, as Bryan Stanley Johnson claims, all representation is inevitably a form of falsification—regardless of who is doing the storytelling—then we, as scholars, should be a little more careful of the tales that we choose to tell and in whose voice they are being told. Recognizing that much comes down to the act of choice[32] prompts us to adopt a rather more humble scholarly approach than we often find in the work of liberal humanist mind-readers in our field; for, despite the proclaimed and often much celebrated empathy for their subjects of study, like everyone else they have no choice but to deploy concepts and interests alien to their object of study; it's just that they seem to assume that their language and their interests are coterminous with reality and universally shared, which supposedly allows them unimpeded access

[31] It is worth noting that, when responding to an earlier version of this essay that was presented as a public lecture at Trinity College in Toronto, Jeppe Sinding Jensen thought the image of a cannibal to be far more apt than a ventriloquist.

[32] Although his thoughts on religion being "solely the creation of the scholar's study" have certainly influenced my own work in profound ways, I have come to think that the far more important insight contained in the opening pages to J. Z. Smith's *Imagining Religion* appear a little lower on the page, concerning this topic of choice: "The student of religion must be able to articulate clearly why 'this' rather than 'that' was chosen as an exemplum. His primary skill is concentrated in this choice" (1982, xi).

to the grieving widower's heart.[33] And it's just this self-serving assumption, obviously detected by those research subjects who fail to recognize themselves in the supposed mirror held up to them by liberal humanists, that likely angers some people so much; the limits of the liberal humanist bait and switch are more than apparent to them.

So, to return to some of the rhetorical questions posed earlier, I fear that I have gone on far too long with hints, and, instead, owe readers a straightforward answer: so here it is. When it comes to the liberal humanists whom I have studied, they diligently work to sanction those Others either toward whom they already feel affinity or toward whom they feel very little estrangement—those Others whose differences from some posited "us" and our interests and norms can either be explained away or, because they strike us as utterly inconsequential, simply overlooked altogether. It is easy, of course, to tolerate those whom one feels to be of no import. However, when the differences of historical existence cannot be ignored, when the estrangements are painfully apparent because they strike at what the classic Marxist might once have termed the base, then we instead understand these other Others to have relinquished their right to be taken seriously as conversation partners, for they have committed the mortal sin of taking themselves as seriously as we take ourselves; in so doing, they call into question our self-declared right to set the parameters for what gets to count as "decency" and "civility."[34] In response, we withhold the classifications "religion," "faithful," and "spiritual" and excommunicate them from the body of the faithful, giving these people new names, all depending on the degree to which some posited "us" feels estranged from, or threatened by, "them": they can be classified as mildly curious and tolerated as exotic specimens, they can be understood as deviants and thereby diagnosed and deprogrammed, or portrayed as outrightly dangerous and attacked or jailed as enemies.[35]

My suspicion, then, is that scholars in the liberal humanist tradition never have to think twice about whom to include in their list of the faithful, for

[33] As noted in my brief reply to Orsi's review (2004), that a hypothetical grieving widower, among others, is used as a trope in an essay meant to score rhetorical points strikes me as begging a series of crucial questions concerning just what type of morality Orsi implies.

[34] See Colas ([1992] 1997) for an excellent study on the politics of discourses on civility.

[35] Despite the universalist rhetoric of the humanist position that undergirds the liberal democratic nation-state, there are far too many examples of how the so-called humanity of anyone can easily be defined away, especially those known as "cult fanatics" and "political extremists"—those who, despite holding the sort of "deep beliefs" that we are so often told we ought to respect and take seriously, happen to hold the wrong set of deep beliefs.

they are already seated with them at their kitchen table, swapping stories, and enjoying their no doubt kind hospitality. Only those who are bold enough to involve themselves actively in contesting how our world works need to be explained and thereby saved from themselves, for their all too apparent interests prevent us from ever being invited into their homes, prompting us to resolve our differences by defining these other Others out of the tradition of the faithful, by saying to them "You're not in the Word." Their subsequent protestations simply confirm the line that we have drawn. As for those who pose no threat to our world, they are in no position to challenge our representations; we can therefore speak for them, answering "Amen" to our own other words, without ever fearing reprisals, for we resolve our little differences with them by simply ignoring them.

In both cases, our attempt to resolve conflict and difference, to borrow a few words from Courtright, "is not without its price" (2001, 116).[36] In my estimation, the price that we pay when we worry over how scholarship silences the indigenous voice, a concern that prompts us to try to mediate and resolve difference, amounts to (to paraphrase Lincoln's thirteenth thesis [1996, 227]) forfeiting our role of being anything but dedicated disciples to one set of voices, no longer able to be scholars of how the disciplining process happens to take place. But it is a forfeiture that comes with far too high a price: the end of the very institutions in which we carry out our work. It is therefore rather ironic that fretting over erasing Others ends up in our own demise.

Addendum

Those familiar with some of Orsi's more recent work might counter that, whether or not it was relevant for the work that he produced twenty years ago, the foregoing critical response is no longer applicable, perhaps citing as an example his 2022 review essay on Shaul Magid's book, *Meir Kahane: The Public Life and Political Thought of an American Jewish Radial* (2021). There, Orsi makes what those familiar with his earlier work might read as a surprising series of statements concerning the fact that the way that scholars of religion go about their work should "give comfort neither to religious practitioners nor to their adversaries, we will be agents neither of the state nor the temple" (2022, 316). This claim is inspired by Magid's use of the comparative method in examining the degree to which Kahane (1932–1990)—the politically conservative/nationalist American Orthodox rabbi

[36] Courtright is here talking about the resolution of the child/parent conflict as represented in the story of Ganesha.

and cofounder of the Jewish Defense League who was eventually convicted in the United States of domestic terrorism, then immigrated to Israel, was elected to its federal government, and murdered when back in New York by an Egyptian-born American—broadly represents the views of a surprising number of American Jews today. Instead of simply juxtaposing bad religion (Kahane) with good (the way some say Judaism ought to be practiced), as many scholars and certainly pundits might, Orsi praises Magid for finding a number of similarities when comparing Kahane to a variety of other social actors, both from within and outside of Judaism (e.g., Malcolm X). It's therefore no longer about such simplistic good/bad dichotomies, Orsi concludes, which might lead some to decide that he has just undermined the above critique's focus on the role played by the no cost Other, what with Kahane being a social actor who, for many, seems so costly an Other as to not even be mentioned in many contemporary histories of American Judaism.

In reply, I'd argue that, despite appearances, little has changed, since the whole point of such a comparative project seems to be to document and account for "the seepage of Kahane's 'radicalism' in the Jewish 'political and cultural mainstream'" (316; Orsi is here citing the phrasing of Magid [2021, 197]). Accordingly, far from "destabilize[ing] the solidity of the good/bad religion distinction" (316), as Orsi puts it, the project seems to be all about accounting for how and why one has impacted the other (evidence again of just when explanatory work is indeed encouraged in our field). While this may at least move the needle forward somewhat, by seeing these two supposedly distinct domains as not so isolated from one another, it strikes me as conserving the old distinction, nonetheless, by focusing on how one influences the other. In good J. Z. Smithian fashion, Magid is certainly to be commended for, as Orsi put it, "render[ing] Kahane recognizable in the context of his times" (313), doing so by means of his use of the comparative method; but the implication of this work, at least according to this review essay, is not to study the socially formative impact of the good/bad religion distinction itself (as was done so nicely by the contributors to Smith, Führding, Hermann 2020), but, rather, to study the interaction of the two separate domains, a move that conserves the distinction rather than historicizing it as a socially formative rhetorical technique. If I am correct in this reading, then for many scholars of religion today the no cost Other remains the center of our efforts to understand and appreciate—no one here is advocating that we study Kahane in that fashion, after all—while we deploy rigorous explanatory methods to account for Others who bring with them far higher costs.

And, by the way, as I've written elsewhere, the reason that I prefer this word "data" is because it owns (by making apparent) that the frameworks and curiosities that prompt either this or that to seem to stand out as worth examining are brought to the situation by the scholar. Instead of obscuring and thereby naturalizing and authorizing those choices and assumptions, *as if* the world just is naturally interesting in either this or that way, "data," in my reading, ensures that readers feel removed from the supposed authenticity and immediacy of some text, action, or group, keeping ever-present for them that our role as scholars—the questions that we pose when made aware of something—is what constitutes some generic item in someone else's world *as* an object of study in our own. Failing to do this, to draw attention to a scholar's own choices, therefore strikes me as a rather imperialistic move.

References

Bayart, Jean-François. (1996) 2005. *The Illusions of Cultural Identity*. Translated by Steven Randall et al. Chicago: University of Chicago Press.

Borges, Jorge Louis. (1989) 1999. *Collected Fictions*. Translated by Andrew Hurley. New York: Penguin.

Braverman, Amy M. 2004. "The Interpretation of Gods: Do Leading Religious Scholars Err in Their Analysis of Hindu Texts?" *University of Chicago Magazine* (December) 97 (2). http://magazine.uchicago.edu/0412/features/index.shtml.

Cabezón, José Ignacio. 2006. "The Discipline and Its Others: The Dialectic of Alterity in the Study of Religion." *Journal of the American Academy of Religion* 74 (1): 21–38.

Chidester, David. 2003. "'Classify and Conquer': Friedrich Max Müller, Indigenous Religious Traditions, and Imperial Comparative Religion." In *Beyond Primitivism: Indigenous Religious Traditions and Modernity*, edited by Jacob K. Olupona. New York: Routledge.

Colas, Dominique. (1992) 1997. *Civil Society and Fanaticism: Conjoined Histories*. Translated by Amy Jacobs. Stanford, CA: Stanford University Press.

Courtright, Paul B. 1985. *Ganeśa: Lord of Obstacles, Lord of Beginnings*. New York: Oxford University Press.

———. 2001. *Ganeśa: Lord of Obstacles, Lord of Beginnings*. Delhi: Motilal Banarsidass.

———. 2004. "Studying Religion in an Age of Terror." *Religious Studies News* 19 (4): 19.

———. 2006. "The Self-Serving Humility of Disciplining Liberal Humanist Scholars: A Response to Russell McCutcheon." *Journal of the American Academy of Religion* 74 (3): 751–754.

Covington, Dennis. 1995. *Salvation on Sand Mountain: Snake Handling and Redemption in Southern Appalachia*. New York: Penguin.

Dalrymple, William. 2005. "India: The War over History." *New York Review of Books* 52 (6) (April 7): 62–65.

Eliade, Mircea. (1954) 1990. *Yoga: Immortality and Freedom*. Translated by Willard R. Trask. Princeton, NJ: Princeton University Press.

———. (1969) 1984. "A New Humanism." In *The Quest: History and Meaning in Religion*. Chicago: University of Chicago Press.

Godlove, Terry. 1994. "Religious Discourse and First Person Authority." *Method & Theory in the Study of Religion* 6: 147–161.

Hughes, Aaron W., and Russell T. McCutcheon, eds. 2021. *What Is Religion? Debating the Academic Study of Religion*. New York: Oxford University Press.

Johnson, Bryan Stanley. 1973. *Aren't You Rather Young to Be Writing Your Memoirs?* London: Hutchinson.

Juergensmeyer, Mark. (2000) 2001. *Terror in the Mind of God: The Global Rise of Religious Fundamentalism*. Berkeley, CA: University of California Press.

Kripal, Jeffrey. 1995. *Kālī's Child: The Mystical and the Erotic in the Life and Teachings of Ramakrishna*. Chicago: University of Chicago Press.

———. 1998. *Kālī's Child: The Mystical and the Erotic in the Life and Teachings of Ramakrishna*. 2nd ed. Chicago: University of Chicago Press.

Kurson, Ken. 2003. "Professor Denies Justifying 9/11 While Doing Exactly the Same." *Chicago Sun-Times*, March 15. Editorial Letters.

Laine, James. 2003. *Shivaji: Hindu King in Islamic India*. New York: Oxford University Press.

Lincoln, Bruce. 1989. *Discourse and the Construction of Society: Comparative Studies of Myth, Ritual, and Classification*. New York: Oxford University Press.

———. 1996. "Theses on Method." *Method & Theory in the Study of Religion* 8: 225–227.

———. 1999. *Theorizing Myth: Narrative, Ideology, Scholarship*. Chicago: University of Chicago Press.

———. 2003. *Holy Terrors: Thinking about Religion after September 11*. Chicago: University of Chicago Press.

Magid, Shaul. 2021. *Meir Kahane: The Public Life and Political Thought of an American Jewish Radical*. Princeton, NJ: Princeton University Press.

Marty, Martin. 2004. "Scholars of Hinduism Under Attack." *Beliefnet*. http://www.beliefnet.com/story/128/story_12899_1.html. Originally published as "Hyper- and Havoc in Hindu Studies." *Sightings* (May 10, 2004). https://divinity.uchicago.edu/sightings/articles/hyper-and-havoc-hindu-studies-martin-e-marty.

McCutcheon, Russell T. 1997. *Manufacturing Religion: The Discourse on Sui Generis Religion and the Politics of Nostalgia*. New York: Oxford University Press.

———. 2001. *Critics Not Caretakers: Redescribing the Public Study of Religion*. Albany: State University of New York Press.

———. 2003. *The Discipline of Religion: Structure, Meaning, Rhetoric*. London: Routledge.

———. 2004. "A Few Words on the Temptation to Defend the Honor of a Text." *Bulletin of the Council of Societies for the Study of Religion* 33 (3&4): 90–91.
———. 2005a. "Affinities, Benefits, and Costs: The ABCs of Good Scholars Gone Public." *Method & Theory in the Study of Religion* 17 (1): 27–43.
———. 2005b. *Religion and the Domestication of Dissent, or How to Live in a Less than Perfect Nation*. New York: Routledge.
———. 2006. "A Response to Paul Courtright." *Journal of the American Academy of Religion* 74 (3): 755–756.
———. 2015. "It's a Lie. There's No Truth in It! It's a Sin!": The Cost of Saving Others from Themselves." In *Claiming Identity in the Study of Religion: Social and Rhetorical Techniques Examined*, edited by Monica Miller. Sheffield: Equinox.
———. 2018. "Historicizing the Elephant in the Room." In *Irreverence and the Sacred: Critical Studies in the History of Religions*, edited by High Urban and Greg Johnson. New York: Oxford University Press.
———. 2024. *Critics Not Caretakers: Redescribing the Public Study of Religion*. 2nd ed. New York: Routledge.
O'Flaherty, Wendy Doniger. 1986. "The Uses and Misuses of Other People's Myths." *Journal of the American Academy of Religion* 54 (1986): 219–239.
Orsi, Robert A. 1988. *The Madonna of 115th Street: Faith and Community in Italian Harlem, 1880–1950*. New Haven, CT: Yale University Press.
———. 2002. *The Madonna of 115th Street: Faith and Community in Italian Harlem, 1880–1950*. 2nd ed. New Haven, CT: Yale University Press.
———. 2004. "Fair Game." *Bulletin of the Council of Societies for the Study of Religion* 33 (3&4): 87–89.
———. 2005. *Between Heaven and Earth: The Religious Worlds People Make and the Scholars Who Study Them*. Princeton, NJ: Princeton University Press.
———. 2022. "The Study of Religion on the Other Side of the Good Religion/Bad Religion Binary." *Journal of Religious Ethics* 50 (2): 312–317.
Padoux, André. 1987a. "Hindu Tantrism." In *The Encyclopedia of Religion*, vol. 14, edited by Mircea Eliade. New York: Macmillan.
———. 1987b. "Tantrism: An Overview." In *The Encyclopedia of Religion*, vol. 14, edited by Mircea Eliade. New York: Macmillan.
Proudfoot, Wayne. 1985. *Religious Experience*. Berkeley: University of California Press.
Ramey, Steven W. 2015. "Accidental Favorites: The Implicit in the Study of Religion." In *Claiming Identity in the Study of Religion: Social and Rhetorical Techniques Examined*, edited by Monica R. Miller. Sheffield: Equinox.
Sharpe, Eric J. 1986. *Comparative Religion: A History*. LaSalle, IL: Open Court.
Smith, Jonathan Z. 1982. *Imagining Religion: From Babylon to Jonestown*. Chicago: University of Chicago Press.

———. 1996. "Why Imagine Religion?" Unpublished manuscript, author's personal files.

———. 1997. "Are Theological and Religious Studies Compatible?" *Bulletin of the Council of Societies for the Study of Religion* 26 (3): 60–61.

———. 2024. "The Necessary Lie: Duplicity in the Disciplines." In Russell T. McCutcheon, *Studying Religion: An Introduction*. New York: Routledge.

Smith, Leslie Dorrough, Steffen Führding, and Adrian Hermann, eds. 2020. *Hijacked: A Critical Treatment of the Public Rhetoric of Good and Bad Religion*. Sheffield: Equinox.

Smith, Wilfred Cantwell. 1959. "Comparative Religion: Whither—and Why?" In *The History of Religions: Essays in Methodology*, edited by Mircea Eliade and Joseph Kitagawa. Chicago: University of Chicago Press.

Urban, Hugh B. 2001a. *The Economics of Ecstasy: Tantra, Secrecy, and Power in Colonial Bengal*. New York: Oxford University Press.

———. 2001b. *Songs of Ecstasy: Tantric and Devotional Songs from Colonial Bengal*. New York: Oxford University Press.

———. 2003. *Tantra: Sex, Secrecy, Politics and Power in the Study of Religion*. Berkeley: University of California Press.

Vedantam, Shankar. 2004. "Wrath over a Hindu God: U.S. Scholars' Writings Draw Threats from the Faithful." *Washington Post*, April 10: A01. https://www.washingtonpost.com/archive/politics/2004/04/10/wrath-over-a-hindu-god/17ac5b88-7d9d-4a3e-ad41-144f1b1a2e3b/.

White, David G. 2003. *Kiss of the Yoginī: "Tantric Sex" and Its South Asian Contexts*. Chicago: University of Chicago Press.

3
Introduction
Complicating Not Simplifying

Two separate, smaller portions of the following chapter first appeared as posts on my department's sometimes very active blog (making evident that blogging and scholarly writing, let alone teaching, are not so removed as some might claim; between that site and those at Culture on the Edge I have about 1,000 posts living out there on the web). The first of those was posted on November 30, 2012.[1] Prior to enlarging that into what became this chapter, I communicated with the then *JAAR* editor, either over email or in person, on several occasions concerning the criticisms eventually documented here (a chapter that was first published in a 2016 essay collection of my own; its relevance to the theme of this volume suggested to me that it was worth revising and including in this book as well). That my advice, offered as a member of the *JAAR* editorial board at the time, to discontinue the inclusion of aesthetic pieces to open each issue of the journal (first communicated when I initially became aware that poetry was appearing in 2011) had little effect, was what prompted me to write and publish this essay.

The framework for the piece, signaled by its title, was indeed a direct quotation straight from my longtime colleague, Merinda Simmons, who was among those who flew home together from our annual conference in Chicago that year, all of whom I was driving back to Tuscaloosa, an hour's drive from the airport in Birmingham. We were discussing the addition of poetry to each issue of the main U.S. scholarly journal, all of us expressing

[1] Still available, along with a variety of reader comments, at Russell McCutcheon, "And That's Why No One Takes the Humanities Seriously," University of Alabama, "Studying Religion in Culture: Ongoing Discussions at the University of Alabama," November 30, 2012, https://religion.ua.edu/blog/2012/11/30/and-thats-why-no-one-takes-the-humanities-seriously/.

frustration over it, which prompted her to sum it up by flatly stating to everyone in the car: “And that’s why no one takes the humanities seriously.” Her phrasing was something that pretty obviously stuck with me, making its way into that initial blog post just a week or two later. That no one in the car that day was an ardent, quantitative methods person deserves to be said (Merinda’s own Ph.D. is in English, by the way), so the criticism was not coming from a place that romanticized empirical research, lab coats, and the sort of disinterested objectivity that was once thought to come along with all of that. Instead, and despite the different subfields and academic generations represented in the car that day, it was coming from a group that, first off, took seriously the need for self-reflexive work as a scholar and, second, agreed that the things commonly designated by us as being religious, sacred, or holy were all interesting, to be sure (otherwise why study them?), but hardly special or privileged cases. Instead, as many members of our department increasingly refined this teaching and research position over the coming decades, the items that we each study were seen as instances that were exemplary of broad issues of (sometimes surprising) relevance all across culture—not because the sacred lurks all over the place, as many scholars of religion might still assert, but because the basic workings of culture are evident in all human moments, including those that we often call religion. For, regardless of the setting or the moment, we all negotiate issues of rank and authority, claim and contest identities, select and value (or work to forget and thereby minimize) those things known as the past while either anticipating or dreading something known as the future. And so, if religion is not considered to be some unique item that’s set apart from all else, then we should certainly expect to find all of this going on there—even in the very act of designating and then treating something *as* religious, *as* sacred, *as* holy—making anything that we learn about identity or rank at some site known by us as a ritual, a congregation, a temple, or a scripture directly applicable to virtually any other site all across culture. Such is the engine driving my entire argument, hinted at in the following chapter but more than apparent by the close of the book: that generalization from our specialized work is among the things that we have to contribute to higher education today. Sadly, it is a step made by too few of our colleagues.

In the midst of all of this is what I’m calling complication in this chapter, something that I would argue was not happening with the inclusion of poetry or art in our scholarly journal. Instead, such verse was presented as transparently meaningful (at least an artist’s statement accompanied later artwork that also made its way into the journal, one might say at this point), needing no deciphering or contextualization; accordingly, it was not represented there so much as presented, at the opening of an issue of an academic periodical supposedly devoted to the academic study of religion. Given that it is not difficult to study language as a loaded, ideological structure, like any other symbol system, the missed opportunity to complicate the verse (i.e., to treat it as data) signaled to us that the inclusion of the poetry was not meant as an instance of scholarship. These were not moments of literary critical studies, in other words, but, instead, an assertion of taste or an aesthetic sense shared by those making and, I guess, enjoying the selections—for what else was one to do with them? That a system, faulty as it may be, had long ago been derived to govern the selection of content to be published as constituting scholarship—we call it double-blind peer review—is among the techniques that we in the academy have used to distinguish knowledge from opinion. Whether or not the results of such a process are persuasive to everyone, it is nonetheless an effort to moderate and regulate choice and potentially idiosyncratic, unaccountable preference (not unlike the role played by footnotes, as once observed by Bruce Lincoln; see the epilogue, "Scholarship as Myth," to his still important collection, *Theorizing Myth* [1999]). Those of us in the car that day could come up with no such mechanism to determine what counted as an aesthetic worth reproducing in such a journal—other than, as I argue in the following chapter, the close and, to some scholars, even self-evident relationship between what they consider to be the beautiful or the deeply meaningful, on the one hand, and the sacred and its many manifestations, on the other.

And so, the twofold requirements of scholarship that I propose—that it *complicates* the world while *generalizing* its findings to help us to understand something about a variety of other scenarios and situations—were not met whatsoever by this journal's onetime aesthetic initiative. This does not mean that I personally dislike poetry or art in general (I did indeed win a poetry contest at my school in grade 7, thank you very much—and I can still recite it all by heart); it just means that, as a scholar, I think that there needs to be a dependable way to distinguish my own enjoyment of, for example, the short stories of Ray Carver or, let's say, the journalism of Joan Didion, from the work that I produce as a scholar. In this way we can credibly talk about novels and journalism as being something different from the volume that readers now hold in their hands. Now, something that such writers once wrote might be of use to me in doing that academic work, to be sure, as a piece of data, perhaps, or maybe even inspiring or aptly representing an approach that I might adopt in doing that work. I think here of the opening paragraph to Didion's essay "The White Album" and how useful her reference to "the shifting phantasmagoria which is our actual experience" has been on so many past occasions, whether in my writing or as part of my teaching ([1979] 1990, 11). But that relevance is premised on my argumentation, contextualization, and persuasion; it's not asserted by mere citation of it. In fact, no text should be cited in scholarship as if obviously meaningful—it's part of our argument, after all, so what do we make of it? (Yes, we are literally the doers here, *making* something of it.) Only members of dominant discourses can evade that responsibility. Self-evidency is therefore not something on which members of marginal groups can rely; their claims never go without saying, because it is more than apparent to them that *not* everyone knows such-and-such. The same should go for a scholar—in their role as both a researcher *and* a teacher—who aims to support, rather than merely assert, their claims about the world.

So, to bring it back to the task of complication, the inclusion of poetry in the journal struck me as a simplification of what is actually a tangled process of signification that scholars are more than capable of examining and understanding. It therefore seemed to be a moment when, yet again, scholars of religion reneged on their duty as academics, akin to making those sloppy and grandiose claims in the classroom about what Buddhists believe and what Hindus do—universalized assertions that, akin to the work of many of our intellectual predecessors, lack all nuance, specificity, and therefore limit. Happening in a journal whose marketing people have long billed it as "generally considered to be the top academic journal in the field of religious studies" made it all the worse (a claim long present on its website, one with which I do not necessarily agree, despite being honored to have been published in the journal on several past occasions). Correcting this tendency to simplify, in both our classrooms and our publications—to hide the hard work involved in what we do, as Jonathan Z. Smith once put it (Smith 2024)—strikes me as being high on the list of what's needed if we're to continue to persuade colleagues and others well outside our lecture halls that our work is indeed work and that it is worth doing, hearing, and reading—not to mention supporting and, yes, even funding. Complicating our commonsense understanding of ourselves and others, doing so in ways that are understandable to a variety of people (again, something far removed from mere simplification—ask any teacher: effective pedagogy is never simple), and in ways that produce knowledge that sheds light on yet other situations are therefore among the keys to arguing for our continued relevance and place in higher education.

"And That's Why No One Takes the Humanities Seriously"

The very resistance offered by poetry makes it an ideal prey for myth.
—Roland Barthes, "Myth Today" ([1957] 1973, 145)

In the second of its four issues in 2011, what has to be the widest circulating journal in the academic study of religion—the *Journal of the American Academy of Religion* (*JAAR*)—opened with a poem. Titled "Metamorphosis," it was a new poem written by the American Eliza Griswold (b. 1973); its opening reads as follows:[1]

> The mimosa trees misunderstand
> the New Year's heat, and burst
> into mustard tufts across the garden—
> their premature buds, a birth forced
> by the earth's unnaturalness.
> Poor trees, like nine-year-old girls,
> who have to negotiate breasts.

This marked just the second issue for what was then the journal's new editorial team, headed by the scholar of Islam and interreligious dialogue, Amir

[1] In the spring of 2024 Griswold—already a *New York Times* bestselling author, Guggenheim fellow, and recipient of a poetry prize from the American Academy in Rome—was appointed as the director of Princeton University's Program in Journalism. For more information, see "Eliza Griswold Named Director of Princeton University's Program in Journalism," Princeton University Humanities Council, March 28, 2024, https://humanities.princeton.edu/2024/03/28/eliza-griswold-named-director-of-princeton-universitys-program-in-journalism/.

Hussain (who went on to become the president of the American Academy of Religion [in 2023]); the previous issue had, understandably, opened with an editorial thanking the outgoing editors and giving an indication of some of the new editor's goals. Ending his editorial note with his thanks to the various institutions and people who were assisting him in his new role, he saluted two of his mentors at the University of Toronto, the late Wilfred Cantwell Smith (d. 2000) and the late Willard Oxtoby.[2] The editor closes his inaugural editorial by quoting Smith from his 1962 book, *Patterns of Faith around the World*:

> This much at least we may say: that prehistoric burial shows that men and women from the very earliest traces of their beginnings have recognized that there is more to human life than meets the eye, that our total significance is not exhausted within the six feet of space or sixty years of time whereby we each play our part on the stage of earth. The sober observation of the historian now agrees with the insight of the philosopher, and the faith of the saint, that human beings are not human until they have recognized that the proper response to death is poetry, not prose. (W. C. Smith [1962] 1998, 34)

"While I have no desire to turn the *JAAR* into a literary journal," the editor then concludes, "I think that poetry is the proper way to begin." And with that he turns to the poem that opened the first issue for 2011: the late Margaret Avison's seven-stanza poem, "To Wilfred Cantwell Smith," which opens with the following words:

> When asked, What is an intellectual? he said:
> "An intellectual is a participant in his own
> society, listening to people. That kind of truth
> cannot be put anywhere by us, not in words, never
> put in its place. The human mind can apprehend,
> not comprehend."

[2] In the interest of full disclosure, I should note that I too earned my Ph.D. at the University of Toronto, completing it six years ahead of Hussain, and that the late Will Oxtoby (d. 2003) was on my own comprehensive exam committee, was one of three members on my dissertation advisory committee, and that (like Amir, I believe) I was a teaching assistant for the world religions course that he then co-taught with the late Joe O'Connell (d. 2012), a course that comprised the basis for a much-adopted world religions textbook that Oxtoby later produced for Oxford University Press (on whose subsequent editions Hussain has served as a co-editor, after Oxtoby's death).

Despite the editor's stated desire not to turn the periodical into a literary journal, as we already know the following issue, the second for 2011, also opened with a poem. As did the third, which began with a reprint of a poem published in 2002, by Wole Soyinka, a Nigerian who, in 1986, had been awarded the Nobel Prize for Literature. And the last of 2011's quarterly issues also opened with a poem: "Heartease II," by the Jamaican poet, Lorna Goodison. Apart from the first, of course, which was in honor of one of the editor's late mentors and that likely needed some contextualization so that the relevance of the poem was evident to readers of this peer review scholarly journal, none of these poems receive any commentary or elaboration. They are not epigraphs to the issue, as if setting a thematic tone for a set of papers concerning some related topic. Instead, they are simply poems opening each issue of what the editor characterized, in his inaugural editorial, as "the premier journal for the study of religion" (Hussain 2011, 1).

The following year, 2012, this scholarly journal switched from opening each issue with a solitary poem to, instead, beginning with reproductions of art, accompanied this time by a brief statement from the artist, such as Amalia Masa-Bains's work that opens the March 2012 issue. Focusing on what she sees as the interrelations between "land, spirituality, and memory" (Masa-Bains 2012, 3), her art had recently been featured as part of an installation at the 2011 annual meeting of the Academy, in San Francisco, as well as being part of an hour-long conference session one evening.[3] As she said in her artist's statement: "Many of my works were inspired by my own cultural values of the spiritual and the sacred connected to ancient beliefs and indigenous practices revered in the early Chicano/a Movement. My search for the spiritual has been both a personal practice and an artistic

[3] The session, A20–409, took place Sunday, November 20, 2011, from 8:30 to 9:30 P.M., as part of the Arts Series. Titled "Amalia Mesa-Bains: Circle of Ancestors," the installation was described in the conference's program book as follows:

> The Circle of the Ancestors narrates through a circle of chairs eight historic moments through eight historic women our cultural genealogy as Chicanas. The circle refers to the arrangement of the eight chairs facing inward around a spiral of candles placed on the floor. The chair, as a metaphor of the body, recalls the suffering and sacrifice present in the lives of these women. At the same time the circle of chairs is a recalling of the intimacy and collective strength of women's lives in the home, in the fields, even in the Church. The eight figures refer to the ancient, the Mexican Cuatlique, and Coyolxauhui; the Virgen de Guadalupe; the colonial paintings, the Castas; the colonial nun and scholar Sor Juana Inez de la Cruz; the revolutionary woman soldier, Adelita and my own Abuelita (grandmother); the Chicana farm worker; the Pachuca/Chola and my First Holy Communion. The women represented in the chair altars offer us a circle of time where we remember our future, constructing for ourselves a spiritual and cultural genealogy as Mexicana/Chicana women.

form born out of traditional spirituality concerned with home altars, *ofrendas* for the dead, and vernacular forms such as the *capilla* yard shrines and *descansos*, a roadside memorial that is a resting place that marks the site of a death." The editorial that begins the issue in which her art appears, the first issue produced after the San Francisco conference, described how "as academics who study religion, we often focus exclusively on texts, so the creations of Professor Mesa-Bains arouse our appreciation of the nonverbal, including ritual, music, and images as accompaniments to our incalculable destination" (Hussain 2012b, 2).[4] Issues 3 and 4 for 2012 also open with art accompanied by artists' statements;[5] and, if the first of 2013's four issues is any indication, photography comprises the artistic medium of choice for the following year.[6]

To a reader familiar with academic publishing, I think it is unclear why poetry, art, and photography once appeared in this academic journal (let alone as an installation at a national conference of academics). As already noted, they are not connected to any of the scholarly articles in the journal but, instead, stand as a preface to the issue, a speaking beforehand—but don't let the silence that comes with their general lack of context or background fool you, for I think that something is indeed being said by means of these artistic expressions (for why else are they here?).

Because this periodical is devoted to publishing peer reviewed scholarly research on religion, it's not immediately evident why any sort of prefatory

[4] In fact, scholarship on ritual is among the more thriving subfields in the study of religion, dating to the very origins of the field in the nineteenth century. I think here of the work of William Robertson Smith (1846–1894), which proposed that so-called ancient religion was organized around ritual and not belief or doctrine (2002, though first published in 1889). The prominence of such works on ritual, despite the earlier ones often seeing ritual as a secondary site where myths and beliefs were acted out, suggests that the supposedly text-based nature of the entire field is not as apparent as many scholars, such as the editor quoted above, still maintain.

[5] Sandow Birk's art appears in issue 3 (2012), accompanied by his illuminated Quran, in the style of classic copies of the Quran, aimed at "investigating how the message relates to our lives in the United States today" (Birk 2012, 582); and Robert Davidson's Haida-styled artwork opens issue 4 (along with a separate editorial commenting on his art [Hussain 2012a]), along with an artist's statement that concludes: "Since the almost complete destruction of our spirit, our disconnection from our values and beliefs, it is the art that is bringing us back to our roots" (Davidson 2012, 852).

[6] Dorothy Braudy's photographs of various places of worship in the city of Los Angeles open issue 81 (1) (2013), along with her artist's statement; her focus on this subject matter is a result of her "becoming more sensitive to the complex spiritual life of the city." She continues, "I wanted to celebrate the beauty and diversity of Los Angeles, and it seemed to me religion uniquely embodies what seems to make us separate from one another at the same time that each religion calls on us to become our better selves" (Braudy 2013, 2).

message is even needed—editorials rarely appear in journals, except when announcing some change or retraction/correction, or, perhaps, when preparing readers for an issue-wide topic (such as a special issue or a commissioned set of papers). But an editor opening an issue of a journal for specialists in the academic study of religion by trying, as he phrased it, to "arouse our appreciation of the nonverbal" . . . ? Well, I find this very puzzling, for I had thought that our job as academics was *neither* to criticize *nor* to celebrate our object of study, but, instead, to examine whatever we each happen to study in a fashion that is as applicable to the things that we may find personally troubling as it is to those that we support. Such an equal opportunity methodology—the sign, I'd say, of any disciplined approach to the cross-cultural study of human behavior—surely applies in the selection of the scholarly papers to be published in such a journal but I do not see how it can apply when it comes to selecting poetry or art, for I don't suppose that the editor was selecting works which he dislikes,[7] or those which, I suppose, "stifle" our appreciation for the nonverbal, though I would hope that he publishes well-written and soundly argued essays with which he disagrees.[8] So why open yourself to possible critique by including a domain within a peer review journal that entirely bypasses the peer review process—for while there's ideally a way to account rationally for all editorial decisions concerning why certain papers are or are not being published, there's absolutely no accounting for taste, as the old saying goes.[9]

Driving back to Tuscaloosa in November of 2012, from the Birmingham airport, after flying home from the annual meeting of the American

[7] Opening his remarks by saying that he has "admired [her work] for years" Hussain, not long before taking over as editor of *JAAR*, participated in a "conversation" with Griswold, whose poetry opened the second issue for 2011, on September 30, 2010, at the Los Angeles Public Library. Part of the Library's "Interfaith Series," the event was titled "The Tenth Parallel: Dispatches from the Fault Line between Christianity and Islam"; listen to it at Los Angeles Public Library online, http://www.lapl.org/collections-resources/e-media/podcasts/aloud/tenth-parallel-dispatches-fault-line-between (accessed April 19, 2024). Notably, at the seventeen-minute mark, Griswold appreciatively recounts when she first read Mircea Eliade and his concept of the hierophany, and how it helped her to understand herself and her own upbringing in the church (her father, Frank T. Griswold, was the Episcopal Bishop of Chicago [1987–1997]).
[8] Also, in the interest of full disclosure, I have been fortunate enough to have published on a variety of occasions in *JAAR*, including during the tenure of the editor whose choices are under examination here.
[9] Sometimes journal editors reject submissions, much as departments decline hiring someone, due to what is described by them as a "lack of fit"; I find this sort of disclosure, which is nothing but a nondisclosure, very troubling for the manner in which it usually fails to articulate the criteria by which "fit" was measured, a failure that ends up normalizing these criteria by ensuring that they are never disclosed and can never be debated. So, like taste, there's no accounting for "fit."

Academy of Religion in Chicago that year, a few of us were talking in the car about this very topic: our premier journal and its puzzling poetry; all of us were curious why a peer reviewed journal in our field had started doing this. After all, scholarly journals in, say, molecular biology or radiological oncology—fields that study aspects of the human in no less technical and thus specialized ways as the academic study of religion—surely do not open *their* issues by establishing an aesthetic tone for their readers, and even journals in literary studies would publish poetry only inasmuch as it comprised an example of something discussed in one of its articles (what with the scholarly study of poetry being something different from writing poetry itself). Journals in these fields are therefore seen as technical places where research is disseminated to a relatively small group of interested readers—and no one seems to think that they ought to offer apologies for the way this work excludes possible readers who do not possess the necessary technical expertise. At a pause in our conversation, while we drove down I 20/59, my colleague, Merinda Simmons—herself an English Ph.D. but who has been a colleague in our department for her entire career—summed it all up when, from the back seat of my car, she simply said, in a tone of exasperation: "And that's why no one takes the humanities seriously."

Although it was an off-hand comment, it caught my ear. Given that I had by then been on the *JAAR* editorial advisory board since 2008, I had been privy to some conversations on trying to reach new readers—for example, the journal experimented with movie reviews and the board was told by the publisher that readers are more likely to continue reading if something early on in the publication—say, an image or a poem?—grabs their attention (oddly, I had thought that readers kept reading if the articles were intellectually compelling and relevant to their own work). More than likely this accounts for the cover beginning to carry a photograph of some sort as of the first issue of 2016 (Cynthia Eller's first as editor). Because the AAR is the largest society of scholars of religion in the world, and given that subscription to the journal comes along with membership, I can't imagine Oxford University Press, the journal's publisher, pressuring the journal to rebrand itself as more relevant or engaging or open to nonspecialist readers (correction: subscribers)—simplification is, to my way of thinking, the death knell for a scholarly journal (though general applicability—which is not to be confused with simplification—of such specialized research may be, as I argue elsewhere in this volume, how we revive the field). Yet, as we all know, academic publishing has fallen on hard times and so the journal was clearly aiming for new markets, in part, it would seem, by means of a catchy artistic opening to each issue—or so the advisory board had been told. But I have a hunch that more than this is going on—after all, although I agree that, when it comes to commenting on religion's causes or effects, it is rather unfortunate that highly respected scholars working in other fields, such as political theory or sociology, often feel free to draw on what is often their merely Sunday school level of expertise, I hardly think that using poetry to open each issue of our field's main journal will draw them into reading the results of our research. In fact, judging by my colleague's conclusion that this was sufficient evidence why others do not take scholars of religion, in particular, or humanists, in general, seriously, such an editorial policy is probably the last thing that will help to persuade specialists outside our field to see the relevance of the academic study of religion. So, what else might be behind this aesthetic innovation?

As you may know, there's a well-established tradition of scholars of religion who have long asserted, first of all, that (as the American psychologist, William James, might have phrased it in the early twentieth century) religious institutions are simply a secondary site where a prior, pristine and personal, experience is expressed (a key word) publicly and, second, that there's some shared identity between these so-called religious experiences and what they often call aesthetic experience, which is also claimed to exist separately from a specific work of art. The definitive early statement of this position, at least within our field (considered broadly) was made by the German Lutheran theologian, Rudolf Otto, in the opening pages to chapter 3 of his still influential 1923 German book, *Das Heilige*, or more commonly known in English as *The Idea of the Holy*:

> The reader is invited to direct his mind to a moment of deeply-felt religious experience, as little as possible qualified by other forms of consciousness. Whoever cannot do this, whoever knows no such moments in his experience, is requested to read no farther; for it is not easy to discuss questions of religious psychology with one who can recollect the emotions of his adolescence, the discomforts of indigestion, or, say, social feelings, but cannot recall any intrinsically religious feelings. We do not blame such an one, when he tries for himself to advance as far as he can with the help of such principles of explanation as he knows, interpreting "aesthetics" in terms of sensuous pleasure, and "religion" as a function of the gregarious instinct and social standards, or as something more primitive still. But the artist, who for his part has an intimate personal knowledge of the distinctive element in the aesthetic experience, will decline his theories with thanks, and the religious man will reject them even more uncompromisingly. ([1923] 1950, 8)

This argument, of course, has a long history—one that, if effective, allows one to bypass rationalist critiques of religion as being illogical, contradictory, and not premised on empirical evidence by claiming that religious belief and behavior are simply the outward expression of a prior, nonrational, inward sentiment. It is the precursor of today's "I'm spiritual, not religious" claims.

We can trace this argument at least as far back as Friedrich Schleiermacher, the late eighteenth- and early nineteenth-century German Protestant theologian who quite effectively argued against the Enlightenment ideals that often resulted in spirited criticism of religion as mere superstition; much like Otto after him, he did this by holding that religion was first and foremost about "feeling" and as such, was neither a rational nor an irrational element of the human. As Schleiermacher famously phrased it in his *On Religion: Speeches to Its Cultured Despisers* (1799): "Religion's essence is neither thinking nor acting but intuition and feeling. It wishes to intuit the universe, wishes devoutly to overhear the universe's own manifestations and actions, longs to be grasped and filled by the universe's immediate fullness in childlike passivity" ([1799] 1996, 22). As such, and contrary to those of his day whom he labeled the cultured despisers of religion, Schleiermacher concluded that there was no contradiction to be found in a rational person also being a religious person—feelings are nonrational, personal, and thus not prone to logical critique. "Don't tell me how I feel," as the B-movie dialogue might phrase it, is curiously in keeping with Schleiermacher's strategically useful prioritizing of the personal and the nonrational.

And with this move in mind, we fast forward nearly a hundred years after Schleiermacher's death (in 1834) to the publication of Otto's "analysis of such states of the soul" (8), which was significantly subtitled *An Inquiry into the Non-rational Factor in the Idea of the Divine and Its Relation to the Rational.* Although it would not be accurate to maintain that, for a writer such as Otto, an appreciation for the sublime or the beautiful was simply the same as the ability to experience what he called the numinous, usually translated as "the holy"—what he otherwise described as the awe-inspiring mystery of it all—it would be accurate to say that, for such writers, both are at least related analogically inasmuch as both presuppose deeply personal sentiments that are said to transcend argumentation and empirical documentation. "But the artist," as Otto wrote, "who for his part has an intimate personal knowledge of the distinctive element in the aesthetic experience, will decline . . . [the uninformed outsider's] theories with thanks, and the religious man will reject them even more uncompromisingly." Why? Because both have had *the* experience. A unique experience. A private experience. "I can't quite put it into words—but take my word for it, there was an 'it' and I had it. Did you . . . ?"

Before proceeding, I realize that this brief historical survey may, rightly, leave some dissatisfied, inasmuch as I seem to be doing little more than excavating eighteenth- and nineteenth-century windmills for later toppling. So as to assure readers that critiquing the antique strawmen known as Schleiermacher and Otto is not a sly rhetorical trick, I could remind them that both Wilfred Cantwell Smith, still regarded by many as one of the most influential modern scholars of religion, and *JAAR*'s onetime editor presuppose that our object of study transcends rational inquiry and language, for while the former was confident "that there is more to human life than meets the eye" and was cited by the poet as saying that "the human mind can apprehend, not comprehend," the latter wrote, in an already cited editorial, on how such things as "ritual, music, and images are accompaniments to our *incalculable destination*" (emphasis added)—something that seems to be not too far from Otto's notion of the mystery of it all that inspires our awe. Or perhaps I could cite NYU's onetime president and former dean of its School of Law, John Sexton, who appeared as a guest on, of all places, "The Colbert Report," on March 7, 2013, promoting his book, *Baseball as a Road to God* (2013). As described on its publisher's website, the book—which is based on his university course by the same name and on whose reading list William James's once important study of religious experience, from 100 years ago, and Mircea Eliade's *The Sacred and the Profane*, first published fifty-six years ago, both regrettably figure prominently—"is about the elements of our lives that lie beyond what can be captured in words alone—ineffable truths that we know by experience rather than by logic or analysis."[10] But instead

[10] John Sexton, with Thomas Oliphant and Peter J. Schwartz, *Baseball as a Road to God: Seeing beyond the Game* (Avery, 2014), penguinrandomhouse.com, accessed April 17, 2024, https://www.penguinrandomhouse.com/books/310992/baseball-as-a-road-to-god-by-john-sexton/. At the time the class was described (in surprisingly confident terms) as follows on its NYU course page:

> Baseball as a Road to God aims to link literature about our national pastime with the study of philosophy and theology. This seminar aims to blend ideas contained in classic baseball novels such as Coover's *Universal Baseball Association*, Kinsella's *Iowa Baseball Confederation*, and Malamud's *The Natural* with those found in such philosophical/theological works as Eliade's *Sacred and Profane*, Heschel's *God in Search of Man*, and James' [*sic*] *Varieties of Religious Experience*. It discusses such themes as the metaphysics of sports, baseball as a civil religion, the nature of sacred time and space, and the ineffability of the divine. Not for the faint-hearted, this course requires students to read over two dozen works of varying lengths in addition to supplemental readings as they might arise.

of citing the work of a lawyer and university administrator who, like so many other people trained outside our field, dabbles as a scholar of religion, consider a chapter in the wordbook, *The Cambridge Companion to Religious Studies*; written by Robert Orsi, the volume's editor, a well-known and much respected scholar of American religion, and, back in 2003, himself the president of the American Academy of Religion. The chapter in question is titled "The Problem of the Holy" (2012b), and opens with the following three sentences: "Many (not all) scholars of religion become restive sooner or later with the simple sufficiency of explanations of religious phenomena and experiences in terms of the social and psychological. It is not that these scholars of religion propose foregoing social explanations. It is that they recognize that such accounts fall short of the realness of the phenomena they purport to describe and explain in people's experience" (84). While my previous chapter attempted to rebut an earlier version of Orsi's position,[11] suffice it to say here that, as you may have guessed, I am certainly not one of the people who counts among the ranks of his "many"; for, unlike those in the intellectual tradition that stretches from Schleiermacher to Orsi (and which contains the various other examples I've so far cited), I do not think that it is the job of scholars to speculate on matters that they somehow supposed to transcend the horizon of their academic conventions let alone their training and credentials; it is therefore not for the scholar to be faithful to the so-called realness of his or her research subjects' experiences as these people either perceive them or, more accurately, *report* perceiving them when queried (since we do not study experiences or perceptions but, instead, people talking and writing, a simple though crucial distinction; as such, we therefore study discourses *on* experience and *not* experience itself, whatever that may in fact be). After all, people *claim* to believe all sorts of things as being really real and while we, as scholars, likely study all of these things, we often do so with a view to explaining *why* anyone could even conceive of such a thing, much less be persuaded by it. For not everyone who *claims* to hear voices is venerated as a saint. Or, as Freud phrased it in the 1920s, admittedly in a rather provocative fashion, "Am I to be obliged to believe

The course also requires weekly papers. As with any serious commitment of one's time, the rewards of taking a seminar such as this can be great.

The course page was available at New York University Gallatin School of Individualized Study, accessed March 8, 2013, http://gallatin.nyu.edu/academics/courses/detail.SP2012.IDSEM-UG1324.001.html.

[11] Related to this attempt to push back against the dominant approach within the field, see also my introduction to Martin and McCutcheon (2012) for a critique of such traditionalist discourses on experience.

every absurdity? And if not, why this one in particular?" ([1927] 1989, 35). That is, in many cases we feel no special duty to conserve the reality attributed to the claim for, in many of these cases, it so opposes our own commonsense view of the world that we can't be anything but perplexed why anyone would even think *that*—and thus enters the specialist in, say, abnormal psychology. Simply put, even the Vatican's Congregation for the Causes of the Saints (*Congregatio de Causis Sanctorum*) investigates claims to miracles and refuses to legitimize many.

The problem, of course, is how we distinguish between those views that we as scholars routinely explain in mundane terms and those that some of us instead decide to honor by preserving them untouched—to put it in words I quoted earlier, from Wilfred Cantwell Smith: if, as he holds, "an intellectual is a participant in his own society" then do we study those who are familiar to us in ways different from how we study those who are not, because there are many other societies and social standards out there other than our own. While of course taking seriously the claims that people make and the stock that they put into them, I would argue that it is *not* the scholar's task to take sides (or, as per the previous chapter, pick favorites) by determining which claims are credible and which incredible, which groups are normative and which are not; instead, as suggested earlier, we ought to use an equal opportunity method—might this be what we mean when we talk about the work to be carried out by critical thinking in the academy?—to offer accounts for *all* of the claims that we examine and not, as Orsi asserts in his introduction to the volume from which I quoted earlier, to provide people with "assistance with the real religious challenges of their local worlds and with their immediate and personal concerns" (2012a, 9). Contrary to Orsi, I do not think it is for the scholar of religion to offer therapies for just some people's existential, social, political, or economic crises—and I say "just some" because, as suggested just a bit ago, those people with whom we disagree are quickly labeled by us as radical or extremist or dismissed as members of cults or quasi-religious fringe groups, and we, as scholars, would never dream of assisting them with their no doubt equally real (at least to them) concerns. Instead, we study *why* such people even think and act the way that they do. I therefore strongly disagree when Orsi argues that we, as scholars of religion, have a therapeutic responsibility to the wider public; scholars of religion do not exist to, as phrased by the first artist to have her work appear in the journal's pages, help with or even appreciate someone's "search for the spiritual." Rather, as a scholar of religion, I would argue that my responsibility is to take my profession's standards of *argumentation*, *evidence*, and *collegial cooperation* seriously and to see upholding *these* as my duty to the wider public which helps to fund and thereby make my work possible. But I fear that it significantly over-reaches my expertise as a scholar of religion credentialed in a specific domain to claim that I am responsible to help address the existential challenges faced by the people whom I may happen to study or among whom I may happen to live. While I certainly owe to them a fair and thorough description of their claims and their behaviors, descriptions in which they surely ought to be able to recognize themselves, moving from description to comparison and then eventually analysis I am now in the debt of the scholarly traditions in which I do my work.

And I think it is this overly ambitious sense of relevance, based on the presumption that a scholar of religion's object of study transcends all the usual measures of the human, that propels many of my colleagues' overly ambitious sense of scholarly duty—something that I think is rather different from the relevance of our specialized work once it is generalized to other human situations (as I argue to conclude this volume). I am reminded here of a letter that was sent to the program chairs of the American Academy of Religion's various sections by Laurie Zoloth (a University of Chicago ethicist who was then at Northwestern University and who, at the time, was the president-elect of the AAR), concerning the conference theme for the 2014 meeting in San Diego: "Climate Change and the Coming Global Crisis: Religions and Responses." After outlining the threats posed by the facts of climate change, the letter goes on to say: "I *believe* that everyone has a role to play as we try to understand, change, and respond to a warming world, but I *believe* that scholars, who are in full and early possession of *fact*, with opportunities to articulate positions and policies, have a role specific duty to act now" (emphases added). She then outlines her two reasons for these beliefs: "It is our scholarly duty, I would argue, that we bring forward a scholarship from a wide set of traditions that may suggest a meaningful set of actions in response to an unprecedented and shared crisis. Second, there is a normative task. How ought scholars of religious studies behave, meet and live in the world? How do our theoretical concerns influence our academy? Our university, or community of worship? Our annual meeting?"[12] Although I too happen to *believe*—a key term in the memo and one that deserves some critical attention, since, as I've already suggested, people claim to believe all sorts of things—that global warming is happening and that human behavior has played an important, perhaps even definitive, role, I am no climatologist and I can't even name the many different academic specialties that

[12] See Zoloth (2016) for the published version of the paper she delivered in November 2014 as her AAR Presidential Address.

are required to gather the data needed to draw a sensible conclusion on the matter, much less devise a plan to address it. So please be clear—I'm no so-called climate denier; but I have a Ph.D. that, like anyone else with one, is in a precise specialty, credentialing me to make authorized claims within a very specific domain of knowledge, so I sensibly leave to others more qualified than me to pronounce on the so-called "facts" (as they are phrased in the memo) of global warming. Apart from this curious way in which the memo's repeated statements of "belief" routinely slide into proclamations of "fact," I therefore find the well-known fallacy of misplaced authority, and along with it, a misplaced sense of obligation and relevance, running throughout this text, much like the others I've so far surveyed. For only if we presume that (A) the object studied by scholars of religion is somehow necessarily beneficial and that (B) those who study it therefore have some special duty to spread the good news of their findings to the benefit of humankind, would a conference populated by scholars of religion (whether they are humanists, social scientists, or theologians of whatever stripe) be called upon to apply their research to help solve the climate change crisis—in a word, to help save the planet. As human beings concerned with our environment there's likely a strong reason to stop regularly jetting around the globe to read twenty minute papers and cruise the book display; but it is rather dubious to link such a call to our research specialty, what with the problematic assumptions that such a linkage carries, concerning what it is that we study and the cultural authority we therefore supposedly wield.

For an academy of scholars whose mission then was "fostering excellence in the study of religion" (now with the added "and enhance the public understanding of religion"), I find the unproblematized notion of belief employed as if it is an actual motivating source for action, the uncritical notion that those things we call religions are self-evidently a source of hope for people in crisis (more than one theorist would see them as among the sources of these crises!), and the ease with which scholars trained in, say, the careful study of ancient texts or in doing ethnographies of human behavior are assumed to have a special task in addressing climate change all to be extremely troubling. That this sounds remarkably like a restatement of what Eliade called "the new humanism" back in the 1960s—which argued that the scholar of religion's duty was to re-experience past existential situations, encoded in the ancient texts, and thereby give these long extinct values new life today—is even more bothersome to me for it presumes the scholar of religion to be a medium who channels the wisdom of the ancients—a position that, time and time again, has been criticized by a wide variety of scholars, yet it reappears continually.

So, with the AAR's onetime mission in mind—"fostering excellence in the study of religion"—my question is: Just how much excellence are we fostering if no one questions these sorts of claims when they are made by scholars? For without questioning them, why should we take claims of "excellence" seriously and not just read the word as a handy rhetorical tool?

For example, I recall an earlier university where I worked and how, when we discussed the specialty we needed for an open faculty position, someone would inevitably cut off the discussion by saying, rather grandly, that we were simply looking for the cream of the crop, the best applicant—in a word, excellence. It was a pretty useful rhetorical move, of course, since it papered over the disagreements in the room concerning just what excellence meant—after all, best according to what measure? That one happens to share some of the beliefs that are credited with animating our then-president-elect's memo should not, I would hope, prevent scholars of religion from knowing their professional limits or curtail them from questioning the sort of excellence that allows our peers to make such claims.

If we're going to sell the practical utility of the critical thinking that we say we're teaching our students in the humanities, then maybe we should consider applying these skills a little closer to home than we usually do. For whatever one thinks our "scholarly duty" is to the fate of humankind, isn't this at least one that we owe to our own profession—perhaps leaving to our civic duty the diagnosis and correction of the various social ills that we may or may not come to believe in?

Before proceeding, let's pause for a moment and make plain the contours of the dominant approach to the study of religion that is evident in the various examples that I've so far cited, including the analysis from the previous chapter—from poetry in *JAAR* to a former president of the Academy rehabilitating "the holy" as a technical term, and finally, to our current president-elect's invitation to help solve global warming. It presumes, first, that our object of study is individual subjects who each have private experiences that are communicated publicly by means of subsequent actions and sign systems—like sausage pressed out of the meat grinder, these experiences are said to be "expressed" (a frequently used term of importance, I previously suggested); second, these public systems inevitably mire the original experience in ambiguity, such that they must be decoded properly by the careful, authorized interpreter. Third, because these so-called experiences are understood as extra-mundane and thus thought to be of some deep and abiding significance to all of humanity, these interpreters are not only changed themselves by means of their studies but they also have a special responsibility not just to the people whom they study—a responsibility to, as Orsi phrases it in the close to his chapter on the holy, help to "unearth experience from the thick sedimentary strata of language covering it" (2012b, 104)[13]—but also to share this meaning with the entire planet.

Which brings us all the way back to the puzzle of the poetry—something linked, I'd maintain, to that newer component of the Academy's mission: enhancing the public understanding of religion. For apart from the marketing people's desire to grab readers accounting for this artistic innovation within the journal's pages (an experiment that ended as of issue 81 (1) in 2013, as best as I can tell; photos on the journal's cover continue, however),[14] it seems clear to me that the widely shared presumption that aesthetic expression and religious expression both provide some sort of privileged access to those prior, extramundane, experiences explains why *JAAR* once opened with poetry and art. In other words, the thing that is implicitly being said in these prefatory texts is a theory of religion—though I use the word "theory" here in a vague manner, akin to how Orsi used it in describing Rudolf

[13] Orsi is here quoting Ankersmit's *Sublime Historical Experience* (2005).

[14] The cover photos have sometimes been paired with articles in the issue, as in the case of the cover of 86 (4) (2018), with the Wikipedia Commons photograph of a seated nude, dust/ash-covered male Indian sadhu and an apparent female devotee bowing over while seated in front of him, touching his foot—a photo that struck a former colleague, himself a scholar of Hinduism, as rather Orientalist in composition. His brief December 20, 2018, post about this on our department's blog (which I solicited after hearing about his post to this effect on the Religion in South Asia listserve), and which is still available at "Note from the Field," Studying Religion in Culture: Ongoing Discussions at the University of Alabama, December 20, 2018, https://religion.ua.edu/blog/2018/12/20/note-from-the-field/, prompted a rather stern email to me in reply from the journal's editor at the time, Andrea Jain; her message bristled—which I believe would be the correct term, having just re-read her December 22, 2018, email to me—that white male colleagues had suggested that the image that she herself had selected for the cover was Orientalist. Those interested can find and read Llewellyn's post for themselves, to come to their own conclusion about his claim. Of particular interest to me is—thinking back to Orsi's "in other words" from a previous chapter—how the caption for the photo carries an explicitly Eliadean *interpretation* of the image that is represented *as if* it were merely a *description*; for it states that the devotee was touching the man pictured in the photo out of their "desire for proximity to that which is believed to be a conduit for the sacred." (See the above-cited blog post where a photograph and the caption appear; no caption appears on the Wikipedia page which is the source of the photo, leading me to presume that someone associated with the journal's production composed it. Find the original photo at Wikimedia.org, https://upload.wikimedia.org/wikipedia/commons/e/e2/Naga_Sadhu_and_Devotee_-_Gangasagar_Fair_Transit_Camp_-_Kolkata_2013-01-12_2800.JPG. I suspect that few people whom we study would describe the situation anything like this; so, while such an interpretation of the pictured setting may be correct (but who knows a person's desires?), this observer's claim exists at a distance from some presumed authentic Other's self-report that is no more or less great than that of any form of redescriptive scholarship—a point often lost by those in the hermeneutical tradition of the field.

Otto as a "theorist of the holy" (2012c, 86)[15]—that anyone familiar with its usual, scientific usage (signifying a hypothesis that can be empirically tested and thus its results are potentially reproduced) will stop short of calling this a theory or a scholar such as Otto a theorist, much as they would likely prefer not to call the doctrine of irreducible complexity of Intelligent Design a "theory" of the origin of species. Instead, the approach that motivates the inclusion of art that addresses "the search for the sacred" is more akin to the sort of folk psychology that characterizes each of our commonsense view of the world: for we see here the widely held presumption that: (A) individuals preexist groups (despite the fact that individuals are quite obviously the products of those social actions we call pair bonding done according to social conventions we call mating rituals, and then fashioned through styles and standards that are themselves thoroughly social); (B) that these individuals are motivated by private inner states called intentions (despite the fact that we routinely don't ourselves know why we do many of the things that we routinely do, like why we speak German to someone whenever they sneeze or why we sometimes bounce our knee when we sit); and (C) that these intentions are expressed—again, quite literally pushed out from some dynamic but mysterious inner region—into the world of ambiguous public signs which then need to be decoded to ascertain their original meaning (despite the fact that it strikes me as rather uncontroversial to argue that meaning is instead the public result of such things as grammar, that was here long before any of us uttered our first mama or dada, and that without it, all I'm doing when speaking is making noise). Despite these parenthetical examples of how commonsense can be complicated, this is indeed how we often represent our world—somewhat akin to commonsense observation once telling us that it was flat; these assumptions are so basic to our social world that they not only provide the basis for almost every English Literature course you've ever taken (where we were always asked the time-traveling question: "What did Shakespeare *mean* when he wrote . . .") but they also constitute the foundation upon which our legal system is based

[15] As argued in an earlier article, "'My Theory of the Brontosaurus . . .': Postmodernism and 'Theory' of Religion" (reproduced as a chapter in McCutcheon [2001] 2024, 150–175, though originally published in 1997), it appears to me to be worthwhile, for a variety of reasons, to define "theory" in a technical sense, inasmuch as those who seek to define it so widely as to include theologians such as Otto (or Karl Barth, as in the case of an example cited in my earlier article mentioned above) seem to be trying to gain the legitimacy of the narrowly defined technical term (for why else would they be concerned to argue for them having a theory? Why not just call it an approach, viewpoint, interpretation, or just a good guess?) but while applying it to those who would not otherwise qualify as having a scientific theory.

("Did you *intend* to kill? If not, then it's manslaughter.") But is this commonsense worldview of our society, the one in which we all too obviously live (as Smith phrased it), *also* the framework that we, as scholars, ought to be working with qua scholars? For I thought that, as scholars, our goal was, as suggested earlier, to develop what is often a counterintuitive expertise in a specialized domain of knowledge, governed by rules all its own, one that, by definition, reaches a very small number of other qualified specialists yet one generalizable to other human moments. To say it somewhat differently, I presume that our goal, as scholars, ought to be to problematize commonsense viewpoints, much as how, for example, a Marxist analysis of labor makes the seemingly simple idea of money or commodities rather more complicated inasmuch as everyday views of both treat them as concrete things when we might instead understand them as the abstracted tips of a large but generally unseen iceberg of working human subjects. In a word (or two), I take this to be what we mean by critical thinking.

And with the mention of critical thinking—the often called upon skill that seems to be the main thing that we, in the humanities, say we're all selling to prospective students—I wish to close by addressing head on the topic that, along with what I take to be a poor "theory" of religion, seems to have prompted poetry to open our journal: that topic being our way of representing our relevance as members of the humanities. Although many in the humanities would likely agree with those scholars of religion whom I've critiqued, claiming that the disciplines collected together into the humanities are *not* an ad hoc grouping but, instead, all share in nurturing expressions of something nonempirical called the enduring human spirit, when *I* use the word "humanities"—or, to put a finer edge on it, I'd prefer to talk about the human sciences, though I hardly mean the term as it is often used now, to name what we once might have called home economics—I think of a loosely knit collection of disciplined pursuits that focuses on the study of people, the items that they produce, and which they leave behind once they're gone, but doing so to *complicate* and then *generalize* and not to *simplify* things (as I have tried to do with the sudden appearance of poetry in our journal). And those intellectual pursuits that I see as being the humanities do this in a few ways: first, by taking the contingency of historical existence seriously—with a nod to the slogan of the literary critic, Fredric Jameson, "Always historicize!," our motto as relevant humanists should be "Things could have been otherwise" (it would sound so much better in Latin, I know); second, by keeping an eye on both individual agency *and* social structure at the same time, understanding that both are always present, continually informing each other—after all, if you and I are well schooled in the English language, something that long preexisted us and was taught to us within various institutions, like schools or the family, we might eventually begin to tweak it, in some previously unforeseen way, and thereby move the structure in some unanticipated, new direction (in fact, isn't that precisely what jazz is—disciplined variations within a prior structure?); and third, by never forgetting that, while scholars are no less (and, of course, no more) a person than anyone else, they are also not necessarily involved in the social worlds that they happen to be studying, and if they are, then their goal ought to be to use the comparative method to (as many scholars of religion before me have phrased it) juxtapose their familiar alongside the strange, so that something new and exotic can be seen in what had previously only appeared to them to be routine, everyday, and mundane—the creation of knowledge, in a word, presupposes some form of alienation from that which is being studied.

For me, then, the humanities is a designation not so much for a unit of organization within the university but, rather, for a style of scholarship, a set of attitudes, that we should find—but, sadly, too often fail to find—all across the university, regardless of the subject matter under examination. It is a stand adopted by the professor in class, the researcher in scholarship, the colleague in conversation, and not something determined by the supposed existential value or deep meaning of the topic that happens to catch our eye. Somewhat akin to the starting point of the literary movement that we associate with the phrase, "the death of the author"—in which the idea of long-past authors leaving symbolic clues in a text concerning their intentions and meanings is re-thought, resulting in the notion of the author being seen to be a perpetual construct of subsequent readers, each of whose idea of the author overlaps little, if at all, with some actual human being who wrote the text—I see the object of study, whatever it is, not as defining the approach that ought to be taken when it is examined. Rather, the starting point of scholarship, for me, is that theories and prior interests make things curious, whereby just some of the many things in our world *become* more or less interesting to us, turning mere stuff into something worth paying attention to. I therefore side with Humpty Dumpty over Alice (in *Through the Looking Glass* [1871]): we are the master and not the objects that we study: "'When I use a word,' Humpty Dumpty said in a rather scornful tone, 'it means just what I choose it to mean—neither more nor less.' 'The question is,' said Alice, 'whether you can make words mean so many different things.' 'The question is,' said Humpty Dumpty, 'which is to be master—that's all.'" This is the attitude that I'd say characterizes the humanities as I would like to see them practiced—an attitude that would likely not conclude that poetry will entice people to read our research or that this genre will somehow more accurately represent reality in some natural or presignified state. It is an attitude that would instead tackle the appearance of poetry in a prose academic journal such as *JAAR* in order to examine how signification itself functions. For then, along with someone like Roland Barthes perhaps, we might conclude that, despite the poet's apparent effort to "regain an infra-signification, a pre-semiological state of language . . . , to reach not the meaning of words, but the meaning of things themselves" (much as Smith and Hussain both suggest in their commentary on poetry's power to transcend mere prose in its ability to speak truth), "the very resistance offered by poetry makes it an ideal prey for myth: the apparent lack of order of signs, which is the poetic facet of an essential order, is captured by myth, and transformed into an empty signifier, which will serve to *signify* poetry" (Barthes [1957] 1973, 145–146). "By fiercely refusing myth"—or what Barthes otherwise calls "the essentialist ambitions of poetry" (145)—"poetry surrenders to it bound hand and foot" (146).[16] But to make such inquiries of poetry in *JAAR*, to see this strategic dodge around the apparent limitations of prose as itself being of political curiosity, requires an attitude far different from the scholarly tradition in the study of religion that I've rehearsed in this chapter, which strikes me as nothing more than an intellectual posture in which empathetic observers were trained to recognize religion in the behaviors of others who strike the observer as safe and tolerable, and to describe it in a way conducive to the interests of those who claimed to have experienced the acceptably ineffable "it." This sort of scholarship strikes me as uninteresting and, to be honest, rather boring, inasmuch as it passively awaits self-evidences to pass by.

As an example of what it is that the alternative scholar that I'm proposing ought to be doing, consider the late Jonathan Z. Smith, who was, perhaps, the most influential scholar of religion in recent years, and yet one who has also written widely, throughout his long career, on higher education and pedagogy (e.g., Smith 2013). That he mainly taught introductory courses all throughout his career, focusing his teaching career mainly on general, undergraduate education, and, at the same time, became one of the most rigorous and prolific writers in the field, is what, for me, sets Smith apart. And it is with the introductory course in mind—not a survey, mind you, but, as Smith was always careful to distinguish in his choice of words, an introduction, an initiation into a domain of knowledge, much as someone might introduce a new species into a specific environment—that I think we can best see what

[16] My thanks to Kathryn Stockton, of the University of Utah's Department of English, for prompting me to consider how a Barthean, for example, might find the appearance of poetry curious rather than merely assuming it to be expressive of some otherwise hidden truth.

I have in mind when I think of the humanities as a practice that *complicates* and then *generalizes*.

In an essay that had once been used by the University of Chicago to help train incoming graduate students to become teachers, and which he (or his widow, Elaine, after his death) was generous enough to allow me to use as an afterword in my own introductory book (Smith 2024), Smith argued that the introductory course is not a place to simplify (as many assume it to be, such as those who teach surveys of English literature or world civilizations that pack in as much as they can in how many ever weeks they have at their disposal); for such an approach unnecessarily hides from our students (not to mention parents, taxpayers, and legislators, to name only three other stakeholders in public education who often question our contributions) the hard work required to make certain human beliefs, behaviors, and institutions stand out as interesting, curious, and thus worth studying. The contestable human interests and choices—of those who made the texts that we read or devised the steps of the dances that we observe; of those who remembered, continually revised, and rehearsed them; of the Professor who made the syllabus that included them; of the publisher that made the standardized exam that came with the textbook that includes them; or of the politicians who created and police the standards that assess whether you've learned the correct way to study them—all of these are generally hidden from sight when we simplify. And we do ourselves no favors, Smith argued, when this is the picture of our profession that we present to our students. In that essay, he writes:

> In the name of simplification we treat theory as if it was fact. We treat difficult, complex, controversial, theoretical entities as if they were self-evident parts of the universe that we inhabit. Students coming out of introductory courses in the humanities know that there is such a thing as an author's intention, and they regularly and effortlessly recover it from a text they are looking at. Students in introductory social sciences know that there is such a thing as society that functions and they effortlessly observe it doing so. Students in introductory sciences are wedded without their knowing it to a tradition of induction from naked facts, in what Nietzsche called "the myth of the immaculate perception."[17] Indeed, I've often argued when teaching in the social sciences Core that if I could only have

[17] See *Thus Spoke Zarathustra* ([1833–1835] 1984), Book Two: Of Immaculate Perception: "To be happy in gazing, with benumbed will, without the grasping and greed of egotism—cold and ashen in body but with intoxicated moon eyes! For me the dearest things would be to love the earth as the moon loves it, and to touch its beauty with the eyes alone—thus the seduced one seduces himself. And let this thing be called by me immaculate perception of all things: that I

> the first week of Chemistry 101, my job would be infinitely easier because at least we would have raised the possibility that one wears eyeglasses when one gazes at the naked facts. (2024, 150)

That my own interest happens to revolve around the category religion itself—its history and the utility of using it, in this or that way, to name parts of our social world in distinction from yet other parts—means that the taken-for-granted knowledge of my students, their folk knowledge about what is and what is not religion, if you will, is the very thing that I wish them to examine ("Know thyself," as the old saying goes, gets written now as "Make data of thyself"). So it means that my own work in the classroom involves starting out by asking questions that assume my students to be the experts—for they already know what religion is—but then slowly complicating the narrative that they arrived with in my class, doing so in a way that, if I'm successful, will eventually have them looking back on the world as they once described it and being rather dissatisfied with how easily understood they thought it was. And because many of my colleagues throughout the field are from the same culture as my students, and have thus acquired the same commonsense or folk knowledge that allows them to confidently name this or that *as* religion (as pure, as authentic, as original, as apolitical, as personal, etc.), much of my writing adopts the same approach: take a simple thing, like say, a brief, that two-page 1893 U.S. Supreme Court decision I've so often cited, the one on whether a tomato is a fruit or a vegetable (i.e., *Nix v. Hedden* 149 U.S. 304 [1893]), but then generalize from what we learn studying it and so, use it as an opportunity to complicate other things, occupying possibly analogous sites, considerably, so that we can see some of the intricacies of the social situations of which this or that seemingly simplistic artifact is just a hint. The high court's decision—like any artifact of human beings—might end up being not nearly as simple or as isolated as it seemed, making it much more interesting to us.

While being no Platonist myself, I find this approach, ironically perhaps, to be in-step with the Socratic method that is much valued by traditional, Renaissance-inspired humanists, those who assume that we are here to teach students the tools necessary for learning the art of living well—except *now* we seek complex answers to simple, seemingly naive opening questions. "Of all the ways to live, dear Euthyphro, which will count as living well?" Now there's a question that opens all sorts of things to discuss and examine.

---

desire nothing of things, except that I may lie down before them like a mirror with a hundred eyes" (145).

I recall talking, a few years back, to a mathematician on my campus and asking him what he was teaching that semester. "A course on deriving proofs," he replied, and, without me asking any further questions, he went on to express his frustration with the fact that the students were finding it very difficult. While many of them were quite advanced in terms of working within the rules of mathematics (i.e., those taken-for-granted tennis lines that we call axioms), few of them were able to consider that the rules themselves were historical products (i.e., the artifacts of past agents working within structured settings not of their making) that could be argued for or critiqued. $1+1=2$ was, for them, the simple fact of the matter. These were the students, I presume, that Smith would have liked to get his hands on, during the first week of Chemistry 101, to suggest to them that, in order to get on with the business of talking about the content of any class, a number of interconnected assumptions needed to be in place, assumptions that are themselves historical products, our possessions, and not something already encoded in the world that we are seeking to describe. I try to do much the same when, as I've discussed in print on a variety of prior occasions, I still bring to my introductory students' attention D. G. Burnett's wonderful book, *Trying Leviathan* (2007), which focuses on an 1818 New York state "trial that pitted the new sciences of taxonomy against the then-popular—and biblically sanctioned—view that the whale was a fish" (to quote from the publisher's blurb). For if I can persuade my students that the self-evidency of their judgment that a whale is a mammal has something to do with onetime (but now exotically curious) commonsense, to yet other people long before us, that it was simply a big fish (after all, as Herman Melville has Ishmael state in *Moby Dick*: "Be it known that, waiving all argument, I take the good old fashioned ground that a whale is a fish, and call upon holy Jonah to back me"), then I will have succeeded in complicating their taken-for-granted world and, perhaps, have made them curious as to how elaborately authorized, and endlessly repeated, systems of classification, made by the people and for the people, make it possible for us to move around efficiently by taking for granted that green means go and red means stop. And this is something that's just as applicable to classifying tomatoes as it is to defining religion.

For the last time I checked, the world struck me as pretty complicated, for example, an ally one day is an enemy the next, and your freedom fighters are apparently terrorists to me. It is a complication harnessed, often with the same dubious success of weather forecasts and stock market predictions, by our tireless efforts to simplify (what we euphemistically call understanding, translation, and interpretation, but also meaning, intention, prediction, tradition, heritage, fate, etc.). Studying people and their efforts to simplify—like those scholars who see religion as the public product of inner experiences and meanings, akin to the apparent truth spoken by the poet[18]—therefore requires us to muddy the waters considerably, to identify yesterday's choices and contests, so that, perhaps, students can be empowered to consider which decisions they wish to make tomorrow.

The humanities, as I understand them, therefore ensure that our students become players, whatever way they choose to play the game—and whichever the game. The first step toward that is for the professor to stop professing (something I see an awful lot of in those ambitious claims of duty and deep meaning) and, instead, to assume the Socratic role of the strategic but modest inquirer about things we all supposedly take for granted—such as asking misleadingly simple questions like what is justice or maybe even religion. The trick is in slowly persuading students that their supposed expertise is itself the thing that should attract their attention. If done well, they might declare a major in the study of religion rather than running off, as poor Euthyphro did when Plato's Socrates asked him one too many questions about defining piety.

If you're able to do this in a classroom or while editing an academic journal then you're in the humanities, at least in my books, and I believe that you'll be taken seriously by your students, their families, and your colleagues. But if you're able to do that while teaching the proofs to math students then you're also in the humanities (maybe rephrased as what used to be called the liberal arts), regardless of how an institution happens to divide up the bureaucratic pie for ease of managing its people and its payroll. But if all you're able to do is represent back to your readers or your students their own taken-for-granted assumptions about the world and themselves—maybe by starting an academic journal off with some poetry that you and whomever shares your sensibilities all happen to like—thereby assuring them that they are right, that those other people are outrageously wrong, and that the world is easily understood, then you're not in the humanities and I see little reason to take you seriously.

[18] At the 5:06 point in the previously mentioned "conversation" between Hussain and Griswold, the former asserts that "poets tell the truth about the world," reminiscent of his use of the already cited poem in honor of Smith's: "That kind of truth cannot be put anywhere by us, not in words, never put in its place."

References

Ankersmit, F. R. 2005. *Sublime Historical Experience*. Stanford, CA: Stanford University Press.

Barthes, Roland. (1957) 1973. *Mythologies*. Translated by Annette Lavers. London: Paladin.

Birk, Sandow. 2012. "Artist's Statement: American Qur'an." *Journal of the American Academy of Religion* 80 (3): 581–586.

Braudy, Dorothy. 2013. "Artist's Statement: Sacred Los Angeles." *Journal of the American Academy of Religion* 81 (1): 1–5.

Burnett, D. Graham. 2007. *Trying Leviathan: The Nineteenth-Century New York Court Case That Put the Whale on Trial and Challenged the Order of Nature*. Princeton, NJ: Princeton University Press.

Davidson, Robert. 2012. "Artist's Statement." *Journal of the American Academy of Religion* 80 (4): 852–855.

Didion, Joan. (1979) 1990. "The White Album." In *The White Album*. New York: Farrar, Straus and Giroux.

Freud, Sigmund. (1927) 1989. *The Future of an Illusion*. Translated by James Strachey and introduced by Peter Gay. New York: W. W. Norton.

Hussain, Amir. 2011. Editor's note. *Journal of the American Academy of Religion* 79 (1): 1–3.

———. 2012a. "Editor's Note: Robert Davidson, Haida Artist." *Journal of the American Academy of Religion* 80 (4): 848–851.

———. 2012b. "Editor's Note: Something Observed." *Journal of the American Academy of Religion* 80 (1): 1–2.

Lincoln, Bruce. 1999. *Theorizing Myth: Narrative, Ideology, Scholarship*. Chicago: University of Chicago Press.

Martin, Craig, and Russell T. McCutcheon, eds. 2012. *Religious Experience: A Reader*. With Leslie Dorrough Smith. New York: Routledge.

Masa-Bains, Amalia. 2012. "Artist's Statement." *Journal of the American Academy of Religion* 80 (1): 3–6.

McCutcheon, Russell T. 1997. "'My Theory of the Brontosaurus': Postmodernism and 'Theory' of Religion." *Studies in Religion/Sciences Religieuses* 26 (1): 3–23.

———. (2001) 2024. *Critics Not Caretakers: Redescribing the Public Study of Religion*. 2nd ed. New York: Routledge.

———. 2016. *A Modest Proposal on Method: Essaying the Study of Religion*. Leiden: Brill.

Nietzsche, Friedrich. (1833–1835) 1984. *Thus Spoke Zarathustra: A Book for Everyone and No One*. Introduced and translated by R. J. Hollingdale. New York: Penguin.

Orsi, Robert A., ed. 2012a. *The Cambridge Companion to Religious Studies*. New York: Cambridge University Press.

———. 2012b. Introduction. In *The Cambridge Companion to Religious Studies*, edited by R. A. Orsi. New York: Cambridge University Press.

———. 2012c. "The Problem of the Holy." In *The Cambridge Companion to Religious Studies*, edited by R. A. Orsi. New York: Cambridge University Press.

Otto, Rudolf. (1923) 1950. *The Idea of the Holy: An Inquiry into the Non-rational Factor in the Idea of the Divine and Its Relation to the Rational*. Translated by John W. Harvey. London: Oxford University Press.

Schleiermacher, Friedrich. (1799) 1996. *On Religion: Speeches to Its Cultured Despisers*. 2nd ed. Edited by Richard Crouter. Cambridge: Cambridge University Press.

Sexton, John. 2013. *Baseball as a Road to God: Seeing beyond the Game*. New York: Gotham Books.

Smith, Jonathan Z. 2013. *On Teaching Religion*. Edited by Christopher Lehrich. New York: Oxford University Press.

———. 2024. "The Necessary Lie: Duplicity in the Disciplines." In R. T. McCutcheon, *Studying Religion: An Introduction*. 3rd ed. New York: Routledge.

Smith, Wilfred Cantwell. (1962) 1998. *Patterns of Faith around the World*. Oxford: Oneworld.

Smith, William Robertson. (1889) 2002. *Religion of the Semites*. Introduced by Robert A. Segal. Piscataway, NJ: Transaction.

Zoloth, Laurie. 2016. "Interrupting Your Life: An Ethics for the Coming Storm." *Journal of the American Academy of Religion* 84 (1): 3–24.

4 Introduction

Scrutinizing Structures

When Aaron Hughes and I originally co-wrote the essay that predated its version as a chapter here—an essay that, in part, resulted from Aaron's shock upon learning, for the first time, that a private academic society existed in our field (from my work on the history of the field I was already acquainted with it)—we were mulling over seeing it as part of a larger joint project on the current field. Though such a project may still be in our future, we instead decided to write the following and submit it to the *Journal of the American Academy of Religion*, which has long described itself as the premier academic journal in the field of religious studies. (Given the variety of specialties that comprise the field, many of which are represented by peer review journals of their own, such a claim is difficult to take too seriously as anything but a marketing ploy.) Should the term "generalist" have been added to that description—a term that we both value and hardly suggest as any sort of slight—then, perhaps, it could at least be billed more plausibly as the widest-circulating generalist journal in the field today. After all, given just the population of the United States and the American Academy of Religion's (AAR) rather broad understanding of the field (thereby allowing it to include members who are openly and unapologetically theological while also being home to humanistic and social scientific scholars) it stands to reason that the *JAAR* probably now goes to more mailboxes than any other single periodical in the field today. (There was a time when the onetime *Bulletin of the Council of Societies for the Study of Religion* was the widest-circulating periodical in the field, given that it went to all of the members of the various societies that constituted the Council of Societies for the Study of Religion's (CSSR) membership, which once included the American Academy of Religion, the Society of Biblical Literature, the Society for the Scientific Study of Religion, etc.) And so, agree or not with the self-conception that the journal may have under any one of its editorial teams, it still understandably strikes many as a desirable place to publish their work.

And so it did for us too.

Although we admit that we were not optimistic for the fate of the submission that predated the version as a chapter in this volume, on April 27, 2017, we sent it off nonetheless, hoping that an essay examining how our field works—using, but not limited to, one specific case study within the field—might catch the attention of readers and, perhaps, spark a bit of a debate. It was therefore not surprising, though still disappointing to us, to receive an email back on May 5, 2017 (making evident to us that the submission never made it to the peer review process) that stated that the submission "was not suitable for publication" in the journal. (See the introduction to McCutcheon 2024, which documents a surprisingly similar story concerning the current *JAAR* editorial team and the out-of-hand rejection of a co-written paper on the need to revise graduate education in our field.) The reason that was cited struck us as rather interesting and, though it was surely in an unintended manner, we read it as providing further evidence to support the paper's thesis on how members of an academic discipline police its limits, often in undisclosed ways. For, after citing the journal's mission statement (a statement with which we admit we were completely unfamiliar at the time, not knowing how long it had existed, let alone in the current form)—"This international quarterly journal publishes top scholarly articles that cover the full range of world religious traditions together with provocative studies of the methodologies by which these traditions are explored"—we were informed in the email that because our paper did not discuss a methodology relevant to the study of religions, it was not suited to *JAAR*, though, we were told, it might find a home at the more professionally oriented *Religious Studies News* (the AAR's onetime quarterly newspaper, but now the periodically used online site, devoted to more professional issues in the field).

With that mission statement in mind, the stated reason for rejecting the paper outright was therefore that, while obviously not on descriptive information relevant to understanding one or more world religions (such as an essay on, let's say, ritual in this or that tradition), it didn't even examine broader methodological issues of relevance to studying world religions (e.g., discussing, say, a theory of ritual or way to study myths) that could then be applied to, as the mission statement phrased it, "the full range of world religious traditions." While the field's still dominant world religions paradigm is prominent in the mission statement and thus the supposed reason for rejection, what we find far more curious is that the so-called premier academic journal in the field of religious studies was said to limit itself to this one conception of the study of religion. For, at least in our reading, it clearly does not—or at least has not; yet, *on this occasion, it did.* To rephrase: a quick look through the table of contents over the years makes evident that while descriptive or comparative articles on items of relevance to one or more of the world's religions obviously dominate the journal's pages, there are plenty of articles and book reviews on things of wider relevance to the workings of the field at large. We could, of course, cite many (if not most) of the AAR presidential addresses themselves, printed annually in the journal, inasmuch as they are often on field-wide or even professional topics that are (i) neither concerned with descriptive items from the world religions (ii) nor concerned with honing a methodology useful in their study.[1] Or perhaps we could instead cite some of our own past appearances in the journal, such as my own early (and perhaps provocative, judging by the published replies that it provoked) article on the scholar of religion as a public intellectual (1997)—which was neither descriptive of the world religions nor focused on methodologies useful in their study. Instead, recognizing that allowances may reasonably be made for presidential addresses (which the journal is presumably required to publish each year, even if that requirement remains unarticulated) and also noting that the journal's self-conception may have changed over the past twenty years, what I'd simply prefer to cite is the then editor's own published statement, included in the second issue produced under her leadership: "Keep those submissions coming in: *JAAR* publishes in all areas of interest to scholars of religion" (Eller 2016, 285). (Thanks to Matthew Baldwin for reminding us of this statement.) Of course, should one narrowly define what counts as a scholar of religion to someone solely studying things classified as the world's religions, or approaches that are useful in their study, then we acknowledge that there's little contradiction between this statement and the rationale given to us for rejecting our submission. But not only does such a narrow definition strikes me as extremely odd and difficult to defend; based on such a restrictive understanding, it is unclear if that editor's own past work would count as scholarship on religion.

[1] Case in point, consider just Thomas Tweed's 2015 address, published in *JAAR* 84 (2) (2016), "Valuing the Study of Religion: Improving Difficult Dialogues within and beyond the AAR's 'Big Tent,'" which was on the long-standing religious-studies-versus-theology debate, or even Laurie Zoloth's address, from the prior year but published in 84 (1) (2016), 3–24, "Interrupting Your Life: An Ethics for the Coming Storm," concerned with global warming and, or so she argued, the specific moral duty scholars of religion might have in helping to solve it. The list could go on and on, of course.

So, on the one hand, we have an incoming editor's extremely (and, I think, laudably) broad statement concerning the scope of the journal—*in all areas* of interest to scholars of religion (emphasis added)—while on the other we have a rather narrow, extremely traditional understanding of the field, one in which an article on, say, the now much-studied Nones would likely not find a home, given that they are (at least not yet) not considered a world religion and thus even an article refining how they're studied would also not be ruled in bounds. And, we would imagine, neither would an article on a theory of religion as a human phenomenon nor an article critiquing the world religions paradigm itself, inasmuch as both fail to focus on—in this strict reading of the mission statement—some discrete element among, or approach used to understand, "the full range of world religious traditions." Today, I should add, the journal describes itself pretty much the same, though with slight revision: "This international quarterly journal publishes top scholarly articles that cover the full range of world religious traditions together with provocative studies of the methodologies by which these traditions are explored" (see the "About the Journal" page at its website). It should be noted, however, that by means of the current editorial team's addition of the "Discussing the Discipline" article genre the journal can (and, in fact, does) routinely publish items well outside this narrow understanding of the journal's scope. Case in point: in *JAAR* 91 (3) (2023) two essays appear under this rubric, one on the theological significance of the history of science for the founder of the Templeton foundation and the other on the category "sect."

But it is precisely the strategic wiggle room provided by the oscillation—when needed, that is, *and that's the crucial element here*—between the simultaneously held narrow and the broad mission that should attract our attention. It brings to mind a comment from the late Burton Mack, sometime ago, concerning this thing that we might just call culture being the creation of a tactical middle space. Our classificatory systems, Mack argued, "function . . . at a certain distance from the actual state of affairs experienced in the daily round. They articulate a displaced system (imaginary, ideal, 'sacred,' marked off) as a counterpoint to the ways things usually go. The inevitable incongruence between the symbol system and the daily round provides a space for discourse. It is the space within which the negotiations fundamental to social intercourse take place—reflection, critique, rationalization, compromise, play, humor, and so forth" ([1988] 1991, 21). To press this a little further, inasmuch as one might not assume the unproblematic existence of an actual state of affairs that can be juxtaposed to our classification systems, we might instead say that something called an actual state of affairs (i.e., an academic discipline, perhaps) becomes possible for social actors to imagine, to inhabit, and then to act within, only inasmuch as they employ a nimble classification system that functions as a handy sliding scale. It is in relation to the opposed, abstract boundaries that some new action or previously unanticipated situation is plotted, thereby allowing it to be known and understood inasmuch as it can now be judged to be more or less relevant and closer to or further from some hypothetical standard (whatever one wishes to call the undisclosed ideal or norm about which the one making the judgments aims). For only now can something be earlier or later, taller or shorter—not to mention accepted or rejected.

Case in point: consider a situation in which an article critical of what is portrayed as the rhetoric (as opposed to, say, the value) of collegiality is submitted to a journal representative of the dominant tradition in the field—a field where some influential members' position in a private society are used as a primary e.g. What does an editor do with such an unanticipated development? There are a variety of options, undoubtedly; one among them is to invoke a specific understanding of the journal's pliable mission so as to exclude it from consideration while advising its authors to consider placing it in a venue of lesser significance where fewer will likely read it.

So, it strikes me that our experience with this submission and its quick and outright rejection—conveyed here anecdotally, of course—nicely exemplifies how the rhetoric of collegiality works. For while the journal, seeing itself as broad in scope, regularly publishes articles, review essays, and book reviews on topics far wider than what we assume many would be surprised to learn is its supposedly highly focused mission, a narrow orthodoxy can be invoked whenever a strict adherence to the letter of the law is seen as advantageous, for whatever reason. (Interesting fact: just a short time after the rejection, one of us was invited by this very journal to be an external reader on a paper that was neither on the world religions nor a methodology useful in their study; rest assured that the return comment recommended publication, thereby refusing to flatter the suspect mission statement with continued relevance.) It's a convenient interpretive oscillation that is indicative of any number of social situations, making our experience hardly unique. Consider a traffic cop on the lookout for speeders; this would be a pretty mundane instance of the same strategy, since we all know that not everyone going 70 or 75 mph in a 65-mph zone is ticketed. Instead, the sliding scale of more or less lawful comes into play, managed by a variety of factors—one of which is the officer's situated judgment at the time, along with disposition, inclination, intentions, and biases.

The rhetoric of collegiality, as argued in this chapter, functions in just this manner; it is a handy device, a sliding scale that social actors in a position of authority can invoke as they wish, to regulate an unanticipated situation, helping them to judge someone as either merely quirky (and thus tolerable) or inappropriate (and thus intolerable). Those not in power have long known of the existence of such tools, of course; although we, the authors of the following chapter, are both white males, we could easily cite the reports of female friends who routinely find that exhibiting anything near the qualities of their male co-workers lands them in the midst of characterizations of being bossy and pushy as opposed to being portrayed as (in the case of their male counterparts) self-motivated go-getters. In fact, just as we were finalizing this chapter's earlier version, this was made evident in some media representations of a rigorous line of questioning, during a U.S. Senate hearing featuring the then U.S. attorney general Jeff Sessions, by a then female U.S. senator (Kamala Harris, Dem., from California, who later became the vice president of the United States). She was portrayed as "hysterical" despite her demeanor being no worse, or perhaps even less robust, than that of some of her male colleagues on the committee.[2] But this is not a double standard, as it is often popularly understood—for, more accurately, there are an infinite number of standards and gradations, any of which can be operationalized at any given moment; it is therefore best understood as the undisclosed and thus utterly flexible manner in which unanticipated or oppositional situations are policed by interested and authoritative social actors. We see this in that police officer with a radar gun making a judgment call no less than a professor going over a final grade sheet and looking for reasons to be (or not to be) generous with students whose grades are on the cusp. And we see it when assessing the relevance of submissions to a journal just as we find it present when faculty members try to ascertain the relevance and worth (and thus employability) of those who are junior to them. Making the criteria by which we, as scholars, navigate these inevitable judgments as public (and thus testable and refutable) as possible is the crux of this chapter's argument. As for the inclusion of this essay as a chapter in this particular collection? My hope is that it makes plain the strategic work that needs to be done, at a wide array of sites, by anyone trying to change how an academic field works (e.g., how it trains its students, the futures for which it trains those students, the point of the scholarship it produces and disseminates, etc.). There are interests being satisfied by the field's current rationale, methods, and configuration and the gatekeepers are astute at doing their job; structural change can indeed happen, but it will never come easily.

[2] For example, see this discussion in the article by Leinz Vales, "Columnist Kirsten Powers: How Was Sen. Harris 'Hysterical?'" CNN.com, June 14, 2017, http://www.cnn.com/2017/06/13/politics/powers-miller-kamala-harris-hysterical-sessions-hearing-ac360-cnntv/index.html.

The Gatekeeping Rhetoric of Collegiality in the Study of Religion

CO-AUTHORED WITH AARON W. HUGHES

Reverence is a religious, and not a scholarly virtue. When good manners and good conscience cannot be reconciled, the demands of the latter ought to prevail.

—Bruce Lincoln, "Theses on Method" (1996, 227)

"Collegiality" is a term that is often invoked in the hallowed halls of academe. Although we often judge children on whether "they get along together" or "play well with others," that we would likely never judge working-class occupations in terms of such a thing as collegiality, or even call the people with whom we worked so-called blue collar jobs "colleagues," is something worth considering—that is, the terms carry undisclosed class connotations of gentility and fine breeding, suggesting, right from the outset, that this seemingly innocuous term (which is used elsewhere in this volume, undoubtedly) is doing some undisclosed heavy lifting. Of course, many regard it as the foundation stone upon which is erected all that we do as professors along with the genteel ethos that governs our interactions both with our data and with one another. Yet, it is a term that is as opaque as it is imprecise—perhaps the very characteristics that account for its wide use when describing (and thereby assessing) the performance and thus status and even job security of faculty members.

The term's imprecision, however, provides a convenient site to interrogate some of the undisclosed (and, because of that, unchecked) social, political, economic, and intellectual processes that drive our field—an examination that has taken place in other fields, of course, but which has yet to focus on our own. (We think here of the work done by those elsewhere, in the past few decades, examining the labor conditions of higher education; generally speaking, this is not the sort of work one finds tackled by many scholars of religion [see McCutcheon 2024 for an effort to reverse this trend]). For, as many have argued, it is these often-hidden standards that comingle to create an orthodoxy, the breach of which, by means of actions labeled as "uncollegial," can lead to disciplinary censure and even ostracization—everything from the more mild rejection of a submitted paper to the far more significant loss of a career or reputation. It therefore seems to be one of the major reasons for the inherent conservatism of many disciplines and intellectual fields of study—a significant mechanism used in the reproduction of a (usually speaking hierarchical) status quo. Religious studies, our own academic home, for example, is ostensibly invested in understanding (i.e., recovering the otherwise obscured meaning of) the lives of religious practitioners. If one undermines such efforts, for instance, by calling attention instead to the meta or nonagential structural processes that make the study of religion possible in the first place let alone our ability to designate people *as* religious or *as* practitioners—thereby querying what we usually take for granted and often overlook—one risks transgressing a set of firmly established conventions and boundaries, inasmuch as (or so one might be told) the field's members study religion, not "religion" and much less themselves as scholars of religion. Such transgression is not uncommonly met with accusations of failing to be sufficiently collegial, or of being its antonym, to wit, too critical (a term that we propose as the current inheritor of the once used derogatory term "reductionistic"; for more on our sense of what it means to be critical, as well as various other usages, see Hughes and McCutcheon 2022, 52–57), leading to portraits of one being "out to destroy the field or a particular subfield therein." Indeed, even an article like the present one, one devoted to the trope and rhetoric of collegiality, may well be met in certain quarters with the charge of being uncollegial.

In religious studies, not unlike any other discipline, undisclosed standards of collegiality set the tone of the conversation, in this case about religion, myth, ritual, tradition, et cetera, and what it means to study such things. Those standards dictate that we, as scholars, ought to understand the meaning of, to thereby experience for ourselves and more than likely appreciate (also known as "take seriously"), religion, religious actions, religious organizations, and religious devotees (notably by developing a way to amplify their own understanding of their supposed intentions and meanings). Such scholars therefore endeavor not to offend the religious subjects whom we are ostensibly charged to study (via detailing what are now termed their lived experiences or embodied practices).[1] Offend believers, either by offering a counter reading of their understanding of their scriptures or their rituals, or by studying the possibly unarticulated reasons for them representing things as they do, and, so the story goes, we offend one another and thus the profession itself (inasmuch as religion is often defined as a universal core of meaningful human nature—a definition that actively implicates scholars, inasmuch as they are human beings too, in their objects of study). In sum, to improperly engage in the study of religion one is seen as breaking the unwritten code of collegiality by not having sufficient respect for the rules that ostensibly govern our collective guild.[2]

An instance of this understanding of collegiality may be found in the work of the important scholar of American religion and onetime president of the American Academy of Religion (2003), Robert A. Orsi, someone whose general hermeneutic of understanding so-called lived religion has become increasingly influential.[3] His method focuses less on theory, we would argue, than it does on what some might characterize as post-theoretical observations. For it is now relatively easy to find a generation of scholars who would argue that, having gone through what some might term the fires of the 1990s and 2000s in which critical, theoretical issues were emphasized in the study of religion, we now need to return to what might be termed thick descriptive studies, hence this term "post-theoretical." For example, consider Kathryn Lofton, herself an influential scholar and founding/current co-editor of the series mentioned in the previous note; near the opening of part one of a three-part interview, she says as follows: "My generation of Religious

[1] See Taira (2022) for a refreshingly different (i.e., discursive) sense of what it means to "take religions seriously."

[2] A suitable example would be the earlier chapter detailing Orsi's criticism of my approach; see also some of Hughes's work (e.g., 2012, 2013) that seeks to showcase the identity politics that resides at the heart of much of Islamic studies and Jewish studies as well.

[3] Witness, for example, the description of a book series at the University of Chicago Press established around the time when this chapter was first written, that curiously seemed to pride itself on asserting that religion is "more than a discursive concept or cultural idiom." In full its mission was originally described as follows: "It will nurture authorial reflexivity, documentary intensity, and genealogical responsibility. The series presumes no inaugurating definition of religion other than what it is not: it is not reducible to demographics, doctrines, or cognitive mechanics. It is more than a discursive concept or cultural idiom. It is something that can be named only with a precise and poetic wrestling with the nature of its naming" (online at "Class 200: New Studies in Religion," University of Chicago Press, http://press.uchicago.edu/ucp/books/series/CLA200.html). Although the series is described differently (i.e., rather more vaguely) today, it remains firmly centered, as it phrases it, in humanistic inquiry.

Studies . . . were just drowning, somewhat productively, in the postcolonial critique; we were all avid readers of Tomoko Masuzawa and Timothy Fitzgerald and Russell McCutcheon, and we felt the words that we'd been handed by our teachers were filled with contradictions, lies and empires that had not been identified. . . . But it also then, once we all started to be teachers . . . the vocabulary that we were given was so critical we had a hard time making cases for ourselves in that deconstructive idiom." The "turn" in the field (away from that deconstructive idiom) that they then go on to discuss could be summed up by the interview's opening allusion to the TV character of Leslie Knope (played by the American comedian Amy Poehler), from *Parks and Recreation* (2009–15), whom Lofton characterizes as "piercing through the presumption of cynicism." Whether cynicism best characterizes the work of Masuzawa, Fitzgerald, or myself is, of course, open to debate; in fact, such a characterization may tell us far more about some readers' goals for their own version of the academic study of religion and how they feel impeded by such critical works.[4]

Returning to Orsi, he conceives of the scholar of religion's role in the following terms: "Once religion is understood as a web not of meanings but of relationships between heaven and earth, then scholars of religion take their places as participants in these networks too, together with the saints and in the company of practitioners. We get caught up in these bonds, whether we want to or not" (Orsi 2005, 5). As should have been evident from the earlier chapter that examined his work in some detail, religious practitioners and scholars of religion, at least on Orsi's reading, are all involved in what we might aptly term a mutually collegial relationship—with this term, "collegial" stretching now rather further than the boundary of the educational institution implied by the term's etymology (originally from the Latin *collegium*, meaning guild, community, or just society, thereby implying the group of people with whom one works in such institutions [i.e., colleagues]). Scholars, operating in this vein, are said to respect religious practitioners and the latter, in turn, allow the former into their world of meaning, as colleagues. In studying the religious, inasmuch as it is presumed here to be a transhuman universal, we would then seem to better and more fully understand ourselves (itself a classically humanistic model). Within such a framework, when scholars overstep their bounds (by studying the religious in terms other

[4] For all three parts to this 2015 interview, hosted by Marko Geslani, see "Religion in the Post-Colonial Humanities: An Interview with Kathryn Lofton," *Sacred Matters Magazine*, accessed June 20, 2024, https://sacredmattersmagazine.com/religion-in-the-post-colonial-humanities-an-interview-with-kathryn-lofton-part-1/.

than their own) they are judged to have acted in bad faith and are considered poor guests in other people's worlds (and even improper inhabitants of their own).[5]

Collegiality in this guest/host model, then, seems to name the parameters of our field's first principles, its very conditions of possibility. Here, again, collegiality is used synonymously with terms such as "respect," "empathy," "understanding," "propriety," "peer," and "appreciation." One transgresses such virtues at one's peril (risking being called impious, in a long past era, a reductionist, more recently, or now, a cynic, an imperialist, or even worse). Indeed, the deck would seem to be stacked against those who do not perform work in this manner (thereby limiting it simply to description) or who do not act, to use Orsi's words once again, as "practitioners." Undermine religious belief (by, for instance, querying its conditions of possibility rather than taking it as a self-evident given) and one risks being represented as difficult, overly critical, or, more specifically, as "uncollegial." This sense of collegiality in the academic study of religion has therefore led to the formation of an inherently conservative field wherein scholars are expected to conserve a certain sort of folksy relation to the peoples or traditions whom they happen to study, in which they are discouraged from straying too far beyond the path trod by their academic predecessors, and in which a certain gentility of interaction among peers is presumed to be the norm (in fact, even our professional disagreements cannot be too animated and our intellectual convictions must be worn lightly).[6] Yet while many regard collegiality as a virtue, that which permits self-governance and respectful cohabitation within a

[5] Those social actors not prepared to invite the scholar in, or those with whom the scholar fails to identify enough to presume this method is even worth using, are defined out of their religiousness, of course, and termed such things as radicals or extremists and studied in a rather different manner.

[6] In fact, I'd go so far as to suggest that among the reasons my own work has stood out for some readers is because it has contravened such rules from the outset, by, for example, tackling problems that I find in the work not just of onetime leading lights of the field but also contemporary scholars, thereby naming names, as it were. This may help to explain why, of all the things that could be said about my work, my disagreement with Orsi from fifteen years ago mainly comprises the short Wikipedia entry someone created on me. It is worth saying that contravening such rules of what we might just call collegial decorum must itself happen within rather precise parameters; otherwise, it will not be read and answered (even if angrily, as has often happened during my career) but, instead, mainly ignored and dismissed. As I've aged in this profession I've not only found that among the rules of decorum is the general inability to offer critiques of any sort of those who are in positions judged by others to be inferior to one's own, so-called punching down but also that the increasing scarcity of academic jobs has led to a wariness to offer critiques of any sort; it would seem that the latter is out of concern for how such work might limit one's own career opportunities. An increasing conservatism within the field therefore attends, or so I would argue, the economically inspired decline of the profession.

shared academic pursuit, we regard collegiality as the silencing of critique, as a strategic boundary maintenance device, and, thus, as a hindrance to a broader sense of academic freedom. What's more, if our argument is persuasive, then it is worth considering that collegiality, being the product of the status quo and a device used to conserve its hold on power, is an activity that is maintained and patrolled on a variety of seemingly innocuous occasions, such as the venerable institutions as "blind" peer- and tenure-review.[7] In such situations uncollegiality is often pointed out anonymously and sometimes in what we would claim to be the most uncollegial of fashions (collegiality, after all, applies differently to those in positions of power), all the while paradoxically occurring under the guise of being collegial.

While we certainly place a high value on the necessity of professionalism, academic self-governance, and the value of respect, as one might commonly define it, in carrying out scholarly discourses and participating in the life of the profession as well as a department or university (along with a variety of other values that we also prize, e.g., accuracy, rigor, transparency, etc.), we therefore wish to suggest that lurking behind uses of the word "collegiality," a term that drives the professional study of religion along with much work in the academy, are a host of undisclosed and hardly self-evident meta-professional issues. For while scholarship and engaging effectiveness in the classroom can, to whatever extent, be measured and quantified, collegiality cannot. It, thus, functions discursively, defined and used at will to deprive or admit access to the profession. At risk of appearing uncollegial to some, our task in this chapter is to explore some of these meta-professional issues, trying to illumine the fault lines that lurk beneath disciplinary collegiality. Our contention is that as long as an undefined notion of collegiality can be used arbitrarily to dismiss or marginalize individuals, then institutions—universities, professional organizations, departments, and so on—of higher education will never truly be collegial (as we will later attempt to redefine the term). For it is our hope that such open and explicit scrutiny of this usually undisclosed gatekeeping device will strike readers as constituting collegiality in its best sense: that of being a co-inhabitant of our field, that is, a colleague and thus one who holds peers to high standards of evidence

[7] Case in point, one of us recently co-authored an unsolicited reply to what they considered to be a very poorly written and argued article published in a leading journal and, upon submission of it to the journal, it was initially rejected by the reviewers for being overly pedantic, too critical and, in the editors' reading, condescending. That the critical reply was rigorous and thoroughgoing is not in doubt, but it was also professional in tone and composition; that this was ruled out of bounds is the issue, we contend, in need of examination.

and argumentation in hopes of them doing likewise (what we think of when we recall Bruce Lincoln's challenge, in the closing chapter to his *Theorizing Myth*, for scholars to "show their work").

Although not written in the colloquial style of each of their book's entries, we therefore see this essay as offering an assessment of the discourse on collegiality's doublespeak in a fashion suited to Nelson and Watt's engaging and frankly written *Academic Keywords: A Devil's Dictionary for Higher Education*. Thus, it is an attempt to examine critically, as they describe it, the "vocabulary that reinforces various forms of false consciousness" in our profession (1999, vii).

Case Study in Gatekeeping

In order to move the discussion along, and to provide a specific e.g. where these implicit operations can be made more evident, we wish to begin by focusing on an organization far removed from any personal anecdotes of our own, one that we believe to be exemplary of some of these larger institutional issues. This organization, to be named shortly, is devoted to the academic study of religion; its raison d'être is to hold "meetings on an annual basis, where members present papers on a particular theme. In order to encourage rigorous and substantive engagement, papers tend to be short and discussions tend to be long. In addition to the stated theme of the meeting, discussions also may focus on the challenges of comparative work, the history of the field, and the role of the disciplines in the interdisciplinary field of religion. Occasionally the conversation will also engage the topic of pedagogy in the study of religion within the contemporary American academy." Yes, you are probably thinking to yourself, we know all about the American Academy of Religion (AAR—the largest national professional association in our field). So, what is new here? Well, it turns out that this is not the AAR, but, instead, another U.S. scholarly organization—what some might see as a condensed and rarefied AAR, as it were—that meets separately and whose membership is by invitation only. The little known (at least to some in our field, perhaps) American Society for the Study of Religion (ASSR), is, like its larger counterpart, a society devoted to the study of religion, but unlike the AAR it is restrictive and composed of mid-career and senior scholars who themselves determine those invited into the organization. Founded in 1959, and thus very much associated with the heyday of the Chicago School in the study of religion, ASSR meets annually (at the end of April) when members and invited nonmembers (so-called guests) discuss a particular theme in the academic study of religion.[8] The organization grew out of the Paul Carus Memorial Symposium of 1957, in commemoration of Carus, who had served as the secretary of the World's Parliament of Religions held in Chicago in 1893 (O'Flaherty 1986a, 293). The Symposium proved to be so successful that its attendees, most notably the late Joseph Kitagawa, petitioned the American Council of Learned Societies (ACLS) for membership, at which point the latter organization created ASSR and, for a time, it became the American representative to the International Association for the History of Religions (IAHR—a group comprised of national and regional member societies, one of which is no longer ASSR; it is also no longer a member of the ACLS).

Membership in ASSR, then as now, was thus by invitation only and open to scholars who worked in more than one religion (comparison, presumably, thus being a valued method). Agility in comparison was (and presumably still is?) judged according to the primary source and research languages that prospective members must have acquired.[9] To show that potential members could work competently in two traditions, they were once to be fluent in (at least) two languages. Despite, or perhaps because of, the cross-cultural, comparative nature of the organization, the organizers significantly argued that final term in its ethnonym was to be "religion" (i.e., in the singular) as opposed to the final term of the IAHR's (to wit, religions in the plural). Some of the ASSR's early presidents include such noteworthy scholars in the history of our field: Erwin Goodenough, Mircea Eliade, Wilfred C. Smith, Joseph Campbell, Joseph Kitagawa, and Ninian Smart. Such names, not surprisingly, signal what we see as still being the guiding hermeneutic of the organization (if not, some might claim, the field as a whole).

For the purposes of this essay, what we find most intriguing about the ASSR are the current rules around new membership. According to its website: "New members of the ASSR are elected on an annual basis by vote of the society. They are nominated by current members of the ASSR, and chosen on the basis of their contributions to the field, their achievements and interest in the comparative study of religion, and their record of *collegial*

[8] For example, "secularization and the sacred" (1967); "new modalities of the sacred" (1971); "sacraments" (1987); "embodied mind" (2012), and "race, ecology, and the matter of religion" (2022). A full list of topics may be found at American Society for the Study of Religion, https://assr-religion.org/history.html#programs-anchor (accessed June 21, 2024).

[9] Though it is worth noting that there are a number of scholars of American religion on the ASSR's current membership roles, who presumably need only one research language to carry out their work—in many cases, their native tongue. A list of current members is available on their website.

engagement" (italics added). "Contributions to the field" and scholarly "achievements" are, in our estimation, understandably noted as valid criteria for membership in a professional association, notably one that aims to comprise an honors society of some sort. Although it might seem that these two criteria are verifiable and relatively transparent, it is not entirely clear how one measures "contributions" or "achievements." Are such criteria based on the number of scholarly monographs? Or is it to be measured on some other objective set of metrics, for example, the number of citations found in relevant citation indices or their so-called impact (a measure much valued by university administrators these days)? Perhaps the latter is more important because we note, without judgment, that a number of scholars listed among the society's current members have, as far as we know, produced only one book, whereas it would not be difficult to identify scholars with numerous publications and recognized reputations who are not members of this organization. As with all private clubs, gaining admission is initiated when existing members nominate someone, who must subsequently be ratified by a vote of the entire membership. So what, one might reasonably ask, accounts for the absence of many seemingly qualified members or, to rephrase, what accounts for members, whether mid-career or senior, who, by some measures, have amassed what at first seems to be minimal publication records? Depending on how it is defined, the stated criterion "achievements" surely plays a role—there's more to an academic career than publications, of course, and people preside over national scholarly societies, work on grants committees, chair program units at conferences, edit journals and encyclopedias, and fulfill any number of other crucial professional roles that, though sometimes unsung, surely deserve attention and recognition.

But looking over the list of members and lacking a more specific definition of "achievement" or "contribution" one is quite reasonably left wondering. Is it the case of people inviting their friends or perhaps their own students and advisees, thus indicating that some sort of school of thought has emerged over the decades? Group formation would probably dictate that this is inevitably the case to whatever extent. However, it is nowhere stated if one must share some agreed upon pedigree or methodology in order to be part of the group (apart from the use of the comparative method), and thus it is unclear the degree to which the group's origins dictate where it has ended up. We note that, while interdisciplinary, many members list as their area the once meaningful but, we would argue, now rather ambiguous, even outdated, designator "history of religions" as their area of specialization. As just suggested, perhaps this should not come as a surprise since the organization has had, from its beginning, a distinct University of Chicago connection. That institution is one of the few places in the United States that continues to use the term, implying some sort of genealogical connection to the European model that Eliade, among others, helped to introduce and popularize in North America. As Jerald C. Brauer, former Dean of the Divinity School at the University of Chicago, writes in his forward to Eliade and Kitagawa's once well-known volume, *History of Religions: Essays in Methodology* (written in 1959, the same year as the inaugural meeting of what would become ASSR): "the study of the history of religions appears to be at a critical point in its development" (Brauer 1959, vii), and that the field has much to offer because "the world condition is such that modern man [*sic*], of the East and West [*sic*], is struggling to comprehend this revolutionary age, with its sweeping changes and newly emerging patters of life" (vii). In his Introduction to that volume, Kitagawa—himself among the largely unsung, or so we would claim, players in the field's mid-twentieth-century rise—seeks to define better this field of study: "There are three essential qualities underlying the discipline of the history of religions; First is a sympathetic understanding of religions other than one's own. Second is an attitude of self-criticism, even skepticism, about one's own religious background. And third is the 'scientific' temper" (Kitagawa 1959, 15). Many members of ASSR, to this day, certainly seem to have some relationship to that institution, and even those that do not, such as Richard Hecht (longtime faculty member and onetime Department Chair at the University of California–Santa Barbara), can write, "I was trained as a historian of religions under the influence of Mircea Eliade through my teacher at UCLA Kees W. Bolle. I have become increasingly interested in the deep contextualization of religion in its lived environments and most centrally the intersections of religion, politics, and culture. My work is comparative and multidisciplinary, both of which are essential, in my opinion, to the larger study of religion."[10] It would seem, then, that the spirit of Mircea Eliade, one of the first presidents of the organization, still looms in the background of this organization (despite the claim of many today that the field has left his method far behind).[11]

However, our concern is less with such relative "quantifiable" data used to denote "contributions" and "achievements," though again it is worth

[10] See his faculty description at UC Santa Barbara, Department of Religious Studies, "People: Faculty; Richard D. Hecht," http://www.religion.ucsb.edu/people/faculty/richard-d-hecht/ (accessed June 20, 2024; the current site has rephrased the original text in the third person but, otherwise, remains the same.).

[11] Another way of phrasing this would be to identify the Chicago faculty who are *not* listed among the ranks of the ASSR's members and then trying to account for what a reasonable observer might characterize as their curious absence from the ranks of its membership.

repeating that some members seem only to have a handful of publications to their name (suggesting that these seemingly objective measures are just as ideologically loaded terms as any), than it is with the last stated criterion of membership, italicized by us above: a "record of *collegial* engagement." This criterion seemingly has nothing to do with the manner in which the profession usually assesses scholarship (though the term likely appears on a surprising number of departmental tenure and promotion documents, which, by design, simultaneously disclose—by making standards tangible and public—while also disguising, thereby retaining a degree of ambiguity and thus interpretive "wiggle room" for those in senior positions within the unit). Instead, as we've already argued, it has everything to do with "getting along" with others. Case in point, consider *Wikipedia*, the current go-to source for pretty much everything these days (which, like a dictionary, provides us with the popular or commonsense use of a term), which defines the term in the following manner: "*Collegiality* is the relationship between colleagues. A colleague is a fellow member of the same profession. Colleagues are those explicitly united in a common purpose and respect each other's abilities to work toward that purpose. A colleague is an associate in a profession or in a civil or ecclesiastical office. In a narrower sense, members of the faculty of a university or college are each other's colleagues" (accessed June 22, 2024). Collegiality, as can be seen from this description alone, is a relative term—it names one's place among a group, how one's social interactions are seen *by one's peers*, and thus the extent to which one is understood *by them* to contribute to *what they see as* a common goal. It is therefore rather transparently a term of boundary maintenance. Key synonyms therefore sensibly include "relationship," "common purpose," and "respect." Presumably when one violates these or other related virtues—that is, transgresses the boundaries—one ceases to be judged by others as being collegial. But notice how (usefully) vague these terms are (not unlike "contribution" and "achievement"). What constitutes, for example, an academic relationship? And just what is our common purpose? For in the academic study of religion, not unlike other fields and disciplines in the humanities, there exist numerous ways to carry out our studies—long-standing, heated debates over these very issues are the stuff of which undergrad and grad students alike learn in the method and theory courses that now seem to populate most curriculums. However, if one goes about one's work in ways that others do not—and the question we must ask is which others get to constitute the others of significance here?—is one diverging from a supposedly common purpose and, thus, by implication, uncollegial? Read on one level collegiality would seem to be a key ingredient in the creation of not just a nondescript disciplinary identity but a specific type of disciplinary conformity. For those who explore different explanatory frameworks or who pioneer new methods risk, in the early years of their careers at least, disciplinary censure because they lack sufficient "respect" for preexistent ones (i.e., those of their social superiors, perhaps). The question, then, is whether such people would even have the luxury of being admitted to the profession and thereby having the chance at a career.

Perhaps it is within this context that we can situate the AAR's attempts, from the summer of 2015, to formulate a set of "Responsible Research Practices," which we will discuss in greater detail below.[12] Conscious of the fact that scholars of religion occupy various institutional settings and work with "different methods" of analysis, this document seeks to articulate a set of "standards" that govern all of these diverse constituencies. A quick glance at the actual standards, however, reveal less a respect for what some now term the critical study of religion than it does a need to respect those whom we study. Significantly, however, nowhere is the often-used term "respect"—much like its synonym "collegial"—defined in that document. Are we to respect the canons of scholarship—that which has governed the scholarly life from the earliest period—or are we to respect religion and religious actors or are we to respect one another as scholars? If we do not do so, are we being uncollegial? The epigraph we have opted to use in opening this chapter should make clear where we stand on the topics and thus the position from which we aim to problematize some of our peers' apparent answers to such questions.

If we return to the rules for election to ASSR, as our e.g. for the time being, we might rightly ask, what sort of intellectual work is the phrase "collegial engagement" performing for the current members of this organization? That is a difficult question to answer—we're not quite sure what it means or who gets to decide what it means but also unclear what weight is placed on this one criterion. (Perhaps the fact that we do not somehow already know any of this and are inquiring about it signals, at least to some, our own noncollegial approach to this organization.) It may in fact be the case that the very phrase "collegiality"—as vague as it is nontransparent—is what mainly or even exclusively ends up determining membership. This is a reasonable reading given that there are many long-serving non-AASR members in the academic generation beyond our own as well as our own who have made what at least we see as significant and lasting contributions to the national and

[12] The standards were adopted by the AAR Board in February of 2016; see American Academy of Religion, https://aarweb.org/news/responsible-research-practices/.

international field, at least when compared to many (or at least some) of its current members; it therefore appears fair to inquire if the lack of inclusion of such scholars boils down to the fact that "their record of collegial engagement" was somehow found wanting (meaning either that votes did not go in their favor or, as we think far likelier, that their names were never even brought forward in the first place, being vetted far more informally well before a vote was ever necessary).

It deserves to be said at this point that we agree that, as a private organization, it is surely within ASSR's right to limit membership however it sees fit. However, what work this widely used designation "collegiality" is doing—to disclose while also obscuring—in that limitation process is, for us, the curious question. For, as already noted, we find this term used not just in such private scholarly associations but also in tenure and promotion documents all across the field, let alone surely making its fair share of appearances in the undocumented conversations that help to determine our field's membership.

Collegiality, as we have already mentioned, is the discourse of the powerful or the status quo. It is the way the majority or the influential among us protects their interests, their scholarly and related values, and, ultimately, their place and authority—by finding a peer who "goes along and gets along." Collegiality must, accordingly, be conceived of not as a substantive concept, but, instead, as a socially formative rhetorical trope whose utility comes from it sounding *as if* it names something tangible, measurable, and undisputable. It is, thus, part of a discourse related to authority, that which Lincoln argues "is best understood in relational terms as the effect of a posited, perceived, or institutionally ascribed asymmetry" between an in-group, the status quo, and those that it deems as marginal or threatening players (1994, 4). As part of the production of authority, to which the charge of collegiality/uncollegiality is therefore related, nonverbal instruments and media are also often invoked—a "whole theatrical array of gestures, demeanors, costumes, props, and stage devices," to again use Lincoln's words (1994, 5), come into play when assessing one's collegiality. Peer review, tenure reviews, and reference letters can, as suggested above, count among the more formal elements of these gestures.

Again, as we learn from Lincoln, sometimes the best way to understand a dominant practice and its many interconnected components is to find examples of its failure, allowing us to explore what being collegial entails by, instead, imagining its opposite—a situation in which the normally smooth operations of dominance are called into question. So just what counts as "uncollegial" activity? Rolling one's eyes in a departmental meeting? Interrupting or talking over a colleague? Asking a question of a job candidate out of the ranked order of the group? Critiquing in print the writing of someone with whom one works, criticizing one's departmental peers within earshot of your shared students, or perhaps voting publicly against the majority for a decision of some consequence (whom to tenure or hire, for example)? Refusing a teaching assignment from the Chair perhaps? Maybe using the wrong fork with salad at a banquet? Or what about employing a nonphenomenological approach to the study of religion in one's teaching or writing? Of course, we could multiply examples almost endlessly since, given that the value collegiality is necessarily malleable (since it is undefined), there is no limit to what might be included in its membership. Much the same goes for its binary twin, uncollegial, that is, the economy of collegiality/uncollegiality is utterly and necessarily unregulated. It must be "necessarily" so, we add, if it is to function properly as a coded gatekeeper of the profession useful in who knows what future situations. For, were it to be articulated explicitly—that is, each item defined in a clear and delimited fashion—then the interests that benefit its ostensibly endless adaptability would be too apparent (and, if apparent, then more easily documented and contested; tenure or hiring disputes sometimes land in courts, after all). Rather, eschewing public argumentation or the possibility of reasoned debate, collegiality functions as a kind of shorthand for those who hold (and seek to extend their hold on) institutional authority—something that, should the discourse on collegiality function "properly," cannot be breached or infiltrated.

Collegiality thus signals a kind of authoritarianism. To quote Lincoln, once again: "The exercise of authority depends less upon the 'capacity for reasoned elaboration' as on the *presumption* made by those subject to authority that such a capacity exists, or on their calculated and strategic willingness to pretend they so presume. Authorities need not be able to explain themselves so long as others are sufficiently cowed or respectful that they do not ask for explanation" (1994, 5–6). As a form of doublespeak, then, the appeal to collegiality paradoxically works against what some of us might think we understand by this term—for example, engaging in collaborative work with peers who do not always agree but who do so within a publicly disclosed set of conditions that are open to debate and documentation (again: show your work!)—by creating the material and institutional conditions that are defined only by implying that which it is not. The term, thus, strategically conceals what it otherwise seems to reveal.

Defining an Ill-Defined Term

With the above example in mind, let us return to our initial query: just what is collegiality or what might we instead mean by the use of this term? For, as already suggested, everyone seems to know what it is not: A quarrelsome interlocutor; a rogue colleague; an ungenerous hermeneut. But what else might we mean by collegiality (if we're even able to re-purpose the term, that is, and thereby recover it from the dominants' vocabulary and thus social arsenal), and at what point does one transgress its ill-defined boundaries? Since our main concern is intellectual, professional collegiality, we must necessarily ask whether (or not) collegiality functions as a way to create and enforce scholarly consensus. If so, collegiality is less about social posturing than an attempt to marginalize those who seek to move beyond or outside of what appears to be common scholarly paradigms, by portraying them as "beyond the pale," as unprofessional, and thus falling outside the walls of the institution. (We think here of dismissing a scholar's work as mere journalism, or characterizing an interlocutor as an unscholarly dilettante, for example.) If so, then collegiality implies a certain comfort level with received opinion, and a genuine lack of interest (dare we say fear?) in pushing traditional frameworks or methods in new directions. Charges of uncollegiality, then, might have less to do with actual rancor than they do with perceived threats or suspected challenges to disciplinary hegemony.[13] The goal of such discourses, then, may not be to deal with the eye rolling but, perhaps, in an entirely preventative measure, *to prevent it from ever happening in the first place.* It is thus a device to manage and thereby to create tolerable difference.

It is probably no coincidence, then, that, as already argued, it is precisely the status quo that gets to define both the terms of reference and the various contexts wherein the presupposed virtue of "collegiality" is used. At issue is therefore the very way in which we define scholarship and the purpose and organization of the modern university. Is scholarship, for example, an individual activity (as some might no doubt contend) in which scholars engage in their work independently? Or, do we view the university as a collection of, dare we say, colleagues with shared interests, working toward common goals? Regardless, the discourse on collegiality implies a power relationship between potentially competing parties and, as we have seen, an imbalance

[13] Perhaps it is necessary to add, having introduced this term "rancor," that one of the two authors has experienced physical threats within the profession (i.e., that his house would be burned down, as disclosed to a staff member in the unit by a onetime disgruntled colleague), indicating that we do not enter into this debate on the limits of collegiality lightly.

between the status quo and those that members of the status quo, for whatever reason, deem problematic because they are a threat. It is always this outlier, for example, that is deemed the "uncollegial" one, but never the members of the status quo, regardless of how they may act. For idiosyncratic or anti-social behaviors among its members are, often, accepted and managed by being portrayed as "quirky" or "endearing"—a double standard that makes apparent the politics involved in determining what, or who, is tolerated by whom. In fact, as already noted, anyone drawing attention to the often-unperceived working of this category will likely gain for themselves the designation of being uncooperative, of not going along—in a word, of being uncollegial. Collegiality then becomes the term by which institutions, such as the one used here as a test case, minimize access to those who might otherwise appear to have the proper credentials (when membership is judged by means of seemingly substantive or quantitative criteria). Collegiality, in other words, functions as the undefinable and thus always victorious trump card to deny entry to the otherwise qualified. Somewhat akin to Tillich's rhetorically effective notion of "ultimacy"—useful among scholars of religion even to this day, we might add—one can always imagine a scenario in which subjective judgments can use this discourse to pull rank and thereby win the day.

Collegiality thus functions as yet another example of double-speak within the academy.[14] It becomes the term that can be easily invoked by malevolent colleagues to accuse those with whom they have problems of malfeasance. Consider the case of Robert David (K. C.) Johnson, an American historian at Brooklyn College and the City University of New York Graduate Center. An accomplished historian, Johnson was denied tenure, some years ago, on account of his lack of "collegiality." In what became a national case, that was subsequently overturned due to the national outcry (Smallwood 2003), Johnson cites his criticism of a post–September 11 "teach-in" that he believed was weighted too heavily with panelists hostile to U.S. military response and which offered no supporters of U.S. or Israeli policies. He also raised objections to the hiring of what he considered to be an unqualified woman (who was still ABD at the time and with what he considered to be poor teaching evaluations) for a position in the department. Reflecting on the issue of collegiality after he had been initially denied tenure, he writes:

[14] Another example is the institution of peer review, for inasmuch as the journal editor or acquisition editor privately decides to whom to send the submission, the peer in question may not signify peer of the author under review (as we usually conceive of it) but, instead, a peer of the editor who either disagrees or agrees with the submission. For, even if blind to the reviewer and as well as the author, the assignments are hardly random but, inevitably, interested. This, it seems to us, is the little-known secret being the convention of peer review.

"Academic institutions around the country need to think about how to ensure academic freedom for both tenured and untenured faculty. At Brooklyn, several senior colleagues adopted the same positions that I took regarding both the 'teach-in' and the search; tenure afforded them the freedom to speak out. By soliciting feedback from only those tenured colleagues who disagreed with me on these issues and then basing its denial of my promotion and tenure solely on 'collegiality,' the college, in effect, used tenure as a club to silence a junior faculty member who voiced opinions on controversial issues" (Johnson 2002). For him, the issue revolved around collegiality. Once again, the concept functions as a fuzzy category that is meant to silence any form of dissent. Johnson continues:

> The wholly subjective standard of "collegiality" tempts faculty members, temporarily blinded by the emotionalism of philosophical disputes or interpersonal squabbles, to abandon the academic ideals that scholars have championed for decades. CUNY Trustee Jeffrey Wiesenfeld articulated the point when asked about my case: "Collegiality is an appropriate criterion if I wanted to join a prestigious country club and play well with the other children, but it is not that which is necessary to determine whether someone is a good professor." As for me, I hope that President Kimmich will soon remedy the error of his previous decision, and that I will be able to continue, without this distraction, the scholarship and teaching that I love—to which even those who have opposed me admit I am deeply committed.

Collegiality ostensibly defines what we are as academics in general and as scholars of religion in particular. We all just seem to know what a collegial person is: someone who treats colleagues as peers, as equals (even in disagreement), collaborates with others (critique is a form of collaboration, in the classic experimental or conjecture/refutation model of science, no?), engages productively and constructively in larger discourses (that are governed by disclosed and thus debatable rules), and understands one's own interests in relation to the interests of others (Di Leo 2005a, 5). While collegiality would seem to be obvious when approached in this rather more practical way, its opposite—uncollegiality—is perhaps more difficult to define. Is being "uncollegial" a synonym for being "inflexible," "defensive," or "unwilling or unable to cooperate"? Or, as already suggested, is it something much more sinister and insidious? In fact, could it be that the status quo in our field, ironically perhaps, is uncollegial by virtue of the fact that it does not show its work when it comes to the assessment of peers?

We are hardly the first to suggest that collegiality functions as a "weasel clause," that is, a hidden or deeply buried clause that denies admittance for whatever intangible reason or reasons (e.g., see Di Leo 2005b). As already indicated, it can often function as the nebulous and always unspoken fourth category (after research, teaching, and service) to deny tenure to the otherwise fully deserving—people who, despite professional competencies, the majority just do not like for some inarticulate reason. Case in point, consider "On Collegiality as a Criterion for Faculty Evaluation," the American Association of University Professors' statement (AAUP), where we read:

> Relatively little is to be gained by establishing collegiality as a separate criterion of assessment. A fundamental absence of collegiality will no doubt manifest itself in the dimensions of teaching, scholarship, or, most probably, service, though here we would add that we all know colleagues whose distinctive contribution to their institution or their profession may not lie so much in service as in teaching and research. Professional misconduct or malfeasance should constitute an independently relevant matter for faculty evaluation. So, too, should efforts to obstruct the ability of colleagues to carry out their normal functions, to engage in personal attacks, or to violate ethical standards. The elevation of collegiality into a separate and discrete standard is not only inconsistent with the long-term vigor and health of academic institutions and dangerous to academic freedom, it is also unnecessary.[15]

That the AAUP has taken a position on the nefarious nature of this topic, however, does not mean that collegiality ceases to be invoked in characterizing faculty or evaluating peers. Nor does its continued use mean that it is not uncontested. In fact, some have argued that "collegiality" should in fact be an explicit criterion so that it is at least made transparent to candidates coming up for tenure and promotion and thereby requiring those in power to make clear articulations of its criteria and use (Di Leo 2005b, 101; Connell and Savage 2001a, 2001b). Those who are critical of failing to include collegiality as an explicit criterion often point out that such things as colleagueship, cooperation, and shared stewardship represent the very fabric of the university. While they are aware of the slippery, relative nature of

[15] The statement, dating from 1999 though revised in 2016, can be found online at "Reports and Publications: On Collegiality as a Criterion for Faculty Evaluation," American Association of University Professors, accessed June 18, 2024, https://www.aaup.org/report/collegiality-criterion-faculty-evaluation.

collegiality, they somewhat paradoxically argue that implementing it as an overt criterion will help to reduce that relativity.

And so, we return to our above example, the criteria for membership in an honorary society within our field. The collegiality clause here functions, presumably, as a way to deprive otherwise qualified potential members as somehow being "unfit" based on perceived undesirable personality or intellectual traits. Despite the fulfillment of relevant "contributions to the field" and "their achievements and interest in the comparative study of religion"—after all, who among us is *not* interested in our own field and whose work, much like this very chapter itself, is *not* comparative?—the collegiality clause enables the institution to decline or prevent admittance to, and thereby withhold certain institutional laurels from, those who are judged, by undisclosed criteria, to represent a threat to the usually operating power structure or dynamic of the institution (defined in a specific way, to the advantage of a certain few).

Recommendation

We therefore recommend dropping this language entirely, if what we're engaged in is a profession with public standards of argumentation and evidence (i.e., the public study of religion). That the term appears in the membership criteria for a private organization is, as we noted above, understandable though still lamentable to us; that the term appears in documents related to the far more public profession at large is, however, another matter entirely. We would argue that it functions there just as it does in the ASSR document. Case in point, consider the already mentioned draft statement on research responsibilities that the American Academy of Religion (AAR) released for member comments in the summer of 2015.[16] The second to the last item on the draft document is the only one that concerns our work with students—which is odd, if you think about it, since much of our work as scholars concerns preparing a new generation (aka teaching) to be researchers themselves, so you would think that a statement on research responsibilities would give

[16] See "Responsible Research Practices: A Statement on Standards of Professional Conduct for AAR Members," Religious Studies News, July 7, 2015, http://rsn.aarweb.org/responsible-research-practices-statement-standards-professional-conduct-aar-members for the draft posted in the summer of 2015. This portion of the paper is adapted from part 11 of McCutcheon's multipart blog series, from the summer of 2015, devoted to this draft document; see Russell McCutcheon, "A Response to 'Responsible Research Practices': Index," *Ongoing Discussions at the University of Alabama* (blog), *Studying Religion in Culture*, July 13, 2015, https://religion.ua.edu/blog/2015/07/a-response-to-responsible-research-practices-index/.

some attention to our role mentoring those who will succeed us. But, instead, the only attention to students reads as follows: "When working with student research assistants, professors should strive to act with collegiality, providing clear expectations and following institutional guidelines regarding pay equity, workplace safety, and harassment." Up to this point there had been little to no explicit awareness of the loaded nature of terminology so far used in this draft document, and this undefined use of collegial in its penultimate section is no different. So we have little choice but to accept that the slippery term "collegiality" is used in this earlier draft as if it is self-evidently meaningful, making it yet another example of how the document failed to live up to the standards that (we would hope) many of us routinely work to attain in our own research (e.g., clearly define your terms, recognize which are contested, identify your assumptions and mount a persuasive case for why you use the term as you do, etc.).

Now, this recurring shortcoming suggests to us that this document is merely boilerplate—or, if meant to be substantive, then, in an unintended fashion, it tells us much about what was characterized above as a dominant yet unarticulated consensus (we also termed it a hegemony, of course) that exists within the field (as represented by the committee which drafted these policies) concerning the assumed norms of the profession and their limits. It's for this reason that, in many ways, reading this draft document carefully amounts to a fieldwork experience.

But, returning to that notion of collegiality, what's curious is that amidst the committee's various links to other documents (cited in their footnotes), there's nothing referencing the above-quoted AAUP report on collegiality. Such a citation would be instructive for the committee's casual inclusion of this statement on being collegial toward students/research assistants because near the opening of the AAUP document we read the following: "In recent years, Committee A has become aware of an increasing tendency on the part not only of administrations and governing boards but also of faculty members serving in such roles as department chairs or as members of promotion and tenure committees to add a fourth criterion in faculty evaluation: 'collegiality.' For the reasons set forth in this statement, we view this development as highly unfortunate, and we believe that it should be discouraged." But why is this unfortunate? Our above discussion should make this evident. But if it is not already, then the AAUP document argues that collaboration and cooperation—if this is what we mean by collegiality—already inform our activities in the three traditionally and widely assessed areas of teaching, research, and service (meaning that it's already being tracked and assessed thoroughly), so singling out collegiality as if it is a value that stands apart from these, as some schools and departments do, so as to give it specific attention quite apart from these three areas, suggests that the term is doing unique, nonempirical work.

As phrased by the AAUP document:

> Historically, "collegiality" has not infrequently been associated with ensuring homogeneity, and hence with practices that exclude persons on the basis of their difference from a perceived norm. The invocation of "collegiality" may also threaten academic freedom. In the heat of important decisions regarding promotion or tenure, as well as other matters involving such traditional areas of faculty responsibility as curriculum or academic hiring, collegiality may be confused with the expectation that a faculty member display "enthusiasm" or "dedication," evince "a constructive attitude" that will "foster harmony," or display an excessive deference to administrative or faculty decisions where these may require reasoned discussion. Such expectations are flatly contrary to elementary principles of academic freedom, which protect a faculty member's right to dissent from the judgments of colleagues and administrators.
>
> A distinct criterion of collegiality also holds the potential of chilling faculty debate and discussion. Criticism and opposition do not necessarily conflict with collegiality. Gadflies, critics of institutional practices or collegial norms, even the occasional malcontent, have all been known to play an invaluable and constructive role in the life of academic departments and institutions. They have sometimes proved collegial in the deepest and truest sense. Certainly a college or university replete with genial Babbitts [a conformist businessperson] is not the place to which society is likely to look for leadership.

Given our view of how unstable this signifier, "collegiality," can be, and how its unspecified use can signal possible mischief—especially when used in situations where power relations are askew (in fact, we're not sure when else it would even be used)—we publicized these views when the committee was soliciting input from members of the Academy, asking them to rethink what they intended to say in this item. After all, apart from recommending being collegial and providing clear expectations, all the committee did in that bullet point was provide a list (not unlike their earlier remarks on human subjects research which added nothing not already in place for scholars doing such work) of laws (not just this committee's "guidelines") that already apply to our workplaces. We're not sure, however, that we've gained much by having our main professional association recommend, by means of this document, that, when it comes to research assistants, we should pay attention to issues of pay equity, workplace safety, and harassment.

We are not certain, of course, of the effect of the comments posted online on the shortcomings of the draft statement; neither are we aware of the committee's private discussions and the decision-making that led to the final version of the document.[17] But we do find it significant (and encouraging) that the final version of this document removed any statement on collegiality and, instead, the item on working with research assistants now reads as follows: "When employing student research assistants, professors should acknowledge their contributions, support their emerging research interests, and, where appropriate, consider possibilities for co-authorship. Professors also should provide clear expectations for their research assistants and follow institutional guidelines regarding pay equity, workplace safety, and sexual harassment." Despite what we consider to be an important revision, this research responsibility document still reads to us as uncreative boilerplate (evidenced by the inclusion of a series of undefined technical terms, such as the fifth bullet point's unelaborated admonition to treat people "honestly and fairly"), that, at some future point, might provide legal cover for the Academy should someone accuse it of never telling its members, for instance, not to harass people who work with or for them or to tell the truth.

Also, an earlier suggestion that, for whatever reason, seems to have made its way into the final document, advocated for members of the Academy to regularly co-author articles with our grad students—the job market is now so bad that seeing the AAR take a strong stand on what it means in practice to mentor the next generation of researchers would be helpful, we reasoned. For we are continually amazed by the CVs that come in from some early career people who seem to have never been told that they likely need to be writing and publishing despite also working on their dissertations (at least writing book notes, book reviews, abstracts, anything), as an indication to search committees of their wide interests, the degree to which they have already been professionalized, and their ability to juggle a variety of simultaneous projects. While the sort of continually escalating credential inflation that comes with the so-called buyer's market that we've long seen developing in the humanities is lamentable, it is among the facts that we

[17] After a public session on the draft document at the 2015 annual meeting of the Academy (in Atlanta, that year), which we both attended and during which mostly praise was expressed by the session's attendees, a final version of the document (cited above) was passed by the AAR Board in February 2016.

now live with; so, does graduating doctoral students who have no publications whatsoever (in some cases few if any conference presentations, regardless of whether at the national level or not) amount to responsible mentoring of researchers? Is it evidence of collegial behavior toward those whom we train to follow us? And what of mentoring those with futures outside academia?

But focusing on this responsibility, which is rather specific, and thus easily witnessed or measured, rather than the grandiose aim to attain an undefined and undocumentable collegial attitude, calls upon faculty to do something empirical and public—a fire to which some may not wish their feet to be held. And thus, we return to the ease with which knee-jerk and unelaborated admonitions to be collegial make their way into a field's governance documents. For striving to be collegial, in this un-nuanced and merely rhetorical sense of the term, frees us from, say, co-authoring with our students and writing them into grants, even co-authoring grant applications with them. (Curiously, encouragement to apply for grants to support research, or maybe even to support our students, is mentioned nowhere in the AAR document.) We also no longer need to worry about looking for opportunities to collaborate with other universities in our region, creating informal (or even formal) research networks in order not just to capitalize on resources (given ever-shrinking budgets, at least in many state schools) but for the benefit of our students. Focusing on being collegial removes from consideration the responsibilities a supervisor or member of a supervisory committee has toward a doctoral student—especially when, given our current job market, that dissertation will likely have to be innovative enough to get published so as to give the student as much of a leg up as possible once they graduate and start looking for full-time work. (Or, better yet, generally applicable enough to be relevant for a variety of futures.)

While any talk of students might sound to the committee that drafted this research responsibilities statement like we're inappropriately turning their document into a statement on teaching, we think that's a far too compartmentalized, dare we say uncollegial, view of what we do as scholars. Undergraduate research is a catchphrase that's caught on significantly over the past few years in North American higher ed, but the committee seems not to have thought much about undergrads in their document. We also encouraged them to reconsider that, but to no avail. For what might have been an opportunity to make a bold statement about the minimal conditions that we collectively think ought to exist in our efforts to replenish the institution in which we work with innovative and rigorous researchers who will follow us turned into a boilerplate statement that, in the 2015 annual meeting's session on the document, came down to a committee member saying, as we heard it, that other academic associations have such a document so maybe we should as well.

We think that we, as professionals, can do far better than this if we are prepared to get into the weeds, as they say, and entertain the importance of the details and actions. But, like statements on international human rights, the temptation is to limit our expectation to disembodied and undocumented items (e.g., freedom of belief or this ethereal thing we call conscience as opposed to, say, freedom of association or access to potable water), thereby allowing us to feel good about lofty aspirations that may actually have little consequence (after all *access* to clean water doesn't necessarily mean you'll get a drink). And it is in this context that we have tremendous difficulty with the discourse on collegiality—not collegiality itself, we hope to have shown, when defined as, say, practical mentoring of early career scholars so that they successfully move through their careers and contribute to the institutions in which we all work.

Our analysis and recommendation are therefore simple: collegiality, though commonly used as a form of ideological double-speak that polices the borders, ought instead to require us to take each other seriously *as scholars*, which means both rigorously testing each other's work and using publicly disclosed criteria and assessments, while also diligently working to increase the number of peers we have and with whom we interact as professionals. That, we argue, will benefit the field far more than creating a two-tier system of the privileged elite, presenting their work to each other alone, and everyone else clamoring to get on some other annual meeting program.

References

Brauer, Jerald C. 1959. "Preface." In *The History of Religions: Essays in Methodology*, edited by Mircea Eliade and Joseph M. Kitagawa. Chicago: University of Chicago Press.

Connell, Mary Ann, and Frederick G. Savage. 2001a. "Does Collegiality Count?" *Academe* 87 (6): 37–40.

———. 2001b. "The Role of Collegiality in Higher Education Tenure, Promotion, and Termination Decisions." *Journal of College and University Law* 27 (4): 833–858.

Di Leo, Jeffrey R. 2005a. "Editor's Note." *Symplokē* 13 (1&2): 5–6.

———. 2005b. "Uncollegiality, Tenure and the Weasel Clause." *Symplokē* 13 (1&2): 99–107.

Eller, Cynthia. 2016. "Editor's Note." *Journal of the American Academy of Religion* 84 (2): 285–286.

Hughes, Aaron W. 2012. *Theorizing Islam: Disciplinary Deconstruction and Reconstruction*. Sheffield: Equinox.

———. 2013. *The Study of Judaism: Authenticity, Identity, Scholarship*. Albany: State University of New York Press.

Hughes, Aaron W., and Russell T. McCutcheon. 2022. *Religion in 50 Words: A Critical Vocabulary*. New York: Routledge.

Johnson, Robert David. 2002. "Why I Was Denied Tenure." *History News Network*, December 11. https://www.historynewsnetwork.org/article/why-i-was-denied-tenure.

Kitagawa, Joseph M. 1959. "The History of Religions in America." In *The History of Religions: Essays in Methodology*, edited by Mircea Eliade and Joseph M. Kitagawa. Chicago: University of Chicago Press.

Lincoln, Bruce. 1994. *Authority: Construction and Corrosion*. University of Chicago Press.

———. 1996. "Theses on Method." *Method & Theory in the Study of Religion* 8: 225–227.

Mack, Burton. (1988) 1991. *A Myth of Innocence: Mark and Christian Origins*. Philadelphia: Fortress.

McCutcheon, Russell T. 1997. "A Default of Critical Intelligence? The Scholar of Religion as Public Intellectual." *Journal of the American Academy of Religion* 65 (2): 443–468.

———. 2003. *The Discipline of Religion: Structure, Meaning, Rhetoric*. New York: Routledge.

———. 2006. "'It's a Lie. There's No Truth in It! It's a Sin!': On the Limits of the Humanistic Study of Religion and the Costs of Saving Others from Themselves." *Journal of the American Academy of Religion* 74 (3): 720–750.

———. 2024. *Religious Studies beyond the Discipline: On Earning and Awarding a Humanities Ph.D.* Sheffield: Equinox.

Nelson, Cary, and Stephen Watt, eds. 1999. *Academic Keywords: A Devil's Dictionary for Higher Education*. New York: Routledge.

O'Flaherty, Wendy Doniger. 1986a. "On the ASSR and Joseph Kitagawa." *History of Religions* 25 (4): 293–295.

———. 1986b. "The Uses and Misuses of Other Peoples, Myths." *Journal of the American Academy of Religion* 54 (2): 219–239.

Orsi, Robert A. 2004. "Fair Game." *Bulletin of the Council of Societies for the Study of Religion* 33 (3&4): 87–89.

———. 2005. *Between Heaven and Earth: The Religious Worlds People Make and the Scholars Who Study Them*. Princeton, NJ: Princeton University Press.

Smallwood, Scott. 2003. "Tenure Madness." *Chronicle of Higher Education* (May 23). http://chronicle.com/article/Tenure-Madness/3373.

Taira, Teemu. 2022. *Taking "Religion" Seriously: Essays on the Discursive Study of Religion*. Leiden: Brill.

5
Introduction
Practicing Self-Reflexivity

Generally speaking, in my experience many scholars are rather poorly suited to apply their critical tools to the analysis of their own situations and the institutions in which they themselves work. Perhaps it's because of just how effective academia's so-called life of the mind mythology has been in producing a privileged setting in which some "we" get to study "them," as if our world somehow floated free of the constraints that are so obviously evident in theirs. (That increasingly few scholars today have the privilege of taking their own situations for granted, what with program cuts, department closures, and ever-increasing reliance on contingent faculty, certainly needs to be noted here.) I find that even those in the university today who ardently critique the presumption for disinterested objectivity that once grounded much scholarship are often lacking in the ability to strategically understand the workings of their own settings. But even those who are proficient in the use of such things as critical social theory, which they may employ to examine the often-undisclosed conditions of other people's worlds and how they make them meaningful for themselves, tend not to do so well understanding (let alone effectively operating within) their own situations. I keep coming back to the privilege argument to account for what I see as this shortcoming among scholars; after all, if a fresh carton of milk just keeps appearing in the refrigerator every few days, who will ask questions about how it got there, let alone the wider conditions necessary for milk production, packing, and delivery? It might all be as simple as that old saying, "Out of sight, out of mind"—does the average faculty member (especially one who is tenured, let alone those with senior in rank) really think all that much about, let's say, how their courses get placed into classrooms, the business models adopted by, let's just say, their campus bookstore or their college's online courses, or even how decisions are actually made by the senior administration or by their school's board of trustees (perhaps concerning such things as how tuition revenue is distributed and spent or how open lines are or are not filled)? Odds are that far more faculty do today than in previous decades, I'll grant you that, what with the extent to which colleges, large and small, now seem to be racing each other to drop liberal arts majors (from physics, chemistry, and even math to music, English, and, of course, the study of religion), close units, and, in some cases, terminate faculty. Despite all this, however, there's still a rather good chance that paying attention to practical matters on a campus may be limited to those who are working in schools where faculty already feel that their programs, maybe even their jobs, are in jeopardy. Sadly, like people in a horror movie, we tend to realize far too late that the call is coming from inside our own house.

For yet others, notably those lucky enough to still occupy tenured lines and who happen to work on campuses that, at least for now, seem to be insulated from (either some or maybe all of) the pressures that other schools are experiencing, there's likely little incentive to add to their already crowded to-do lists such things as working to shore up faculty governance on their campus or investigating whether the stats used by your administration include second majors in the count. After all, if I'm being generous and not offering a caricature of (especially the senior tenured) professor said by some to be gardening during what should have been work hours, I would have to say that many of them are already pretty busy, what with their teaching duties (which, depending on their school, can often be three or more different courses per semester) but also with the more than likely increased research and publication expectations that have been placed upon them, as well as the more prominent role played today by their school's desire for external funding—an expectation already making its way into the humanities. Adding to all of this whatever service they may be doing for their own department or for the college at large, let alone the work that they may also perform for a variety of outside bodies with which they may be affiliated (such as a regional or national professional association, perhaps), and you arrive at the proverbial overworked faculty member—and note that so far I've only included their career obligations, not even mentioning family. Accordingly, there's little incentive for many of them to find time to serve on a faculty senate, much less to invest the energy and time needed to work toward remaking it as an effective governing body that informs campus decisions. And so, to be fair, there are likely very good reasons to account for many faculty members' current inability to apply their own critical tools in examining the conditions of possibility at their own colleges. Adding to all of this what is, at least in some places, a post-COVID decline in faculty presence and thus investment in their institutions (prompted, I would argue, by faculty dissatisfaction with how some of their institutions treated them during that time, by which I mean how some colleges approached the virus more as a branding or PR challenge than as a public health issue), and you can see how engagement with their own institution's workings may be at an all-time low among some faculty members.

Another layer to this story is the increasing professionalization of the managerial class on university campuses over the past few decades. Long gone are the days of seeing the role of dean or provost as a service to the college and therefore a role from which one would, after a term or two, step down in order to return to the faculty ranks, as we say. Although there certainly still are exceptions, they merely prove the rule that many university administrators would never dream of returning to full-time teaching and research (which really makes someone like me wonder why they earned a Ph.D. in the first place and what they thought the career was going to be like). Although deans still often come from the ranks of chairs (given the latter's experience handling personnel issues as well as managing budgets), chairs and associate deans alike often aim to become deans or associate vice presidents for research (a now standard role, of varying names, that few campuses had just a decade or so ago); deans are clearly angling to become provosts or vice presidents for academic affairs, busily amassing initiatives on their CVs that may appeal to another campus. And as for provosts? Pretty much all that's left to them on the upward track is to become the president of a university—though horizontal moves are certainly possible at every stage of the administrative game, especially a dean or a provost at a small college moving to the same role at a far larger state school, or maybe an administrator senior enough to retire at one school collecting a pension from there while earning a whole new salary at another college. Case in point, on my own campus, when I announced publicly that I would be stepping down after eighteen years in the role of department chair (beginning in 2001, I was chair for eight years, followed by four years out of the position, and then another decade back in the role), I was told how I really ought to be applying to be a dean elsewhere (of an honors college or a College of Arts & Sciences maybe?) instead of returning to the role of a professor (during all these years, by the way, I regularly taught and carried out research). At one point, when it was plain that I had no interest in serving in any role higher up the administrative ladder, a friend at the time who was himself a member of the senior administration expressed regret that I was making the wrong decision for my career, going so far as to send me job ads for administration positions elsewhere. Perhaps it's the pay boost when you move into the upper administration (which is only in part explained by moving to a twelve-month from the typical nine-month contract for faculty here in the United States) or being free of what some see as onerous research and teaching duties, but, for whatever reason, many people I know in such positions would not dream of returning to the faculty ranks. If for no other reason, it's surely a challenge to return to a faculty position from one that paid rather more.

(Aside: in my years as a chair I found that it provides tremendous freedoms, as long as the person in the role understands how their college works, and thereby sees the inevitable lacuna, gaps, or contradictions in the many systems that comprise a campus, that each might be used to further their unit's interests. While budgets are certainly far larger the higher up the administrative ladder you go, the degree to which you must more strictly follow campus dictates also increases, convincing me long ago that moving above a department chair meant paying far more attention to campus-wide goals than to local needs within the department. For an effective chair must recognize, I've often said, that meeting the needs of their unit does not necessarily [or, rather, often does not] sufficiently overlap with meeting the needs of the university as a whole—something that may finally be more than evident to anyone now paying attention to colleges cutting the liberal arts to "save" the school [an action often necessitated, or so we are told, by financial shortfalls; precisely what past spending led to the deficit is rarely explained in any real detail]. The freedoms to work closely with faculty, staff, and students to accomplish things of importance to them, as long as those efforts do not diminish the unit's ability also to address whatever campus-wide goals are within its abilities to reach, persuaded me quite some time ago that moving any higher up the ladder would immerse me in rather unrewarding work.)

And so, this professionalization of the managerial class, which now also draws on people from well outside higher education or those faculty from the professional schools who also have work experience in the private section (aka the real world), has developed alongside colleges increasingly being run like a business, with power crystallized at the top and held only among the executives (which, it must be noted, is now more often than not found beyond university presidents and, instead, resides with the board to which they report). In such a setting, there are overt and implicit signals regularly sent to faculty members concerning their place on the campus and thus their limited (maybe even minimal) sphere of influence; it is therefore a completely rational reaction, in such situations, for instructors of all ranks to focus on their teaching and their research, leaving it to others to run the place—after all, their input is often not sought, with few on the wider campus nurturing the mechanisms of faculty governance as anything other than performative. It's just such a setting that leads to many faculty seeing the role as chair as a dagger onto which they may have to fall from time to time, one that takes them away from their real work—a representation that I find to diminish its very real importance. This alienation from the workings of the place doesn't mean that faculty are content with how it's being operated, but any grumbling that they might have can be rather far removed from the sort of organized, collective, practical action capable of impacting it in some fashion. After all, many U.S. campuses tend not to have faculty who are unionized, of course, and the American Association of University Professors (AAUP), while laudable in many ways, seems incapable of meeting all of the needs of faculty today.

But why do I open this chapter in this way? My hope is that it quickly becomes apparent once one begins to read it; it was originally written as a response to a plenary address delivered as part of a remote annual conference (that took place in November of 2021, during the height of COVID protocols); the conference theme was devoted to a variety of crises—or better yet, at least as I read the call for papers that circulated several months prior, devoted to the very designation "crisis" and its practical effects. But the inability of some in attendance to keep their eyes on the *discourse* on crisis, and instead to focus on so-called *actual* crises that, justifiably they would no doubt argue, preoccupied them was illuminating to me, if disappointing as well. It confirmed the unenviable situation that many faculty are now in: all consumed by the challenges of their circumstances, they may feel little recourse but to stare into the light of the oncoming train, failing to know how to get out of its way let alone understand why it was coming for them in the first place. If nothing else, then, my hope is that the following chapter narrates the difficult position in which many faculty members now find themselves, yes, but also that it suggests why using their critical intelligence even in such situations may serve them well.

Now, in saying this I don't wish to spin some tale of free-wheeling creative agency that someone might be able to exercise if they just got it right; as I've written on a variety of past occasions, I presume from the outside that we are all agents, yes indeed, but acting within an array of structures not of our making. (There's a history in our field of ignoring structures and emphasizing individual agency, I should add.) But since I presume that prior agents made those structures—not that they were all aware of each other, however, or working in coordinated ways—then the systems in which we live and work are necessarily changeable things, what with them being historical, social products. Our agency, as constrained as it may be (i.e., always is), nonetheless has effect, can collaborate with the agency of others, and can achieve a variety of results—but usually arriving at ends that are rather different from those intended, to be sure, since the effects of collective action result from a variety of actors each with (maybe complementary but maybe contradictory) goals of their own. For this reason, I tend to talk of structures as being nonagential (i.e., the English language doesn't do things or have intentions, after all) even though they are nothing if not the products of previous agents who were themselves working with yet prior systems, and so on, and so on. It seems to me that someone who understands social life to be working in this manner, with agency and structure as but two sides of the same always spinning coin, may be in a strategic position to find opportunities where others just see a headlight bearing down on them—they may even be a chair or an undergraduate director finding a gap in a system that allows them to do something inventive and beneficial for their peers or their students. For while we may not be able to derail the much larger economic or political conditions impacting higher education today, let alone our own dean's decisions (which most often follow dictates set well above them in the hierarchy), perhaps we can stall it; maybe we can then regroup and succeed in a new way. (Department closed? Then can you form a center and retain all of your faculty lines, as the former Department of Religious Studies at the University of Miami of Ohio did not long ago, as I recall.) Or, for those paying attention to trends in higher ed but who are fortunately not part of any cuts (for now), can you read the coffee grounds and make proactive changes that may benefit the unit when and if talk of "rationalizing" campus comes to town? As the direct beneficiary of such strategic action, I would hope that faculty members who have so far not paid much attention to the structures in which we all work to begin to see the incentive for swimming against what I recognize as the considerable stream of duties and responsibilities that are already squarely in their laps, adding to their list a focus on how their campus works, how it is situated within regional or even national economics or politics, and how they, working in concert with others in their unit, can enhance or maybe even protect some of their own work conditions—minimally, perhaps, but sometimes far more than that.

To return to the chapter to come, more often than you might realize, I think being in the position to try to do any of this means shifting one's gaze to the discourse around whatever it is that you might be focusing on; for unless you think and act like the world is just naturally comprised of self-evidencies and inevitabilities—and I fully recognize that some do indeed think this—it could be seen as sensible to instead ask about the often unapparent conditions that prompt us to see the world in this or that way (i.e., for the public, politicians, and even some administrators so easily to be able to represent the humanities as irrelevant and ill-equipped to prepare a student for that so-called real world). Understanding those parameters, even in our own world of academia, is probably the first step to effectively pushing back; our time, energy, and resources are not unlimited, after all, so intervening at strategic sites to maximize effect is necessary, and that won't come from failing to understand the structures in which we're all working. So, applying our critical tools to examine our own situations ought to be a real priority for each of us—let's just call that the sort of self-reflexivity that many of us have been championing for the past few decades. But now it's a self-examination that's aimed at our own institutions and work conditions rather than just at the habits of thought that animate our scholarship.

Scholars Are People Too

The (Sometimes) Difficult Shift to the Discourse of Crisis

During the Q&A that followed the North American Association for the Study of Religion's 2021 virtual plenary address by Aaron Hughes I could not help but think of a March 29, 2005, episode (season 1, episode 2, titled "Diversity Day") of the U.S. adaptation of the originally British television series, *The Office*—an episode that has stuck with me, perhaps because of what I take to be the subtle but nonetheless sophisticated theoretical point that it makes (and maybe also because of the series' constant re-runs on U.S. television throughout the COVID pandemic).[1] In the episode's subplot, Jim Halpert—the likable paper salesman who is secretly in love with Pam Beesly, the receptionist (and she with him as well)—has an absolutely terrible day in which he is repeatedly interrupted while trying to finalize an annual sales call that, in the past, has dependably resulted in a quarter of his year's commissions. (He even has a small bottle of champagne, in his office desk drawer, in anticipation of celebrating the sale.) And then, when he finally gets through to the client, after repeated delays and frustrations from his workmates as well as from his less than accommodating boss, it turns out that his arch nemesis in the office, Dwight Schrute, has made the call and made the sale—and made the commission. Although it may go without saying, it's a bad day for Jim. In fact, we might even go so far as to call it a "financial crisis," what with the amount of annual salary that was on the line from this one sales call.

But those who are familiar with this episode know that at the end of the work day, after participating in what turns out to be an inane and, by some contemporary standards, an outrightly offensive diversity training session at

[1] The description of this episode is adapted from my own afterword to McCutcheon (2015).

work (in fact, the episode's main plot is so problematic by the standards of many contemporary viewers that it's now being reported that streaming services may skip over it entirely when playing the series, regardless of it being an obvious parody), Pam, who happens to have been seated next to Jim in the conference room, has fallen asleep with her head resting on his shoulder.

> The meeting ends.
>
> The room empties.
>
> Alone, the two of them remain seated in the room, Pam still asleep.
>
> Jim looks at the camera, aware he's being filmed of course, unsure what to do.
>
> He softly wakes her.
>
> She rises, self-conscious and a little chagrined, fixing her hair.
>
> She leaves the room.
>
> He remains, alone in the chair.

From there we cut to the confessional-shot, where an actor, seated alone in a spare office at the paper company, sometimes speaks directly to the filmmakers, in character, debriefing on the day's events—don't forget, the staff of this office all know that they're being filmed for what is said to be a public television documentary on a local business. And now viewers learn that what had been Jim's terrible, horrible, no good, very bad day has suddenly been transformed, in a way that he could never have imagined just moments before. "Umm . . . not a bad day . . ." he says to the film crew, with a small but self-satisfied grin.

And, just like that, his day has utterly changed, right before our very eyes; there's no longer a financial crisis—though, sure, he's still lost a considerable portion of his annual salary. But his focus, his priorities, and thus the way that he sorts through the day's many events when making sense of it all has all been recalibrated; he's created a whole new narrative basis for an answer to the perennial question: "How was your day?"

I draw on this example from recent popular culture as a place where Hughes's plenary address helps us considerably to see what is going on; for, as he argued (but now in my words), crises exist at the level of discourse, among a group whose members share affinities, share narratives, and share goals—and thus share the identities that might then result. Change any of those elements and, suddenly, either it's not such a bad day or it's a date that—to borrow from then U.S. president Franklin D. Roosevelt's still well-known December 8, 1941, address to Congress, asking it to declare war on Japan—"will live in infamy."

But in response to the critical tools that Hughes offered to his listeners, to examine how such things as rhetorics of crisis work—*when* they're invoked, *why* they're invoked, *who* gets to invoke them, and *what* might be accomplished by asserting such claims—we instead learned, at a variety of points during the Q&A, about the various *actual* crises that seem to preoccupy those who were in attendance remotely: from the crisis of the scientific study of religion to various crises of the contemporary corporatized university and, yes, even the crisis of Donald Trump's place in American politics at that time, not to mention some ill-defined things said to be "existential crises." So, instead of following Hughes and examining *why* and for *whom* such issues or events count *as* crises, and what might be gained by describing them as such—critical questions that, in my hearing, his paper encouraged us to ask—many in the audience struck me as being a little dumbfounded that someone would apparently deny that each of these were in fact *real* crises, and thus moments of such *undebatable* consequence that to label them in any other way, or to overlook them altogether, was somehow to diminish not just these set-apart moments or the situations themselves but, more importantly perhaps, also those who are so deeply concerned about them.

And that, in my estimation, was where the conference's opening session ended—with both the virtual Q&A and the Zoom session's chat active with a variety of participants affirming each other via their judgments that this or that was indeed an *actual* crisis and with Hughes, at least in my reading, somehow taking the fall for the sort of critical analysis that he had placed before us and expected us to use. What's more, judging by some of the panels and paper titles that, at least at that point in the conference, were yet to come that weekend, it seemed entirely likely to me that the divide that was so obvious during that opening session—between those interested in studying the *discourse* on crisis, on the one hand, and those simply making claims about *actual* crises, on the other—would likely continue. And that prediction proved entirely correct; for while a number of contributions to the weekend's program attempted to keep our eyes firmly on what is at stake in either framing (or denying to frame) something *as* a crisis (to draw on Lauren Horn Griffin's apt phrasing of the issue from her response to Hughes's opening paper), yet others skipped over this critical step entirely and went straight to making claims about various crises, with an interest in how they should properly be addressed or assessing how others have (or have not) responded to them.

I find this divergence, especially in a NAASR meeting of all places—an organization famed for its critical analysis—rather problematic and worth thinking about; hence the inclusion of this chapter here. For Hughes's paper struck me as entirely in keeping with the organization's call for papers for that year's program. As posted on the NAASR website, it asked the following two questions: "What happens when we classify something as a "crisis"? . . . How does this designation illuminate or obscure certain political or ideological dynamics?" Judging by such a call it therefore seemed to me that the meeting would be about the *discourse* on crisis, a theme that prompted me to agree to the kind invitation to join the opening panel as a respondent. Case in point: instead of claiming that U.S. president Donald Trump signifies a crisis of American democracy, a scholar in the tradition presumed in the call and assumed in Hughes's address could instead ask for *whom* is Trump's continued involvement in U.S. politics a crisis? After all, for roughly half the country (at the time when Aaron's paper was presented) it still seemed that this was not the case whatsoever; as reported in a Quinnipiac poll on October 19, 2021, 78 percent of registered Republicans favored Trump running for president again in 2024 and 41 percent of Americans surveyed responded that he has had what they characterize as a mainly positive effect on U.S. politics—that he was reelected in 2024 with 312 Electoral College votes (though with slightly less than 50% of the popular vote) makes this point even better.[2] Perhaps it was the ambivalence of the electorate, or maybe a concern for what the designation of something as a crisis would entail for the American body politic, that kept pundits from ever declaring that a "constitutional crisis" was taking place in Trump's first four years in office—despite what many agree to have been his flouting of long-standing norms and possibly even federal laws (cases dropped upon his reelection, of course). Moreover, I'm not even sure what those in that NAASR session who were *not* American (after all, NAASR attracts a wide array of participants, especially given the ease of joining that year's virtual sessions let alone the "North American" in its title) even made of the ease with which specifically U.S. politics was, once again, self-evidently of importance to us—that is, just which "us" is necessary for all of this crisis rhetoric to be invoked and to work? For, as Hughes so rightly pointed out, for an extremely small segment of international society the global COVID-19 pandemic at the time had been a financial windfall and thus anything but a crisis; for, just as in times of

[2] See "78% Of Republicans Want to See Trump Run for President in 2024, Quinnipiac University National Poll Finds; Americans Now Split on Border Wall as Opposition Softens," Quinnipiac University Poll, October 19, 2021, https://poll.qu.edu/poll-release?releaseid=3825.

war, certain sectors of the economy do exceedingly well at times such as these. Consider, for instance, that in an article from April 30, 2021, *Forbes* magazine reported that Jeff Bezos's wealth had increased by $86 billion since January 2020—due in large part to the mass move to online shopping throughout the pandemic.[3] So, theorizing efforts to designate either Trump's first presidency or the pandemic, let alone anything else, as "a crisis," and thereby trying to determine what's entailed in this act, and thus what it triggers or prompts when it is or is not used, is what I heard Hughes to be inviting the scholars in attendance to consider. So the fact that his paper had such an uphill climb during parts of the Q&A—when, to my ears at least, some of the participants in that evening's session seemed to be personally affronted that someone might suggest that, for instance, the pandemic was not an obvious example of a real crisis, what with how, at the minimum, it had turned many of our lives upside down (notably those of academic parents, let alone those who had fallen ill—or far worse), is therefore something to mull over in earnest as we continue to examine what's happening at this particular moment in our scholarly organizations, our universities, and even our society writ large.[4]

And mulling this over is something that I would like to do here, just a little, to try to make sense of the angry response that Hughes's paper evoked on the part of at least some of those who joined that evening's session—a response that was significant enough that it continued to be discussed throughout not only the rest of the panel that comprised replies to his plenary but also during the remainder of the meeting's weekend. What I hope becomes evident in the foregoing is that I have no interest in judging my colleagues or assigning blame; instead, I am quite interested in how this discrete and, for some, possibly forgettable moment might tell us something about the situation in which our profession now finds itself—an insight gained by applying a dose of self-reflexive social theory, since, as a colleague recently phrased it to me, scholars are people too.

What made the reaction to Hughes's paper stand out for me was that it seemed curiously similar to how many people once responded (and still respond) to so-called reductionists when they dared to study the claims,

[3] Chase Peterson-Withorn, "How Much Money America's Billionaires Have Made during the Covid-19 Pandemic," *Forbes*, April 30, 2021, https://www.forbes.com/sites/chasewithorn/2021/04/30/american-billionaires-have-gotten-12-trillion-richer-during-the-pandemic/.

[4] That Hughes signaled early on in his address that evening that the pandemic had had a significant impact on scholars, and that he is himself a parent of two with who knows what parenting challenges of his own at the time, seems not to have been something those who reacted negatively necessarily knew or dwelled upon.

actions, and organizations of those who were identified (sometimes, though not always, self-identified) *as* religious, but doing so in ways that were not already offered or sanctioned by either these people themselves or the scholars who are sympathetic to them (often comprising such people's self-represented spokespeople). As anyone familiar with our field's mid-twentieth-century history will know, such scholars are often met with harsh criticism, given that their methods are said to demean the religious people under study by failing to, as the old saying went, "take religion seriously." (See Pritchard 2010 on this particular claim, who argues: "'Taking seriously' is a controlled experiment in which risks are alluded to but ultimately avoided" [1089].) As evident from an earlier chapter, I have had this very complaint leveled at my own work throughout my career, such as Robert Orsi's (2004) onetime criticism of my use of the supposedly dehumanizing word "data" when discussing the human moments or situations that a scholar of religion might study.[5] What was of note, then, was that what struck me as Hughes's rather less than controversial effort to persuade us to stand back and examine when and how the rhetoric of crisis is used was, apparently, likewise seen by some as a threat to those in attendance who were presumably using occasions *designated as* crises in their own socially formative acts of self-identification. To rephrase it, his paper presented a threat to what they either presumed or wished to be seen as an unquestioned social consensus that such-and-such a circumstance was intolerable, a dire threat, a defining moment, or a unique challenge. And, in response, those sharing this presumption, and thus those wishing to signal a set of shared affinities, quickly rallied to support one another against the perceived threat of, well, scholarly analysis, doing so either vocally or in the virtual meeting's chat.

What I assume was threatening about the method that Hughes proposed—a form of scholarship, I should add, that surely is commonplace in the work of virtually all NAASR members, *at least when they are studying "them" (whether ancient or contemporary) and "their" normative claims, modes of authority, social organizations, etc.*—was that it linked the claim that something, such as the pandemic, was a crisis to contingent, contextual circumstances and social interests, notably of those who were making such a claim and thus strategically using such a designation. For this approach relativizes

[5] As I wrote in the previous chapter, the word "data" remains important in my work because it keeps ever present the important realization that the scholar's curiosities, assumptions, and methods produce the items on which we work and thus that they are not naturally occurring or self-evidently interesting items. My concern is that those who fail to use this term often fail to recognize that there is nothing authentic or necessarily important about that which happens to be the focus of the scholar's attention.

a seemingly self-evident claim (in that crises are now seen as being relative to the interests of those naming things or moments as such)—claims that, when such rhetorics are working properly among like-interested speakers and listeners, do quite the opposite: they effectively mark an occasion or an issue *as* anything but relative, that is, a moment or situation is instead represented as unique, enduring, and especially dire, representing it as a circumstance that must be met with not just consequential but also coordinated action (e.g., from responses to the climate crisis and the pandemic's supply-chain crisis to the crisis at the border and even the crisis of the humanities job market in academia). Hughes's proposed methodological shift, however, required a degree of self-reflexivity that, though now assumed by many to be widely adopted across much of academia, turned out to be a little too challenging (because too close to home, perhaps) for some that evening; for inquiring into the interests of those making such claims, looking at the classifier rather than that which carries their label, and asking what might be gained or at least accomplished by such a designation, prevents the otherwise smooth workings of this rhetoric and thereby calls into question the seemingly self-evident affinities and identities that it helps to shape. And this—not unlike studying what others see as their unique and deeply meaningful religious claims as if they are nothing more or less than ordinary social or political claims and practices—is understandably perceived as a threat to those invested in making such claims, sharing such affinities, and reproducing such identities.

Simply put, the response of some to the plenary address was an occasion when we saw the usually undisclosed limits of what are for many the otherwise unproblematic (or what, by now, some colleagues may even see as somewhat pedestrian) theses on method once offered by Bruce Lincoln; but, as it turns out, they're not pedestrian at all, for on this occasion there was a pronounced failure (to adapt the language of his thirteenth and final thesis) to distinguish between asserting the existence of "a crisis," on the one hand, and adopting the stance of scholars who study how both "crisis-claims" and "regimes of crisis" function to make happenings into crises. It therefore occurred to me as a moment when, as Lincoln notes, "one has ceased to function as historian or scholar."

What makes this failure even more interesting to me is that, as already suggested, this shift in scholarship (i.e., from studying truth to truth claims and, most broadly, regimes of truth, as Lincoln put it) is usually rather uncontroversial for the so-called critical scholars of religion who often comprise NAASR's membership—but that evening we saw that this turns out to depend upon what or whom one might be studying. Consider the ease with which a critical scholar would probably understand not just the perhaps inconsequential e.g. of Jim Halpert's day, cited at the outset of this brief chapter, but, for instance, a more impactful designation such as, say, calling something "a coup," aiming to see it too as being far from an innocently descriptive term that's somehow directly linked to a so-called actual fact on the ground (i.e., an actual coup). To press this point, consider the international news stories not just about what went on in Egypt in early July 2013[6] but, more specifically, about the U.S. reaction to what went on. With around $1.5 billion in annual U.S. foreign aid on the line at that time (second then only to its annual aide to Israel), the Obama administration's reaction was curiously (or predictably?—now *that's* the question that Hughes helps us to answer) focused on how to classify—and thereby how to understand and react to—what just happened. Sure, an Egyptian general had stepped in front of a television camera to make an unanticipated speech, the duly elected (though then widely unpopular) president had been deposed and detained by the military, a number of his party's senior leadership were also detained, the constitution was suspended, and military officers swore in their own pick as interim president. Accordingly, it looked an awful lot like a coup, and it sure smelled like a coup, yes—but was it a coup? Or to be more specific in our question, why was the U.S. government at the time so careful *not* to designate these events *as* a coup?

To answer this, we would be wise to heed Hughes's advice and ask some questions about the context of such a classificatory judgment, including the implications for social actors who do or do not make such a call. We could then inquire into the legal context (making the discourse on coups just as relative as the discourse on crises): the United States' Foreign Assistance Act of 1961 (22 USC)—specifically, chapter 91, subchapter II, section 8422 (Authorization of Assistance) reads as follows:

> (3) Additional authority
>
> Except as provided in sections 2753 and 2799aa–1 of this title, the second section 620J [1] of the Foreign Assistance Act of 1961 (as added by Public Law 110–161) [22 U.S.C. 2378d], and any provision of an Act making appropriations for the Department of State, foreign operations, and related programs that *restricts assistance to the government of any country whose duly elected head of government is deposed by military coup or decree*, and except as otherwise provided in this subchapter, amounts authorized to be made

[6] See the *New York Times*' coverage, David D. Kirkpatrick, "Army Ousts Egypt's President; Morsi Is Taken into Military Custody," *New York Times*, July 3, 2013, https://www.nytimes.com/2013/07/04/world/middleeast/egypt.html.

> available to carry out paragraph (2) for fiscal years 2010 and 2011 are authorized to be made available notwithstanding any other provision of law. (emphasis added)[7]

"Military intervention,"[8] "national reconciliation," and "popular uprising" therefore sounded to some like pretty good choices when the alternative of classifying it as a coup entailed criminalizing what had just happened with this very strategic U.S. ally in the Middle East.

Though, to be honest, I'm not entirely sure why reporters were so focused on the rhetorical contortions among government spokespeople at the time, working to avoid the "c" word—or why all the contortions to begin with—since section 2753 of the law states the following as being among its four conditions for exemption:

> (a) Prerequisites for consent by President; report to Congress
>
> No defense article or defense service shall be sold or leased by the United States Government under this chapter to any country or international organization, and no agreement shall be entered into for a cooperative project (as defined in section 2767 of this title), unless—
>
> (1) the President finds that the furnishing of defense articles and defense services to such country or international organization will strengthen the security of the United States and promote world peace.

Thus, it turns out that all it takes is for the U.S. president to determine that such international developments are in the United States' interest to support the action and, voila, what at first blush seemed like a coup that would end U.S. funding is now a populist uprising that the United States supports.[9]

Now, I assume that many will find this brief example, perhaps not unlike my opening pop culture e.g., unhelpful because it is so obviously the case that, as scholars interested in how classification systems work might say,

[7] Find the law at "22 U.S. Code § 8422 - Authorization of Assistance," Cornell Law School, Legal Information Institute, accessed June 20, 2024, https://www.law.cornell.edu/uscode/text/22/8422.
[8] This was *The Guardian*'s choice for its headline; see Ian Black, "Egypt's Revolution and Diplomacy: When a Coup Is a 'Military Intervention,'" July 4, 2013, accessed June 20, 2024, https://www.theguardian.com/world/2013/jul/04/egypt-revolution-coup-military-intervention-analysis.
[9] The above example is taken from a blog post of my own from July 5, 2013, found at Russell McCutcheon, "The C-Word: Obama Avoids Calling Egyptian Leader's Ouster a Coup," *Culture on the Edge* (blog), accessed June 21, 2024, https://edge.ua.edu/russell-mccutcheon/the-c-word/.

coups exist in discourse—discourses that certainly have practical effects. But shift to another c-word (i.e., crisis) and we quickly learn that a shift to discourse at this point is apparently a little more difficult for some to make. For even if unwilling to follow Hughes and his focus on the rhetoric of crisis, there's surely agreement on the part of many that there's much we can learn from the discourse around classifying something *as* a coup in U.S. law, not unlike what we might glean from the recent tendency to label (and thereby delegitimize) governments with which our own disagrees as "regimes" or, as we saw with President George W. Bush's administration, tactically devising/deploying the term "enhanced interrogation techniques" to avoid the implications of such actions being understood as internationally outlawed "torture"—not to mention the practical implications of naming something *as* a religion (as opposed to politics), *as* a myth (as opposed to history or a fairy tale), *as* a ritual (as opposed to a habit), *as* sacred (as opposed to secular), et cetera. For in each of these cases we likely all agree that, upon closer inspection, the seemingly stable, descriptive term turns out to be a socially formative category used for strategic purposes and effects, by situated and always invested social actors. The challenge for scholars, however, is to see this happening no less when, for instance, the "crisis of academic labor" is discussed, despite many of our own affinities with those who represent and experience the recent and current humanities job market as such. After all, our own investments should not cloud our ability to make critical judgments about our own circumstances. This is what I take the often difficult task of self-reflexivity to mean, at least at its best.

But, as troublesome as I thought some of my colleagues' failure on this point was—what with how it demonstrated the limits of so-called critical thinking when self-interest and self-identity are on the line—I must repeat that I do not wish my comments concerning that evening's Q&A to be read as a criticism of those who seemed to have been bothered by Hughes's comment on how even the so-called crisis of the pandemic will pass and is therefore relative to the changeable interests of specific social actors who name it as such;[10] instead, as someone interested in the history of our field and the contemporary conditions in which the study of religion takes shape, I'd like to propose that we further theorize this situation to better understand

[10] Watching news coverage of the tornadoes that devastated parts of the United States (from Arkansas to Illinois) just weeks after Hughes's paper and hearing various governors say, in response, such things as "We shall rebuild, we shall overcome this," I could not help but think of Hughes's effort to relativize crisis rhetorics. And, as devastating as I admit that the pandemic was for so many worldwide, now, with the benefit of hindsight, it would be interesting to hear how those in attendance at the NAASR paper that evening think of those few years.

the moment in which academics (or the smaller sample size of those scholars of religion joining that session) now find themselves, what with the crisis in the humanities in which many of us all agree we are currently immersed. To rephrase: what wider factors (not unlike that U.S. law inspiring rather artful uses of the word "coup" a few years ago) contributed not only to that situation being read as what I've characterized as an offense to some in that virtual room a few years ago but also in our current moment in higher education; it's a question in need of asking given that Hughes's paper struck yet others, as I've already noted, as making a rather basic, though nonetheless important, point. After all, could the banner of "crisis in the humanities" that so many of us are flying be serving as a rallying cry to assemble those being impacted by budget cuts and move them toward some sort of coordinated action (like writing and publishing a book such as this with some suggested responses to it all)?

I'd therefore like to close this brief ethnography of a plenary session by suggesting that the two or so years of remote teaching, in circumstances that many scholars found to be rather trying, while juggling commitments outside their profession's usual tasks that regularly impinged on their work in ways that they previously had not (e.g., the lack of in-person elementary schools and child care due to COVID-19 protocols in those institutions) created a set of conditions in which academics (or, more properly, certain subsets of scholars, particularly those in the United States), already long feeling pressure from declining government budgets and increased work expectations, reached what they considered to be a breaking point—evidenced in the speed with which Hughes's critically minded approach, often unproblematically adopted by many in the room when studying others, was heard by some as a threat requiring a coordinated response.

In making this claim one cannot help but acknowledge the privilege of academics during that time; for unlike so-called frontline workers (nurses, doctors, fire fighters, delivery people, postal workers, etc.), academics in full-time positions were in large part able to adapt to the remote environment—though part-time and non–tenure track instructors often paid the high price of universities unsure of their COVID-era enrollments and budgets by failing to have their employment continued. Thus, we must consider a surprisingly wide continuum of what the "pandemic crisis" was for a variety of different actors here in the United States—and that includes academia. And it is an even wider continuum if we do just a little cross-cultural work and include the many other national settings in our analysis (a breadth made all the greater when we study its impact on those outside North America and western Europe). But, as we all likely know, privilege, like the rhetorics examined herein, is a relative thing, and thus those in tenured positions who were academic parents working at home no doubt felt considerable daily stress juggling work and family life (likely in constant fear for their own children's health, let alone their need for schooling and social interaction while carrying out their work from their living rooms and kitchens). And it seems that this was among the subsets in attendance during Hughes's session who evidently did not feel that their concerns and additional labor were being acknowledged by means of the relativizing analysis that others were adopting toward the "pandemic crisis."

My sense is that their concerns were also heightened because, in many cases, it seems that their employers (a university's higher administration) had often not taken the threats of COVID-19 seriously enough, at least in some faculty members' estimation. In the United States at least, where even public colleges' funding models often have them competing with each other for the much-needed tuition revenue associated with incoming first year students, practical and sometimes extensive COVID-19 precautions on campus (everything from plexiglass installed in classrooms to testing, contact tracing, and vaccination programs) were sometimes seen by faculty to conflict with some schools' "business as usual" messages that were simultaneously being sent to parents and students. The potential contradiction between these two approaches—one designed to limit the health risk of exposure on campus while the other intended to limit the financial risk of students sitting out the year or going elsewhere and thereby jeopardizing a school's operating budget—seems to have put many faculty members in the difficult (if sometimes untenable) position of caring for their own safety (and thus their family's as well) while also trying to meet (or not contravene too obviously) what some faculty saw as the unrealistic expectations of at least a subset of administrators and even students (such as those wishing to attend classes in-person from the start of it all, and even doing so unmasked, with no disclosures concerning immunization status once the vaccines were developed and rolled out). Add to this some faculty members' presence in regions of the country where state governments had banned more proactive avoidance measures on the part of employers (such as hastily enacted laws against mandating either masks or vaccinations) and one arrives at a nearly two-year period of compounding daily anxiety for many faculty members. Taking into account the hierarchical nature of authority on a university campus, and (in some cases, at least) the lack of effective faculty governance and thus participation in administrative decision making (i.e., weak and merely symbolic faculty senates), and I believe that we arrive at a point where the perceived lack of affirmation or recognition in a venue where many in attendance are assumed to be professional peers (i.e., a scholarly conference) leads to a moment when the usually operating compartmentalization and self-censorship of professional life were abandoned.

Should my analysis be persuasive, then the conclusion that I reach is that the response during that evening's Q&A had little, if anything, to do with Hughes's comments or approach—one with which it should be clear that I, and undoubtedly many others, fully agree and therefore see as utterly uncontroversial. Instead, the evening's session provided an opportunity for some participants to focus on, whether intentionally or not, a long-standing (and, in my opinion, quite legitimate) anxiety, responding in the more egalitarian setting of a group of generally like-minded scholars by saying things that, for purposes of maintaining their professional status at work, they likely were not able to say (at least publicly) in their workplaces or to some of their peers let alone their superiors—be that person a department chair, an associate dean, a dean, a provost, et cetera. Unbeknownst to the NAASR organizers, the conference—the second consecutive of its annual meetings to be virtual due to what many members saw to be health threats associated with travel—along with its theme and Hughes's plenary, thus provided a safe place for alienated faculty from across the ranks to vent and identify with one another; more than likely it was a much-needed opportunity, but one that, quite unfortunately, happened at Hughes's expense.

The moral of the story is that scholars are themselves no different from the people whom they study; for we deploy the usual set of techniques to establish group identity and to nurture what we take to be shared affinities and common alienations. Our critical intelligence, as useful as it is when engaging in the study of distant peoples and places—whether chronologically or geographically—can sometimes be of surprisingly little assistance when those things that we ourselves value feel under threat, even if that threat comes from the (reasonably) critical gaze of a colleague. While I would encourage scholars of religion to be rather more bold and uncompromising in the application of such critical, self-reflexive scholarship—even when it is felt to be applied uncomfortably close to home—we can at least take away something from this episode to help us understand the push-back that our work often receives either from the people being studied or, as is more likely, from those of our colleagues who hold them dear.

References

Lincoln, Bruce. 1996. "Theses on Method." *Method & Theory in the Study of Religion* 8 (3): 225–227.

McCutcheon, Russell T. 2006. "'It's a Lie. There's No Truth in It! It's a Sin!': On the Limits of the Humanistic Study of Religion and the Costs of Saving Others from Themselves." *Journal of the American Academy of Religion* 74 (3): 720–750.

———, ed. 2015. *Fabricating Origins*. Sheffield: Equinox.

Orsi, Robert A. 2004. "Fair Game." *Bulletin of the Council of Societies for the Study of Religion* 33 (3&4): 87–89.

Pritchard, Elizabeth A. 2010. "Seriously, What Does 'Taking Religion Seriously' Mean?" *Journal of the American Academy of Religion* 78 (4): 1087–1111.

6
Introduction
Redescribing Claims

The following chapter's original version, which was co-authored with Andie Alexander, was written for what later turned out to be the first volume of Brad Stoddard and Craig Martin's *Stereotyping Religion* (2017), a book written for a wide audience (hence its lack of notes and direct quotations and citations) and intended to unpack what the editors identified as clichés in the field. Assuming that a cliché is an overused phrase that, because of this, has been vacated of specificity, then saying that someone is "spiritual but not religious" justifiably made it to the editors' list (one that also included such now commonsense items as "religious are mutually exclusive" and "everyone has a faith"). As mentioned at the start of the book, among the problems with such a claim, at least as it is routinely studied by scholars, is that the terms of the debate are usually set by those who make such claims, as if these words all correspond to stable, obvious entities in the world or, better put, private affectations somewhere inside people's hearts. (See also McCutcheon 2018, a companion piece to the following chapter, for further elaboration on the discourse on spirituality.) To rephrase: instead of seeing these words as socially formative—that is, as proactively doing work to fashion the appearance of a certain sort of social world, a type of doing that dates to pretty much just the past forty years or so—scholars studying the so-called unchurched, those commonly designated now as the Nones, or simply the nonreligious, often fail to complicate this now popular phrase. It's relevance here, and thus the reason for including this as a chapter here, concerns how the essay models for readers the way to go about doing a redescription—something required of scholarship, some of us would argue, and also a skill of wide applicability.

By this term "redescription" I mean nothing more or less than what the late Jonathan Z. Smith would often discuss as the process by which we should go about our work, steps aimed at refining our writing and our teaching while also ensuring that scholars do something other than merely repeat or just paraphrase what the people whom they're studying might already be saying about themselves and their worlds (at least when prompted by our curiosities and thus our questions). As Aaron Hughes and I phrased it not too long ago in an entry on this very topic: "The act of redescription—taking an initial folk or idiosyncratic description and then reframing it in a different and more analytic register—is central to the academic enterprise of the Humanities and should, in theory, be especially so within the study of religion. At its most basic level, it means not taking at face value what the people we study, as well as their texts, report. Instead, it involves using such data as a way to uncover other, and sometimes initially unapparent, aspects of human creativity" (2022, 240). This means that, as I've been persuaded by Smith, scholarship begins with a rigorous description of some exemplum followed by a comparison of it to something else that's equally well described—a comparison animated by the scholar's own imagination and not constrained by qualities supposedly inherent to the items being placed side by side. Thus, there is no need to compare, let's say, scriptures to scripture; instead, as Smith would make evident, there's likely something to be gained by comparing, let's say, canons to recipes—if, by a gain in knowledge, we mean understanding something new about the human as opposed to seeing things within the orbit of religion as special cases that stand apart from all else. In light of the previously unrecognized similarities *and* differences that such novel or even provocative comparisons may make apparent—after all, it's all human doings, no?—the scholar is now in the position to return to the original item with new eyes, as it were, and thus able to say something novel about it, perhaps even to reclassify it as an instance of something rather different than how it might have originally appeared to us; "authorized lists" would be a new way to see canons after comparing them to recipes, no? And this result is not without value to us, what with Smith once observing that "the list is, perhaps, the most archaic and pervasive genre of genres" (1982, 44). Seeing the things that we study in such a new light and learning something new in the process is what we mean by comparatively driven redescription.

Case in point: someone reports to us that they're spiritual but not religious. What do we, as scholars, make of this? Do we hear such people much as scholars such as Robert Fuller once did—whose book *Spiritual but Not Religious: Understanding Unchurched America* (2001) played an important role in normalizing work among scholars of religion on such groups—and conclude that their disclosures concern a form of religious belief operating outside the strictures of traditional denominations? To the degree that such an approach still presupposes a dynamic inner domain (responsible for housing religious experiences, or so the old story goes) that is sometimes expressed only secondarily in public (the domain of so-called organized religions), it does not really vary all that much from the world as presupposed and then presented by many of the people whom we study; remember, leading members of the field have long presumed that because the essence of religion resides in either personal beliefs or experiences, it forever remains unavailable to the scholar and all we have to study are its mere manifestations (hence the long dominant phenomenological and hermeneutical traditions in the field). Yet this is a position little different from how the people whom we study already talk, what with the frequency of their discourse on faith as being some sort of nonrational, pre-social sensibility. So, instead of trying to understand unchurched belief, that is, spirituality, in this manner, perhaps there's something else for scholars to study here, something apparent only if we compare this way of talking about the world to other instances where a dynamic inner domain is prioritized as causal of subsequent public representations. For then we might come to see that "spiritual but not religious" claims are not innocently representative of supposed inner states that we call belief or faith but that they're exactly that—claims! And as claims they are evidence that, at least for the speaker, there's something competitive at stake, something up for grabs and to which it is worth their staking a claim (thinking back to old gold rush days of marking the territory over which you've claimed rights). And as claims they are public, social disclosures akin to declarations, speech acts that have effect in a world of contesting proclamations and competing assertions of ownership. Accordingly, once redescribed in this fashion, the ground shifts considerably, and, upon hearing or reading, "I'm spiritual but not religious," a scholar is now prepared to study a social occasion where something practical and tangible might be at stake rather than trying to intuit or speculate on someone's supposedly inner states or feelings. And voila, a onetime cliché is seen as significant in a whole new way.

With just this shift in mind, I think of Chris Cotter's book, *The Critical Study of Non-Religion: Discourse, Identification and Locality* (2020), one very much concerned with the discrete situations in which people make such disclosures as opposed to speculating on the internal dispositions that supposedly pair up with their words. Case in point: one of the people whom he interviewed was identified as a Celtic studies student at the University of Edinburgh named Niamh; when queried she disclosed that among her reasons for identifying religiously as she does—an identity that certainly shows evidence of a wide mix of sources and influences—was that she aimed *not* to be associated with the identity of her grandmother who, she states, "had done so much damage" (2020, 4). Accordingly, Cotter concludes that claims of nonreligion (among which "I'm spiritual but not religious" would count) should be studied akin to how Jean-François Bayart (e.g., [1996] 2005) studies identity more generally: as but one strategy, deployed in a discrete situation and in response to a specific other, that can result in the impression of either a distinct or shared identity being formed. These are socially formative claims, not neutrally descriptive reports.

My hope is that this illustration, elaborated in far more detail in the chapter to follow, provides a useful example of what a redescriptive move entails; animated at the scholar's curiosities, complicated by novel comparative work, the familiar comes to be seen in a rather new way, shedding light on something that we may have never before thought all that much about—at least not in this or that way (such as a biblical canon turning out to have an awful lot to do with all sorts of other lists that people, whether today and through the ages, have made and then policed and authorized against all competitors). That this skill—the ability to manage inventive comparisons so as to say something new about the world—may be among the most useful that we teach to our students and fine-tune in our research, and thus something of wide application (if we can just get over the habit of thinking that scholarship is a discrete activity only of relevance if practiced behind ivory-covered walls), is a topic to be explored in far more detail in the concluding chapter.

The Situated Nature of "I'm Spiritual but Not Religious" Claims

CO-AUTHORED WITH ANDIE R. ALEXANDER

It's relatively easy these days to overhear someone saying or to read someone writing: "I'm spiritual but not religious"—usually just abbreviated as SBNR. But in our experience it's not the sort of thing people just go around saying, unprompted; for, much like declaring your love of chocolate, where you're originally from, or your college major, it's usually stated as an answer to questions, asked and answered in a specific situation—such as the time that one of us was shopping for furniture in a new city, having just moved there. Learning that we were new to town, the salesperson inquired, "Have you found a church-home yet?" There's a variety of answers to such a question, to be sure, from "Yes I have" to "No, but can you suggest one?" or "I don't believe in God" or maybe even the more politic response that was in fact offered, "I study it all day so that's more than enough for me." Among the many other imaginable answers to this query today would certainly be, "No; I'm spiritual but not religious."

This chapter is curious to figure out what might be going on in that moment, during such an exchange. And, given our experience studying human behavior, our hunch is that the social actors involved don't necessarily know all that might be involved in these seemingly simple questions and answers. In a word, we mean to set out to *redescribe* such claims.

So, right off the bat, the first thing to be noted when we consider this now common phrasing is that claiming "I'm spiritual but not religious" (much like saying or writing *anything*—but more on this later) is the tip of a social moment, evidence of a specific situation in which a speaker is interacting with someone—someone with expectations, hence the question that elicited this particular reply. (No doubt that store clerk, who was probably not satisfied with the answer provided that day, had a church recommendation ready at hand, if that's where the conversation had gone. The question more than likely was not, in other words, an idle inquiry or an opportunity just to make conversation.) Now, of course, this is not something that anyone is probably thinking to themselves when they might offer this now common claim in reply to someone; that is, when they answer, "I'm spiritual but not religious," our guess is that such speakers, if we're to imagine what their own self-representation might be, likely think that they're making a claim about some interior state or awareness that they possess or have experienced—call it spirituality, perhaps, or maybe even faith—that, again they likely presume, somehow operates outside of, or prior to, the restrictions of various institutional settings—something that, if pressed further, they might designate as either "church" or "religion." So, when that salesperson long ago inquired if you've "found a church-home"—implying an institution with membership and regular attendance, as well as sets of rituals and periodic ceremonies and social occasions, e.g., pot-luck suppers and church socials, etc.—this reply makes a claim that all of these institutional trappings are somehow just that—trappings, and therefore nonessential; instead, a claim is being made that there is something that predates all of these documentable instances and social memberships, thereby operating outside of and prior to them all, some interior disposition unique to certain people, maybe some insight or affectation that, whether complementary with "going to church" (or mosque, synagogue, or temple, to be sure), certainly does not require it. (In fact, some might go so far as to claim that the institution limits or stifles it.) It's an answer that, to the one making the claim, therefore seems to involve (either explicitly or implicitly) a bit of an arm wrestling match, for it takes a widely accepted notion of religion (i.e., church attendance) and somehow one ups it, as if one can have all of the benefits of some sort of deep interconnection with a creator or the entire universe (or however we might broadly define this word "religion") but without having to get dressed up each week.

But regardless of what those who say (or identify as) SBNR might be thinking (or how the store clerk might have heard it, if that's what we had answered), to the scholar of religion not content merely to describe how people already talk about themselves (or, better put, how *we*, as outsiders to the occasions under study, might imagine or even elicit such reports, not unlike the previously mentioned example of the caption to a photo on the cover of a journal, the one representing a scholarly claim very much in Eliade's tradition but *as if* it were merely a description), there are some interesting things going on here that should cause us to pause for a moment and not simply accept the view that, while this thing we call religion is boringly lodged within repetitive rituals and traditions, some alternative thing that is called spirituality is somehow in-step with each of our truest, deepest, and most authentic and unique selves. For it does not take long to realize that the way that this term "spirituality" is now being used—again, as if it names some pre-social and thus institution-free insight or feeling (dare we call it spirit?) that someone just has or somehow senses—is itself part of a tradition and, yes, like all institutions, has a history and conditions that determine its use. It's therefore no little irony—and this is *precisely* what makes all of this so interesting to look at in a new way—that from *within* tradition and *within* history people who speak this way are making claims that are said to be free of tradition and untainted by history.

Case in point: think back to the opening of this chapter, when we imagined someone replying "I'm spiritual but not religious." Not only should we take seriously the social moment of the exchange; that is, as far as we know people don't go around spontaneously saying such things to one another instead, this is part of a conversation. But, to press this point further, we must keep in mind that this is, of course, language and none of us made up our own language (if we had then we certainly wouldn't be talking with anyone else). Instead, we were all *taught* a language—we memorized vocabulary and spelling, along with all of the rules of its grammar and syntax (who among us doesn't know "i before e except after c . . ."?)—all of which pre-dated us (considerably). Members of a previous generation (or even our older siblings) leaned in close and rubbed our little tummies and whispered things in our ears; they told us that "the farmer drives a tractor" while flipping through the pages of a picture book, singing the ABCs song with us, and they eagerly awaited our words to grow more complex—words spoken in whatever language into which we happen to have been born. It's therefore no coincidence that it's probably the case that most who will read this text are native English speakers. So, the irony grows even deeper, even richer, making it all the more fascinating, when we consider that a speaker who claims to be SBNR seems to think that they're making a tradition-free, authentic claim about some prior, interior dimension that they possess *but they do so in the most tradition-bound of settings: language.* For if you stop and think about reading this very text, and all of the rules that the writer and reader must share and follow in order for it to seem to make sense to all of us—despite having never met each other and, for all you know, living thousands of miles apart and being members of drastically different generations—well, it can lead one to find very curious anyone who claims that they can somehow opt out of institutions and traditions.

(Come to think of it, don't institutions have an institutionalized way to leave them? This suggests that we never really can leave institutions behind, for in opting out, in the proper or improper way, we further mire ourselves within them. Yet another irony.)

So, rather than assuming, as those who claim such a status apparently do, that only one side of the SBNR divide is somehow authentic, pure, and thus pre-social, it may make more sense to conclude that what we may have on our hands, whenever we hear or read someone claiming to be SBNR, is a glimpse into a social moment when members of one tradition, embedded within institutions with which they're familiar, contest others, within yet other social situations, while, in the process, seeking to authorize themselves and their setting. But in order to reach that conclusion—in order to develop a social theory of SBNR discourses—we need to back up a bit and reconsider the very model of meaning-making that many of us walk around with in our daily lives; for asserting that a pre-social moment of pure spirituality exists is something that we can claim *only* if we assume that language is a neutral medium by means of which we *express* (and that's a key word, to which we will return) things that are already somewhere inside our heads, things that we commonly call "meanings." But if that's not the way that meaning-making actually works (and the fact that we commonly call it meaning-*making* is already a clue to rethinking the clichés that attend much research around SBNR claims—for our labor may be involved more than we know, making us hardly passive observers in the process), then maybe there's a way to hear or read "I'm spiritual but not religious" differently, in order to see this claim as part of the mundane, day-to-day arm wrestling match that is social and historical life.

Knowing that's where we're going in this chapter, let's back up and start over again, but this time in order to think in a more focused manner about just how meaning works; we don't imply anything terribly sophisticated, just everyday meanings, such as reading signs downtown or reading a friend's body language. Or maybe the act of reading itself, as you're doing now, looking over these inked and printed markings that we call letters, punctuation, and words. Or consider talking and listening, in the most mundane of ways—riding a bus we hear a bell ring and know that it means the bus is making a stop. But do you remember the first time that you rode a public transit bus . . . ? Did you instinctively know what the ding meant? Or that it even was a signal of some sort? Our guess is that you did not; as with language, we all needed to be trained, by others who came before us, those who already knew the ropes, as it were (a saying many claim to go back to experienced sailors who already know the rigging on a ship). So, as stated above, the difference between how we commonly think about this process, on the one hand, and, on the other, how we might understand this process of meaning-making when we don't assume that we're already familiar with it, may help us to unpack what's going on when someone distinguishes (and then ranks—a crucial element of most distinctions) spirituality from religion.

Let us then reconsider the work involved in everyday conversations. Oftentimes we have varying types of conversations, all depending on the audience with whom we are speaking. That is, the way in which one would greet an old friend is likely quite different from how that same person would greet their professor, dentist, or supervisor at work. There would likely be a level of formality employed when conversing with members of the latter group—maybe we'd signal this by means of a title—that was not included when meeting the long-time friend. That is to say that our ways of communicating are dependent on the specific situations and the degree of familiarity with a particular audience or conversation partner. So, contrary to our commonsense model, one that assumes meanings are first on the inside and are only later projected outward into the public domain (a key aspect of SBNR claims), it may instead be that, despite how we commonly think of it, language is not some neutral medium that merely carries our interior meanings; instead, the very things that we call meanings might be the product of the situation itself—making meaning a far more social thing than we had at first imagined.

Thinking ahead: if the situation (e.g., meeting your sibling at the mall versus meeting the mayor in the townhall) dictates how we talk, then what might the implications be for those situations that lead to SBNR claims . . . ?

This situatedness is probably evident to anyone studying a foreign language. At the undergraduate level, many of us who went to university were required to take several semesters of a foreign language as part of the core curriculum of our degree (a requirement now disappearing as college after college is deciding to cut such requirements in favor of a slimmed-down core). As an undergraduate at the University of Alabama, one of us studied Italian to fulfill those requirements. Throughout the semesters of language training, we quickly learned that translation from Italian to English and from English to Italian was not, as we had at first assumed, a one-to-one correspondence, as if merely converting inches to millimeters or kilos to pounds. That is, rarely is there a verbatim translation of one language into another—for the words work within entirely different structures (i.e., the rules of each language) and so are not necessarily ordered or structured in the same way and the grammar and syntax likely vary, sometimes closely related (languages, after all, do influence one another) and sometimes drastically different. When these sentences, words, phrases, and clauses fail to line up exactly the translator must sometimes do some artful work of their own so as to move the meaning they derive from one sentence to an entirely different rule system. To anyone who immerses themselves in this task it soon becomes very apparent that different languages (especially languages that do not share a common ancestor), each with different rules, make different meanings possible; so what soon becomes apparent is that the widespread model which assumes a common, static, inner meaning that is later *expressed* (there's that word again), in one code there and another here, quickly fails. Instead, when matched up against each other, the systems are separated by gaps, leaving considerable room for ambiguity and difference when they are compared (as a translator might)—like the time one of us had a book translated into modern Greek and were told that there was no available word in Greek to convey all that the technical term "discourse" (an English translation of a French original) has come to mean for current scholars; for, when used in certain scholarly traditions, it means so much more than just talking.

Varying interpretations of sentences and the many different word choices are why many language teachers warn students against using Google Translate to aid in their homework assignments. For, despite how grammatically accurate the sentence translated in this manner may seem, a particular translation may not fit the situation and therefore would be graded by the professor as incorrect. For instance, consider this example of an English to Italian translation: after typing this sentence into the Google Translate box,

> We are going to the square for ice cream this afternoon.

Google provides us with the following Italian translation:

> *Stiamo andando al quadrato per gelato questo pomeriggio.*

Following our commonsense model of language and meaning (which, to remind you, assumes a universal meaning exists on the inside of our heads and which is then expressed), this translation is a word-for-word match and, technically, correct by Italian grammatical standards; however, if you were to use this sentence in conversation, you would likely receive some funny looks from the people with whom you're speaking. For while the sentence does make rudimentary sense, some of the words used would likely give away the speaker as an outsider or non-native, because the language and structure aren't quite right. For example, in Italian conversation, as we were taught in class, gerunds (words that look like verbs but are not) are often dropped and are replaced with the present active voice ("We go"). So, in casual Italian conversation, one would not necessarily say *Stiamo andando* ("We are going"); instead, one would more than likely say *Andiamo* ("We go"). Furthermore, "the square" mentioned in the English sentence (e.g., a town square) can, indeed, translate to *al quadrato*, but would more accurately translate to *alla piazza* (also, "the square"), referring to the town center where one would likely find a few ice cream shops (or *gelaterie*). What's more, the end of this example sentence, *questo pomeriggio*, is a literal translation of "this afternoon," but in Italian, the more common conversational form would literally translate to "in the afternoon" or *nel pomeriggio*. So, while this Google translation certainly isn't wrong, if used, the sentence would show a lack of fluency and constitute evidence that you failed to possess the understanding that a native speaker or well-trained student might have.

So instead of:

Stiamo andando al quadrato per gelato questo pomeriggio.

the more appropriate version of this sentence would be:

Andiamo alla piazza per gelato nel pomeriggio.

While the Google translation may be grammatically accurate, that version is not necessarily appropriate for certain situations (such as speaking to an actual Italian with whom you'd like to go for ice cream—though, what we call ice cream and what they call gelato are hardly the same thing, *which again makes our point*!). From this we can see how quite a bit of work, even art, goes into moving from one language to another—students in language classes have surely experienced this frustration on more than one occasion—and that translations, more often than not, require a great deal of interpretation to create the right meaning for any given circumstance.

What's the moral of the story? Translation, as many before us have argued, is best thought of not as a mere conversion or a search for the matching words (i.e., "How do you say X in your language?") but, rather, a creative move between different code systems that each make different meanings possible. Skilled translators, then, are people who are prepared to make leaps more creative than just knowing that 0.621371 kilometers precisely equals a mile, and thus they're bold enough to let go of some things that are inexpressible in one language (e.g., we have ice cream, not gelato) in order to hold on to, in some newly reshaped form, yet others. For, like that old saying goes, there is indeed something lost in the translation—not the meaning but, rather, the ability to frame, even to make, certain meanings.

Considering the level of (often unrecognized) work that goes into even just everyday conversation—that is, speakers engaging with one another in particular ways depending on their audience and situation—we can see how very simple exchanges are an excellent place to revise the way that we usually think about meaning (and thus the commonsense model, so essential to SBNR claims, that assumes significance is internal and is only secondarily pushed out into the world). Since we're already knee-deep in the example of Italian conversation, let's stay there and consider a standard Italian greeting, one that many of us are likely familiar with: "Ciao." If asked what *ciao* meant, anyone with a rudimentary knowledge of Italian would likely tell you that it *means* "hello"; but, then again, much like "*aloha*" in Hawaiian or "*salut*" in French, they might tell you that it also means the exact opposite: "goodbye." (Question: How does one know when it means which?) But some might tell you that *ciao* is an informal greeting, much like "hey, how's it going!" or "what's up?"—a greeting that requires the intended audience only to repeat the exact same word back as the response: "Ciao!" (Come to think of it, this is not all that different from answering "How's it going?" whenever someone passes you and poses the informal English greeting, "How's it going?") So, depending on the situation—that is, whether one is arriving, leaving, or just passing a friend (as opposed to your boss!) on the sidewalk—*ciao* can have all sorts of meanings and can be translated, or interpreted, differently for each.

While this may seem at face value to be all too obvious, this simple social exchange (a greeting) can help us to reconsider the level of work that goes into everyday conversation—that is, it's not a matter of actors *expressing* in public meanings that are already in their heads but, rather, making up meanings as they go based on the all too public situation in which they're embedded. (And that's precisely how we figure out if *ciao* means hello or goodbye.) Of course, the work that this takes does not necessarily seem to be all that labor-intensive, for native or fluent speakers converse easily, virtually unthinkingly, because they are extremely well trained—they're benefiting from work invested over the course of their entire lives or perhaps years of study and immersion. (Such as those who are reading these very words.) So, for one to adequately translate this social exchange of an informal *ciao*, one must determine the fitting meaning (hello, goodbye, etc.) for a given situation, since it would look a bit strange if a movie subtitle translated *ciao* as "hello" if the speaker said it as they were exiting the movie scene, no? Thus, despite the simplicity of *ciao*, definitionally speaking, it nicely illustrates an important point: the situatedness of the conversation and those doing the speaking determine which meaning we should or should not use and understand.

Or, for another example, consider a common phrase that we have at the University of Alabama: "Roll Tide." While to many people this phrase would likely be directly associated with the Crimson Tide (that is, the long-standing nickname for the university's football team, which is said to roll over other teams as if it were a tide rushing ashore, clad in our school colors), to a native Alabamian and, more especially, to anyone affiliated with the University of Alabama (such as a student or football fan), this phrase, "Roll Tide," is highly versatile inasmuch as it can have any number of meanings. Perhaps some readers are aware of the U.S. sports channel ESPN and its onetime series of humorous commercials, which included the "Roll Tide" commercial which aired back in 2010. In this short commercial, we see many instances of people in the state saying "Roll Tide" to one another, yet the intended meaning varies widely with each usage—that is, in each situation. Aside from meaning something akin to "Go team," it can also be used as a passing greeting, for saying thank you, or, as pictured in the commercial, to conclude a wedding speech and even by a preacher ending his eulogy for an ardent fan of the team. Much like the Italian *ciao*, then, the meaning of "Roll Tide" is necessarily dependent on the social situation, since it can be used in any number of ways—ways that would unlikely translate well to anyone unfamiliar with any of these interactions. For an outsider, as with outsiders to any language, the phrase would be odd if not unintelligible. Yet when speaking to members of an in-group—that is, people who either interact in this way or are at least familiar with this social interaction—this phrase, "Roll Tide," serves as a way to reinforce a particular social identity that a discrete group of speakers may both adopt (or have thrust upon them, of course) and thus share; it amounts to a form of social grooming—"I identify with the University of Alabama, do you?" it asks, awaiting the "Roll Tide" reply if the answer is yes. (Here's another exchange where exactly same thing is said by both parties, without a feeling of redundancy resulting for either.) However, if one were to say "Roll Tide" to a student or person affiliated with Auburn University—Alabama's rival in-state school—such a recipient of that "Roll Tide" would likely retort (in jest or, perhaps, in anger!) with Auburn's own phrase, "War Eagle" (a reference to their school mascot) and so, rather than establishing a connection with that person, the phrase "Roll Tide" would now function to signify a divide. And while it's important to recognize that neither of these phrases really *mean* anything—they are just words associated with the schools' sports teams and do not necessarily signify anything in particular—a specific meaning ("We're allies!" or "We're antagonists!") can be created, all depending on the situation and social actors involved. For it can be a congratulatory statement, a way to bond with others, or a way to mark difference; but this is only evident when we—the users of language—understand and analyze meaning based on the situated (and observable) social interaction as opposed to inherent value. Put differently, much like translating that sentence from English to Italian, we must consider the setting, the speakers who are interacting, and the structure (and thus limits) of the language in which they're working, for the meaning produced can vary with each.

These examples, though straightforward in many ways, hopefully begin to highlight the complexity of meaning—that is, thinking back to the start of this chapter, to begin to make the point that meaning, let alone identity or value, might not somehow pre-exist language, and thus might not be floating privately and spontaneously in the speaker's mind, disengaged from the world until it is spoken or written; for it turns out to be just as much rooted in a social and historical context as are all conversations or all interactions with a text. In fact, since we were all taught language by others, who came before us, you could even go so far as to say that talking to yourself (or thinking a thought) is still very much part of a social exchange and thus a conversation—a conversation with all who came before you and who developed the language that you now speak (and, yes, tweak as well).

So, when we explore the largely unnoticed—or perhaps ignored or, better put, just unrecognized, since we're each just so used to doing what we do (and it is a *doing*!)—work that helps to establish the apparent self-evidency of those sounds that we make, such as "*Ciao*" or "Roll Tide," then we can begin to see the thing that we might at first have taken to be interior, that is meaning, in a whole new light: as a social process of meaning-*making*, a type of shared and always public labor that, depending on how it is done, has practical effect, such as distinguishing a this from that, or an us from a them—such as that Auburn fan not looking too kindly on the "Roll Tide" greeting.

So now, thinking back to where we started this chapter, maybe readers can see why we took that detour to rethink—dare we say redescribe—how meaning works. For if we start *not* with the lone individual thinking (and thereby owning) their solitary thoughts and then pushing them outward (literally, what the English word "express" has traditionally meant) into the world, where they're prone to be misinterpreted by those who hear them but who don't properly understand the speaker's intentions ("That's not what I meant!"), but, instead, reconceive all speakers and writers as always involved in an ongoing, public conversation with others, with all parties involved in the meaning-making, since they all work with an already-made and necessarily shared script and set of rules—a script and rules that make certain things possible to think and say and other things impossible (after all, you can't play ping pong on a tennis court no matter how similar the games appear)—then what do we make of someone who comes along and says: "I'm spiritual but not religious"? For, as already suggested, this claim (at least as it seems to be understood by some who make such claims) seems to signify that there exists something pre-social, something this person (and not that—the one who simply identifies as being religious, presumably) possesses or experiences something that is (more) deeply significant because it is outside of (i.e., pre-existing) all institutional constraints. While our commonsense way of understanding ourselves might suggest that such a claim is sensible—lots of people seem to think it sensible to say it, and many scholars seem to just accept this as fact inasmuch as they mostly fail to scrutinize such claims all that closely—the excursion we just took into an alternative way of thinking about meaning now suggests that such assumptions are rather problematic, at least at the level of scholarly analysis, inasmuch as they seem to take the social work and thus institution-specific setting of all meaning-making as invisible, as if the work and the changeable situations were not even part of it. And, failing to see all the social actors and social work that necessarily came before them, they seem to assume that they came up with it all on their own and that they stand apart, as distinct and individual, from the many others who make it possible for each of us to make sounds and markings that our peers take to be meaningful. (For instance, are we making the meaning as we operationalize a set of English-language rules to type this very line or are readers making the meaning as they bring a set of rules to bear while reading it?) What's more, there are many ways of understanding how to be authentically SBNR, which further demonstrates the continued social contest and arm-wrestling involved in maintaining (because it too requires work) some notion of spirituality as distinct and private, pre-existing the social and the institutional.

And of all the things that scholars do it's likely not incorrect to say that it is our job to try to recover the work that others sometimes overlook, which is another way of saying that our job is to *historicize* the things that we study—that is, to study such things as *human* things, that is, as sites of labor, agreement, contest, negotiation, collaboration, and dispute. So, for instance, instead of taking the idea of the nation for granted, and thus assuming that all human beings ought to identify by means of a nationality (e.g., "I'm Dutch" or "You're Brazilian"), the scholar who studies nationalism would instead be interested in such things as when people first started to organize and identify in this manner; after all, it isn't difficult to study old texts and to see people identifying in rather different social ways, often doing so on a far more local basis than the large-scale national identities that most of us now assume that we all possess and share with so many others. For such a scholar, the idea of the nation would be seen as the result of human ingenuity and human labor—a way of naming and organizing ourselves that *we* came up with just a few hundred years ago, that *we* put in place, and that *we* continue to reproduce and even tweak. (Have you ever asked yourself why nations develop pledges, flags, and anthems, and then ensure that young children pay close attention to these? There's more work taking place than you might imagine.) This is what we mean by historicizing: not just to place the items that we study into historical contexts but also to assume that all things human had beginnings, require tending, and, sooner or later, will have an end. (No one identifies as Prussian anymore, right?) So, when it comes to people who claim to possess a deep and pre-social experience that is somehow superior to those who unthinkingly participate in mere rituals and ceremonies, an experience that transcends time and place, in what new ways might we, as scholars, hear or read such claims if we are instead persuaded that all meaning-making and all of the identities and values that result from such actions—which includes the very act of claiming "I'm spiritual but not religious" in response to some query—are the result of social actors situated within institutions and traditions?

Well, as should be evident by this point in the chapter, we might come to hear such claims as not being much different from saying "Roll Tide." For in both cases—once we assume that all meaning-making is a form of situated, social, and thus collaborative human labor taking place in settings not of the actors' making—a limit is being drawn which includes those who identify with this way of talking and this way of acting—both of which exclude all those who do not. To rephrase, if we assume that all human beings are situated within institutions (though not always the same institutions, of course; *and that's a key point*—it's a competitive environment) then how might we authorize those situations that we take for granted, those into which we were born or, for whatever reason and in response to whatever forces, have opted to join? And, conversely, how might we deauthorize their competitors; for, as just noted, there's many ways of organizing ourselves socially, politically, economically, and so how will we give those we favor a competitive advantage?

One way is to use rhetoric—to use language to accomplish specific social things, to help make certain sorts of worlds more persuasive and legitimate.

For example, have you ever heard someone say "Well, it goes without saying that . . ."? If whatever they were talking about truly "went without saying" then why do they follow up that opening by saying the thing that apparently doesn't have to be said? "It goes without saying that cheetahs are the fastest land animal." We'd suggest that the opening to that sentence is a tactical, rhetorical move in what is actually a debate (in this case, about quick animals), though the speaker is working very hard come out on top by stopping the debate before it even starts. For if "everybody knows . . ." something or if "it's commonsense that . . ." then you've increased the odds that someone present will decline to challenge the point, since by doing so they risk falling well outside the circle of the common and the everybody who apparently knows otherwise (according to the speaker). The claim, then, can be heard as a way to preempt the contest by portraying anyone who adopts an alternative position as speaking nonsense and therefore falling outside the group. For no one ever says, "It goes without saying that we need to breathe." Why? Because it actually does go without saying—that is, we more than likely don't have to persuade each other to breathe and thus we generally don't debate the merits of breathing. (There is no anti-breathing lobby in government, right?) But when it comes to something debatable, something for which there are multiple viable viewpoints—like the meaning of "*Ciao*" or maybe the rate at which different incomes should be taxed—those with something at stake in the debate may try to advance their position by portraying it as being beyond debate. "Because, after all, as pretty much everybody knows . . ."

Another rhetorical technique that's handy at a time like this is trying to erase the history of your claim—that is, to present it as beyond change and thus self-evidently correct. For it likely doesn't help those who, say, wish to portray the nation as a natural and thus inevitable unit of social organization to have it pointed out that nation-states are really not that old and that, previous to such groups being devised, human beings organized themselves socially in far different ways for far longer (e.g., kinship groups or what some call tribes). After all, depending on how long ago your ancestors arrived wherever it is that you now live, there's a rather good chance that they didn't have passports or something that we now call a nationality; they just got on ships there and, if they survived what might have been a treacherous journey, walked ashore here (it was a trip that was not always willingly undertaken, we might add). Or, not too differently, you may opt to create the impression of self-evidency by trying to erase the institutions in which you learned some piece of information. "Everybody knows . . ." is one way to do that, of course, for now it's not just people of a certain class or gender who ought to know something, or those who went to certain schools, are a member of a certain generation, or who worked in certain industries, but apparently everyone, regardless of their situation and background. And, if we're working with that old and still popular (but, as we've argued, rather flawed) model of meaning-making, we might make this very move by positing a pre-institutional and thus private and therefore deeply personal insight, one that doesn't result from students and teachers working within structures to pass along information (and thus people who were taught by yet others who were themselves working within structures, like the structures of language or the structure of the educational system), but which, instead, spontaneously springs to your mind (or your heart—it varies where we tend to place this interior source). Doesn't that sound like a pretty effective way to prioritize one position in an ongoing debate, by portraying it as something other than one among many options? For the result is that we now have the truly lone, original, and rugged individual, on the one hand, i.e., the one who possesses spontaneous, universal wisdom and, on the other, the unfortunates who are lodged in derivative, constricting, unthinking institutions, those who are following the unoriginal lead of others.

As we said before, if heard with a more critical scholarly ear, scholars can begin to see that SBNR claims are evidence of an ongoing arm wrestling match with stakes that the involved actors care about; that's because such a claim is now heard as a strategic move to sanction one social situation, over all others, by positing the existence of a nonnegotiable, pre-social core to our being (like so-called spirituality) that was there before institutions (such as so-called organized religions) were invented.

But, as also argued here, the very language in which these SBNR claims are being made, or even the assumption that people have ethereal spirits that somehow outlive their physical bodies, is itself evidence of an elaborate prior tradition, with institutions of its own, that stretches back centuries is an irony that we best not recognize if we're intent on not troubling such claims. (Case in point: no one today decided on their own that the Latin-based word "spirit" was a good word for the supposedly noncorporeal basis to the human, did they? "Spirituality" only entered English sometime in the late fourteenth century, the etymologists tell us, only about one hundred years after the *spiritus* was adapted to English.) But if, as we also noted earlier, we're scholars—those who seek to historicize the human things that we study—then we can't help but be curious about anyone who claims to supersede the social and the institutional (such as someone who fails to understand that as soon as they say the word "spirituality" they've marked themselves as part of a specific social and linguistic tradition); after all, this amounts to a human being—who, by definition, has a beginning and an end and, in between, occupies a specific setting—who claims to be something more than human. And this curiosity may lead us to ask some interesting questions about why people today even engage in this sort of talk, which in turn might prompt us to become curious about the arm wrestling matches in which they're engaged. For just why, we might ask ourselves, are those institutions widely known as churches, synagogues, temples, mosques, et cetera, which have long been of such central importance to the societies in which they were located, such that virtually everyone might have been said to have belonged to one, now sites from which some people wish to distinguish themselves (hence the fairly recent addition of the qualified "organized" to the noun "religion"—an English term not too much older than the late nineteenth century). What is it about our age that prompts some members of our society to understand themselves as existing apart from it, despite using the same language, economic system, etc. as those from whom they feel alienated?

These are questions worth pursuing, and who knows in what direction such a pursuit will take you, but they're questions that are only possible if we rethink the common assumptions that seem to drive those SBNR claims and much of the work by scholars studying them, that is, those who hear the words as corresponding to some inner spirituality that's qualitatively different from participation in, for example, a worship service—assumptions about the pre-social or even asocial nature of just some ways of being in the world. For if we instead start from the standpoint that it's, well . . . , standpoint all the way down, and that there is nowhere to stand that isn't situated, that isn't invested, that isn't implicated, that isn't part of a prior conversation that we didn't start ourselves, and that isn't therefore part of a social and thus institutional world, then those who talk as if their private, true, or authentic self somehow trumps the so-called derivative forms that other people's lives take will be seen by scholars as fascinating players in an ongoing (but often undisclosed) contest, working with what's at hand, to give their position a competitive edge.

References

Bayart, Jean-François. (1996) 2005. *The Illusion of Cultural Identity.* Translated by Steven Rendall et al. Chicago: University of Chicago Press.

Cotter, Christopher R. 2020. *The Critical Study of Non-Religion: Discourse, Identification and Locality.* London: Bloomsbury.

Fuller, Robert C. 2001. *Spiritual but Not Religious: Understanding Unchurched America.* New York: Oxford University Press.

Hughes, Aaron W., and Russell T. McCutcheon. 2022. *Religion in 50 Words: A Critical Vocabulary.* New York: Routledge.

McCutcheon, Russell T. 2018. "Redescribing Spirituality: The Strategic Use of the Solitary Identifier." In *"Religion" in Theory and Practice: Demystifying the Field for Burgeoning Academics*. Sheffield: Equinox Publishing.

Smith, Jonathan Z. 1982. *Imagining Religion: From Babylon to Jonestown*. Chicago: University of Chicago Press.

Stoddard, Brad, and Craig Martin, eds. 2017. *Stereotyping Religion: Critiquing Clichés*. London: Bloomsbury.

7
Introduction
Relevance through Generalization

This concluding chapter was originally written as the final essay for a special issue of the scholarly journal *Method & Theory in the Study of Religion*, one that I proposed and then guest edited and which focused on the wider contributions of Burton L. Mack (1931–2022); for although he was a noted scholar of Christian origins, I'm convinced that Mack's career-long effort to see the start of the movement that only later came to be known as Christianity in a new, more critical, and therefore scholarly light ought to serve as a model for those of us working to help the study of religion to be seen and then valued for the wider contributions that our students bring with them to a wide array of other domains. The specific contribution that's represented in this chapter—which I add to the list of those already itemized—that is, (i) a disinclination to privilege certain people, settings, or things that we happen to study, (ii) the ability to complicate that which others may seek to simplify and thereby legitimize, (iii) a desire never to take for granted, and thereby normalize, the larger and often unseen structural circumstances, (iv) a recognition of the need for self-examination, and (v) an appetite to create new knowledge by doing something other than merely repeating what the people we study may already be saying about themselves—is what I, like many others well before me, have identified as the skill of generalizing from our specialized work so as to apply our findings in sometimes unexpected places.

Those novel places, at least for scholars such as myself who are working within this one academic field, are more than likely just other subfields, though this alone is a radical enough break with tradition, at least for many of us; think here of your average professor being bold enough to peek into a conference panel, at our large annual meeting each fall, well outside their own specialty, armed only with an inclination that some general points might be gleaned from it and then brought back and applied to their own work. Such a person is a rare breed, in my experience; like tends to congregate with like and so the odds of finding, say, a scholar of Taoism attending a panel on Mormonism, and vice versa, are pretty long indeed. However, even rarer still is the professor who is able to accept, even embrace, that few of their students will ever become specialized scholars in any of the field's many specialties (and this increasing includes most of the doctoral students whom they may supervise, what with the collapse of the humanities academic job market over the past decades) yet who nonetheless understands why what I'm calling a deep dive into advanced research skills, exercised or practiced in either this or that thick data domain, can still have an important impact for the many students whose choices and circumstances may take them far away from academia. Here I do but I don't mean so-called transferable skills, since this phrasing strikes me as being on a par with that once popular way of talking about "alt-ac careers" (i.e., alternative academic careers); for both phrasings strike me as presupposing the norm of futures within academia—although with the possibility of some secondary application elsewhere, of course. But this is something we should no longer assume. (See the pieces collected together in McCutcheon 2024 for a far more detailed examination of this.) As I've written as part of the just cited volume, we need to be frank in recognizing that the only truly alternative career for many graduating doctoral students today is landing a tenure-track position. And so, let's just call them skills, abilities, aptitudes, know-how, contributions, whatever you wish, without the qualifier that references the lecture hall and the research monograph as if they are somehow their proper domain.

When I speak with some academic peers about all of this, not only do I hear laments for the loss of "the life of the mind" that they apparently value so highly (about this I've already written in this volume, I realize, but my repeated comments on this complaint may tell you something about my frustration with this utterly privileged way of talking about our work), but my proposals for graduate training to keep abreast with the world that our students now inhabit are sometimes also greeted with comments that I'm proposing "watering down" graduate school. My critical ear actually hears this retort as "Well . . . , if *I* had to do it then *they* must too"; I have in mind two more years of graduate-level coursework, those language exams and three-hour comprehensive exams, let alone being a teaching assistant but often with little formal mentoring and writing a 300- page dissertation that takes several years to complete (leading to a time-to-doctoral-degree *median* in the humanities of 7.5 years in 2002 and 6.8 years in 2020).[1] That the steps by which old timers earned their own graduate degrees and the requirements that they fulfilled back in the day were themselves historical (i.e., contestable and therefore changeable) conditions is often completely lost on them. After all, as senior as I now am in the field, not even I am old enough to recall using a typewriter for a doctoral dissertation—and inserting, let's say, page 143a to account for a revision or corrected typo but without having to retype the rest of the manuscript—what with desktop personal computers starting to become a commonplace near the end of my B.A. And some years ago, people stopped going into a room by themselves for three hours armed only with a blank pad of paper and a few pens to handwrite a comprehensive exam (which those of us at the University of Toronto in the 1980s and early 1990s did three times in a week, writing one comp in our major area and one in each of our two minor areas). Now? In most places I believe that it has long been all open book, with each exam written at home with a laptop and over twenty-four hours. So, without idealizing our own process and using it as the standard against which everything else is measured, how today does one train students in the kind of advanced research skills indicative of the highest degree a university awards? That's the question we *should* be asking.

Recognizing the continually shrinking chance that our students will follow us into this profession (and, if they ever do, taking into account the high likelihood that many will only gain employment as contingent faculty of various sorts, each largely or even exclusively teaching service courses to professional students, as part of general humanities units into which many of our onetime autonomous departments had long ago been collapsed), how can those changing circumstances inspire revisions to the goals and requirements of doctoral training? That the time is long past for having these conversations in all seriousness is obvious to anyone paying attention, and so entertaining the role to be played by internships, by diverse sorts of assignments in a graduate seminar (of course students need to learn to write well, but is producing an essay the only sort of assignment that we can imagine?), and broadening what counts as evidence of mastery and integration (just why *do* Ph.D. students write a dissertation after all?), is only the tip of what urgently needs to be reimagined. But teaching and inspiring undergraduate

[1] See the American Academy of Arts and Sciences "Humanities Indictors" report *Years to Attainment of a Humanities Doctorate* (based on 2022 data from the National Science Foundation's National Center for Science and Engineering Statistics), posted at "Years to Attainment of a Humanities Doctorate," AMACAD.org, accessed June 26, 2024, https://www.amacad.org/humanities-indicators/higher-education/years-attainment-humanities-doctorate.

students is also part of this, for encouraging some of them to become faculty members someday, meaning suggesting doctoral work to them, does not help any of this at all; certainly, some might, but while I have no desire to throw too much cold water on anyone else's dreams, faculty nonetheless need to intervene far earlier in our students' lives to help them to begin to refine and channel their curiosities, enthusiasms, and growing skills in ways that take into account their present circumstances. While being no ethicist myself, it seems to be something demanded by even the most modest sense of professional standards.

And it is into this context that I come back to this final chapter, one making an argument for the (maybe to some of us, surprisingly) wide applicability of our skills, those that we convey to our students—a relevance evident well outside academia, to be sure. Kicking the habit of seeing what we study as so obviously important that it naturally is worth all of our time is, to me, the lynchpin in all of this, that which—echoing a point made by Mack with regard to how the vast majority of scholars study Christianity, let alone religion as a whole—needs to be addressed in order for any substantial changes in the field to happen. For I tend to think that only in that way will a faculty member learn not to hide behind their specialty and training when it comes to being inventive at whatever level they're teaching. And this inventiveness does not require lessening the depth of the dive that we take into whatever material that happens to enthrall us and some of our students; but it does call upon us to think through just *why* it's important to study and where else (beyond our students' maybe teaching their own versions of the same class in which they enrolled with us) the lessons that are gained from that work can also be applied. I think we're up to the challenge, by the way, since, beneath the veneer of privilege that many scholars undoubtedly cherish, there are some bright and highly motivated people who are well equipped to tackle big topics in order to come up with creative insights—as long as they are able to apply the critical tools that they commonly use to study other people but now to gain a new way of seeing, and hopefully acting within, the institutions that comprise their own social worlds.

Redescribing Our Primary Expertise or, In Praise of Promiscuous Curiosities

> I do think that the task ahead is for the tough minded, not the tender hearted. That is because description is not an innocent activity, and explanation always involves theoretical assumptions. Innocence will have to go, and the theories implicit to our discipline will have to be exposed. Those who are willing to have their models tweaked and twisted will be the ones to reshape the discipline.
>
> —Burton L. Mack, "Caretakers and Critics" (2001, 34)

As I've mentioned on other occasions, during my own doctoral studies at the University of Toronto one of my good friends at the time, Stephen Heathorn (with whom my wife and I were also working as Dons in University College's undergraduate residence system), was pursuing his Ph.D. in history and studying the late nineteenth-century formation of an English national identity, focusing in particular on the role played by mandatory schooling for young children. It was because of conversations at the time with him, on coffee breaks or in the cafeteria, that I ended up reading such scholars of Eric Hobsbawm, E. P. Thompson, Benedict Anderson, et cetera, thereby thickening considerably an early, and eventually a career-long, interest in how groups and identities are created, managed, and, if the conditions are right, eventually internalized and, contrary to how we often think of group identity, only later "expressed," as it is often phrased, as if these apparent feelings and affinities had been lurking somewhere deep inside us all along, just waiting for the chance to be pushed out into the world. As I commented not too long ago (2020, 7), it was also with him that I recall working through some of Michel Foucault's writings, trying to figure out not only precisely what discourses were and how it was that Foucault thought that they functioned but, just as importantly, how such a concept could be applied to make sense of the things that each of us were studying at the time. For although our data, regions, and time periods, not to mention academic disciplines, were obviously rather different—after all, I was in the study of religion and interested in how the field's regnant approach had begun and maintained its dominance—what we nonetheless shared was a set of questions and, increasingly, a set of tools, all of which were animated by a common view as to how the impression of uniformity and permanence was generated within what was actually contingent and internally divided groups (much as all groups are, of course).

If I am to trust my memory, looking back from more than thirty years later, this was one of my early exposures to how stifling the usual silos of an academic field can be, premised, as they often are, on the presumed autonomy and uniqueness of the datum that one happens to be studying and the method that one happens to be using. Or, to put it the other way 'round, I now realize how, early on, my work benefited from taking seriously people who knew far more than I about things well off my radar, since there were often surprising applications and outright overlaps with the matters that preoccupied me. I should therefore add to this memory the now career-long friendship, also begun during graduate school, with Willi Braun—one that led to a wide variety of partnerships: from co-editing *MTSR* for over a decade and then co-editing the *Guide to the Study of Religion* (2000) to our *Festschrift* for J. Z. Smith (2014) and working together again as recently as his own essay collection (2020). This has been a collaboration that has regularly exposed me to work being done in another field well removed from my own: Christian origins; for, as I've also commented previously, I credit Willi with first getting me to read Jonathan Z. Smith back in the mid- to late 1980s. Come to think of it, if you add to this an array of other friendships and working relationships over the years—from (to name only a few) scholars of Hinduism (e.g., Jack Llewellyn and Steven Ramey), of Judaism and Islam (most recently, another of my frequent collaborators, Aaron Hughes), as well as with Americanists (e.g., Julie Ingersoll, Leslie Dorrough Smith, Michael Altman), to those studying race and gender (e.g., Craig Prentiss, Merinda Simmons, Richard Newton, Emily Crews) and classicists as well (e.g., Luther H. Martin, Vaia Touna), et cetera—then you begin to lay bare some of the conditions that led to the creation of a scholar who, though trained initially in the philosophy of religion (taking doctoral courses on the pre-Socratics, Plato, Aristotle, Hume, Kant's first critique, etc.), has morphed into something else entirely, in large part due to some rather promiscuous conversations.

I write "promiscuous" with a nod toward the still widespread assumption that the credibility and thus legitimacy of scholars in our field is to be judged by the fine-grained specificity and pedigree of their work: carried out on this and only this particular fragment of an ancient text or on just that subgroup of people in this delimited time and place. As I've noted elsewhere, this is what I refer to as the "I don't *do* the epistles" model of the field, as was announced, long ago, by a onetime New Testament colleague, as part of a (successful, I might add) rhetorical effort to obtain another faculty hire in a different area of New Testament. Thus, given what I've experienced as the predominance of this model of scholarship, the designation "generalist" can be the kiss of death for an academic career, when one's orthodox colleagues are instead all studying tightly focused elements of a taken-for-granted and thus authoritative taxonomy; in our field that, of course, most often means some specific feature of one or another of the so-called world's religions. And so we arrive at the common structure of our undergraduate and then graduate or postgraduate programs (i.e., initial broad surveys leading to specialized seminars and, eventually, highly technical dissertations, all focused on an increasingly detailed aspect of one or another religion), not to mention the topical division of labor in our profession's journals, publishers' catalogues, scholarly conferences, and even our teaching assignments and job searches (such as they now are), not to mention fellowship and grant opportunities. Even our research and teaching specialties are divided between one or the other of the religions, usually understood as discrete and enduring entities with clear borders, along with their various historical phases and components and also the regions in which they have progressively been found (or manifested and embodied, as some would surely prefer to say—our verbs betray our theories). Case in point: open almost any academic journal in the field and it is quickly apparent from just the table of contents what one might read and what will be completely ignored, that is, articles on this or that topic will only be of relevance to a small band of specialists who have command over their content, since these essays' theses and conclusions will, for the most part, have little to no interest in making broader claims of relevance to the field at large; to press further, in many cases, there might as well not even be such a thing as "the field at large," given that many whose work appears in these journals are content to remain isolated within the technicalities of their discrete domains, rarely, if ever, venturing very far afield from their doctoral training. Reading and working broadly is therefore often not rewarded all that much in a system where, early on, one must choose whether to become let's say, a specialist in ancient Vedic texts (but which one and which hymn in particular?) or an expert on modern diaspora Russian Orthodoxy. (Aside: and so we see the appearance of what for some constitutes the painfully evident gap between teaching and research; for who could teach on topics of such exactitude in, let's say, a first year undergraduate survey course?) Thus, anyone who thinks that having read, for instance, Tomoko Masuzawa (2005, 2014) or Suzanne Owen (2011), let alone some of the chapters in Chris Cotter and David Robertson's edited volume (2016), signals the demise of what many now call the world religions paradigm in our field is in for quite a shock when they look up from those undoubtedly important works and survey the lay of the land in the profession today. For even the world of scholarship is still often divided, along some invisible fault line, between rational Western and esoteric Eastern religions.

This continued emphasis on and dedication to a no doubt hard-won specialization within the so-called religious traditions is, however, all the more curious to me when I think back to the breadth of the authors whom I, at least, recall reading during my own doctoral studies—authors whose works had a fundamental impact on my own studies; sure, I was reading historians of religions whose works I hoped to examine in detail, but I could add so many more cross-disciplinary names to that all too brief list of historians mentioned at the outset, from literary critics, classicists, and anthropologists to scholars working in media studies, the philosophy of science, and political science (Donald Wiebe, once an important member of my doctoral committee, even had me reading Eric Havelock on the history of literacy), all of whom had an impact on my work. What's more, those books line my office shelves to this day, sometimes with me assigning them, all these years later, to my own students. Case in point: consider one that I, like many across the field, have had students read on a variety of occasions over the years: Anderson's still influential 1983 book on nationalism, *Imagined Communities.* What is curious, however, is that few who tackle this still well-known book think of themselves as being Southeast Asianists, despite the fact that this was Anderson's own area; after all, his 1967 dissertation, in government studies at Cornell, was titled "The Pemuda Revolution: Indonesian Politics, 1945–1946" (Tadem 2016, 4; later published by Anderson in 1972). Rather, many readers, as they make their way through his argument, likely grant him the authority of his own expertise and, I conjecture, read rather more quickly over some of the detailed examples that he provides to support his argument; instead, they probably focus mainly on his broader theoretical point (e.g., the interconnected role played by industrialization, the move toward metropolitan centers, print capitalism, and a vernacular language being among the conditions for large-scale shared identities)—one that they may later end up applying to work of their own, undoubtedly carried out in areas that are rather far afield from Anderson's own. I could, of course, add many other instances to support the point that, at least when it comes to certain works in recent scholarship, *everyone is actually a generalist* despite the ever-present rhetoric (and career rewards) of specialization; for we're all happily browsing through works produced in fields in which we each have little to no technical competency *and doing so in search of general insights* (answers to that "so what?" question that Smith would sometimes cite as the driver of scholarship) that can be adopted and brought back to a domain with which they are more familiar. (Ironically, despite the quest for specialization forced upon us as we all trained, wasn't this the reading technique taught to all of us in graduate school, when we were asked to read and digest far more than a person reasonably can, prompting us to read books, in many cases, for their larger, theoretical punchlines?) Is that not why so many in our field who may *not* study, to name but one more example, anything related to gendered identity or who are certainly *not* working in any of the branches of feminist theory, nonetheless so profitably have read such a book as Judith Butler's *Gender Trouble* (1990)? Or, to think back to a rather earlier work, what of Mary Douglas's *Purity and Danger* (1966)? How many of its more than 34,000 citations (according to a quick check of Google Scholar not too long ago) come from sources uninterested in the specifics of her analysis of the Levitical dietary code let alone from anthropologists who also did ethnographic work of their own in what was once known as the Belgian Congo (known since 1964 as the Democratic Republic of the Congo, the region where Douglas carried out fieldwork from 1949 to 1951 and then again in 1953)? Or to pose another: who amongst us assumes that only literary critics trained in the study of eighteenth- and nineteenth-century European literature should dare to read Edward Said's *Orientalism* (1978)? And do you remember how, just a few academic generations ago, pretty much everyone was reading and citing Thomas Kuhn's philosophy of science ([1962] 1970)?

But to do this well, as I assume would be required of someone calling themselves a scholar, that is, to be relentlessly and self-consciously promiscuous, as I'm calling it (adapting, somewhat, what Smith once argued to be "our primary expertise" [1982, xi]), means to me more than mere browsing or worse (at least as Mircea Eliade often put it critically): being but an amateur or a dilettante (someone with superficial or perhaps merely fashionable knowledge [Eliade 1990, 68]); instead, it means making a deliberate shift in one's work, to no longer seeing the datum or the supposed content as our main focus, regardless of the effort expended to master it; but, instead, to understand it as the handy or strategically useful site and thus discrete situation where far larger and transposable questions can be asked and possible answers entertained. The experimental test case or e.g., as Smith would so often phrase it, is no longer assumed to have a significance and thus gravitational force of its own. No doubt, early in one's career many of us were utterly fascinated by something that seemed so unfamiliar, even exotic and thus attractive, to us; as such, and beginning in each of our undergraduate programs, many of us were probably motivated to work in very specific data domains, easily knowing which of the various doctoral areas to eventually apply for grad school—do you work in modern Islam or ancient Mediterranean religions? But, or so my argument goes, a shift is eventually required, in which the topics of our work are now put into the service of a scholar's larger curiosities. What's more, and to drop the other shoe, such a shift means that scholars working with dramatically different examples, each of undoubtedly considerable depth and detail, *can share the same curiosities and tools, and thereby benefit from each other's findings*. (This alternative approach to the usual sense of specialization in our field animates the essays in McCutcheon 2021.)

And this brings me all the way back to the opening remarks concerning the benefits of my early collaborations; for, as may have already been obvious, what united us back then was *not* our data; that is, I did not study late-nineteenth-century English elementary schools (Heathorn 2000), nor did I study feasting rhetoric in the gospel of Luke (Braun 1995). Come to think of it, I do not recall a single person in my large doctoral program who was also in the area in which I was doing my own work—perhaps this was among the incentives for me to see what I now characterize as a shift as being so worthwhile and maybe also among the reasons why those in the better populated and thus more popular subspecialties of the field are usually so well insulated from ever considering making the move. But for that small and diverse subset of students at Toronto back then who somehow found each other, the larger issues that we hoped could be illustrated and investigated at each of our discrete sites is what we shared and what constituted our bond—such issues as how do groups of otherwise diverse people form and then, despite the disagreements that are often all too easy to spot, seem to maintain themselves (or not) over time? It was at the level of shared curiosity and thus theory, then, that we became colleagues and collaborators, *not* at the level of data—despite the pressures of a field and an entire profession that is organized around the privileged datum, as if the questions that we ask of it are secondary and nontransferable and thus inspired by the mere contours of our content.

To be sure, as already hinted at, the specific details of each of our examples (in the service of my argument I'll now resist calling them specialties) can take years to master, something that I dare not minimize or dismiss. Think here of the time and dedication required for language acquisition and mastery let alone for carrying out fieldwork or identifying much less getting to and spending time at archives. (The manner in which COVID protocols put an end to the last two items for almost three years will surely impact scholarship for some time to come.) But the investment of that time is rarely considered worthwhile because of the broad questions about groups of people that it may help us to answer—questions that can very well be of profound interest to scholars who do not share our specialty and who have therefore invested their own time mastering yet other canons or learning much about communities far afield from those with whom we've become familiar. But instead of assuming that some ancient text or a group of contemporary people were obviously interesting and therefore in need of study (a common enough judgment sometimes motivated by a prior affinity that we may bring with us to the work, influenced in many cases by taken-for-granteds of our youth and upbringing), what if we invested the time to acquire the language or the thick descriptive information *because we saw there a site where we might be able to explore a question that struck us as being of broad import or relevance*? If so, then, just as how many of us have read our Anderson, Butler, Douglas, or Said, we might grant to others their expertise, immersed in areas far from our own, and instead read them for the broad argument, the modeled approach, the general insight, and thus the overall theoretical gain that, if we're lucky, might be carried back to an area with which we have our own competencies, making colleagues and collaborators of people who share questions and a means for proposing answers to them instead of just the people who share in the details—after all, to pick just biblical studies, there are many who read and study the exact same texts but do so for such divergent reasons that they hardly see themselves as colleagues. My point? *The data does not unite us even as it is.*

If we went about our work in much the same fashion as many of us have been trained to go about our reading—doing so broadly, somewhat promiscuously, without regard for the usual lines separating disciplines (for yes, my work continues to benefit by what I learn from such wide-ranging authors as Jean-François Bayart, Wendy Brown, Rogers Brubaker, Dominique Colas, Constantin Fasolt, Anthony Giddens, Anthony Grafton, Joan Wallach Scott, etc.)—then we might find that many of us have things in common that we had not previously seen, and thus that we might gain from, to pick a quick example, dropping into a conference session on a topic for which we have no credentials (if by "credential" we mean the old sense of having a Ph.D. in the study of that one verse, that specific moment in history, or that precise spot on the map); for, by stopping by for a while, we signal that the gain in knowledge comes not in the details but in refining and applying the approach to *shared problems* exemplified in diverse, even unexpected, places, something that we may have in common despite the differences in our content choices. For, as already suggested, I would argue that many of us are studying much the same things: how a group forms, how different versions of the group are contested from within and without, how members work against their group's inevitable demise, and how something always arises from their ashes—often with the new members casting backward in time to find some seemingly secure point that might be used to authenticate themselves, as if they'd always been there in the way that they are now. (I think that this is just what Gary Lease had in mind when suggesting that we revive a much earlier nomenclature, by always aiming to write a natural history of our topics [Lease 1994; see *MTSR* 21/2 for a special issue devoted to this essay].)

Which, as a scholar working well outside the study of Christian origins, brings me to an ideal example, from within our broad field, of all of this: the work of the late Burton Mack. Mack's interest in scholarly redescriptions of narratives on origins (as found in Christianity)—in which we come to see origins tales as a socially formative technique for building and then authorizing a certain sort of identity and pedigree *in the present of the writer or the speaker*—turns out to be something of direct relevance to all scholars, at least to the degree that they see their role qua scholar as doing something other than merely repeating what the people under study are already claiming or saying about themselves. That Mack carried out this work at a site no less detailed and difficult to master than any other should be more than obvious to anyone who cannot read Koine Greek—but I recall an aside Jonathan Smith once made, noting that the early Christian texts provided him with a useful place to do his own work because, in part, there was already several hundred years of scholarship in the archive, work that was itself also data for him (there being no better example of the latter point than Smith 1990). As for Mack's questions, though he asked them of this specific content area, they strike me as still being broadly relevant to many of us in the field: what is to be gained for a group's members by positing and then talking about some epic past in this rather than that key?

And that is precisely how I've read Mack all along (thanks, in large part once again, to Willi's sage advice all those years ago in Toronto)—with no illusion of mastery over his material and, instead, with a strong hunch that what he was doing with it might be useful to me back where I was doing my own work. Although I would certainly not go so far as to claim him as my mentor (as did Shekitka recently [2022, 185]—itself an intriguing claim, however, what with the obvious differences in our data), few may know that Mack had a significant impact on my thinking at the time and since (thereby adding him to my own long list of intellectual influences). I first met him in-person briefly at a conference in Philadelphia back in 1995, when I tagged along with Willi and others to attend the Society of Biblical Literature Consultation on Ancient Myths and Modern Theories of Christian Origins—as it was then called, which Mack and a few others established. (That panel was the source for the previously published *MTSR* paper from Mack that opened this set of essays, now thirty years old). Or consider that it was from a 1989 paper of Mack's, then unpublished and originally presented at the faculty/student Seminar on Religion in Society at Wesleyan University, at the invitation of Ron Cameron (on September 14, 1989), that I found the title and, more importantly, the organizing structure for my second book. (Mack's public lecture at Wesleyan was later published in the *CSSR Bulletin* [Mack 2001], which I was editing at the time; leading up to its publication he was concerned with the oral tone of the lecture and wrote to me: "I still wonder a bit about the chattiness of it all. But since some of my most inviting and concluding swipes and metaphors are tied to the occasional context, I'm wondering whether a simple explanation about the occasion would be enough to let it go pretty much as is" [email, November 28, 2000].) My *Critics Not Caretakers* (first published in 2001) is therefore a book far more influenced by a set of issues of relevance to his work in Christian origins than many of its readers more than likely realize. What's more, although they likely are not aware of it, the many who, whether or not in agreement with that book's position, subsequently adopted these terms—that is, critic and caretaker, or a term now preferred by some but which puzzles me: critical caretaker—when discussing issues of stance and perspective in the field, are therefore *working with Mack* inasmuch as he has set the terms of the debate. What's more, his well-known interest in the intertwined critical terms "social formation" and "mythmaking" prompted Willi and me not only to include the former in the *Guide to the Study of Religion* that we devised and then edited but also to invite Mack to flesh out what he meant by this originally Marxist term (Mack 2000). At around the same time, this two-fold focus of his also helped to propel me in my own writing on these topics (e.g., McCutcheon 1998). And, thanks once again to Willi's recommendations, I found Mack's work in *A Myth of Innocence* of such use that it informed my analysis of how a discursive field functions: by setting idealized, binary poles against each other so that a bounded continuum is established, within which variables can inhabit a territory where judgments, disagreements, and alliances "in the daily round," as Mack put it, can be forged—in a word, it's the creation of culture (Mack [1988] 2006, 20; see McCutcheon 2003, 106–107).

Influenced himself in a fundamental way by the work of Jonathan Smith (see Mack 2008 for details of this relationship's beginnings)—as I am myself, which should be all too evident from the thesis of this very chapter—Mack set about using Smith's redescriptive method (on this method, see Hughes and McCutcheon 2022, 240–246 as well as the immediately prior chapter) as a model for other scholars who were equally frustrated by the manner in which participant accounts in the study of Christianity's origins were often passively adopted and used by scholars, as if they were historically accurate and settled narratives, instead of seeing them as archived arm wrestling moments whereby later social competitors jostled among themselves, with each of the tales they spun a proposed way of representing their version of the group as both free of historical baggage and also irresistibly leading to just themselves, their picture of the world, and their place at its head. Or, as Mack put it, to cite *A Myth of Innocence* once again: "The guiding vision [in the scholarly investigation of Christian origins] . . . has been some imagined event of transformation that might account for the spontaneous generation of the radically new perception, social formation, and religion that Christianity is thought to have introduced into the world" (368). That members themselves presume as much about their own group's—let's just say it—magical beginnings may make sense to us; that scholars studying, in this case, Christianity uncritically perpetuate "the big bang concept of Christian origins," as Mack referred to it in the opening of his 1996 *MTSR* paper, is, as Braun so well described it in his introduction to this set of papers, highly suspect.

But people such as I, well outside the study of earliest Christianity, were also paying attention to Mack's critique. For although I never had a seat at the SBL seminar table where this work was taking place, beginning back in 1995 (and, in varying forms, continuing to this day), I was a spectator from the sidelines, attending a variety of their annual working sessions, getting to know such scholars as Ron Cameron, Merrill Miller, Stan Stowers, and Barry Crawford (and later, another generation, including Jennifer Eyl, Erin Roberts, Robyn Faith Walsh, and, at one time, Matthew Baldwin), watching Smith hunched over, hands and chin on cane, as he listened intently to the discussion on the predistributed papers, and following Mack's delicate, often jovial, and always artful wording as he tried to persuade, even cajole—yes, the latter's sense of flattery is intended here—his colleagues to think differently about how it is that scholars study a group's own discourse on where they come from and how they developed over time. That his coaxing of the wider field of New Testament studies did not always pay off was clear and, at times, it was certainly a matter for some frustration for him; I think back on an April 2, 1998, letter that Mack sent to a small group of colleagues, which included a copy of his detailed response to a producer at WGBH Boston concerning their just broadcast *Frontline* television special, "From Jesus to Christ: The First Christians"; his cover letter to colleagues read, in part: "When I saw the script in February 1996, I did some somersaults, for the plans to be interviewed in Boston had already been confirmed, and I couldn't believe my eyes. The script followed the gospel story line as if it were history after all. When I finally got my feet under me, it was clear that [the producer] had been snookered, my work had been misread, and that I did not want to appear to support the program" (personal correspondence).

His frustration with what he read as the wider impact of the Christian myth, as he phrased it (e.g., Mack 2003), on much of contemporary U.S. culture and politics, animated his last few books, some of which first appeared in an Equinox book series that I edited at the time (e.g., Mack 2011). That readers outside the guild would probably not be all that receptive to an approach that historicized some of their cherished origins tales, and, along with them, their current sense of self and the place that they presumed to occupy in the world, must have been known to him, yet he persisted in trying to spread the word about this alternative way of understanding the past and the present. To be sure, it was a difference in approach to origins—what Baldwin once characterized as "the Mackian approach to early Christian literature [that] challenges students of religion to account with greater clarity for the ways myth operates in social formation" (2018, 5)—that was not all that new to some of us; here I think back to Bruce Lincoln's early work on the, as he phrased it, instrumentality of the past (e.g., 1986, 162 f. and 1989, 27 f.]), Masuzawa's own work (e.g., 2000), let alone the groundbreaking contributions of Hayden White in the field of History, decades before; but, to return to my earlier point, for many working exclusively within the field's silos of religious tradition, their elements (i.e., myths, rituals, associations, texts, etc.), their time periods, and regions—those who, like some I've met in any of our subfields, may not have read all that widely beyond their one specialized data domain—this was certainly quite novel and even challenging stuff. It could even be deeply controversial, inasmuch as it threatened to displace long-standing and therefore familiar and comfortable narratives that were preferred by those with certain interests (i.e., "our tradition arose mysteriously, miraculously, and pretty much fully formed, and triumphantly marched through history, much as we see it today, arriving at the present moment . . ."). And, as testified by Andrew Tobolowsky (2023), in an essay reflecting on the relevance of Mack's work, for many it still remains a troubling shift to make, in such a subfield as the study of the Hebrew bible, where the presumption that the texts (known often simply as scriptures, a participant designation that itself comes with a number of complexities for a redescriptive scholar) provide scholars with historical insights into what many call ancient Israel is still dominant, as opposed to reading these origins accounts in the context of work being done well outside this one specialty's immersion in the text, thereby seeing its tales as shedding light on writers and editors in a rather different setting and time who worked with the archive of what they now considered to be their own collective past, all for uses of relevance to their present—a point also apparent in the contemporary groups in India that were recently discussed in an essay by Audrey Truschke (2023).

And it's just that sort of promiscuous reading—a term that I suspect Mack would have relished, what with his focus on social anthropology as but one discipline that might help shed light on what a truly social theory of Christian origins might look like—coupled with a wide-ranging collaboration that I most have in mind when thinking of Mack's enduring contributions to the larger field, which go far beyond how he helped to reinvent the study of Christian origins by trying to get behind the scriptural portrait of events. Singlehandedly he could not undo hundreds of years of specialization, that goes without saying; but in a series of cases and in discrete situations he was himself inspired by people who knew far more about various things than he did and, through his applications of that work to his own domain he modeled for some of us how to do this for ourselves, at times even borrowing from Mack's own scholarship to the benefit of work carried out far from his familiar ground in the New Testament and the Graeco-Roman world. Surely this is why Willi, as I still remember clearly to this day, emailed me in the wake of the terrible 9/11 attacks—events which prompted many outcries and headlines in U.S. and western European media concerning why "they" hate "our freedoms"—suggesting that I read the concluding pages of *A Myth of Innocence*, with a view toward better understanding how identity can rely upon self-representations of groups as ahistorical, unblemished, and therefore above the fray. Those looking for whether the advanced research carried out in our field has relevance and application beyond its specialized borders need look no further; in fact, isn't this the narrative engine that even drives the 1994 film *Forrest Gump*: the well-meaning innocent—"bless his heart . . . ," as we say in my part of the country—doing the best that he can while being propelled through current events by sometimes malevolent forces larger than himself? Given the obvious and wide application of Mack's critique in my own career development, grounded as it is in my own promiscuous reading and collaborations, I highly recommend such an approach to anyone who will listen. For it is just such a shift that much of our department at the University of Alabama has made rather successfully over the past decades, nicely exemplified not only in a graduate program where students are trained to understand that scholars of religion have wide-ranging and perhaps surprising contributions to make (both within and also well outside of academia) but also in a series of collaborative projects among faculty members who each work in drastically different historical periods and geographic regions, from the Culture on the Edge collaboration (edge.ua.edu—an online initiative that has involved a large number of scholars, at varying career stages, elsewhere as well) and a variety of shared publishing projects (e.g., Ramey 2015; Touna and Newton 2023), to the recent, five-year Luce Foundation grant obtained by my colleague, Michael Altman, that resulted in the ongoing multiyear American Examples workshops for early career scholars, which annually involved six other faculty in our department as research, teaching, and public/digital humanities mentors (see Altman 2021 and Choudhury et al. 2022 for the first two of its annual volumes). While the reasons and resources for our reinvention were certainly more diverse than just Mack's implicit influence—to be sure, Smith's work has been an explicit point of inspiration for many of us—much like the manner in which his questions lurk in the background of much of my own early work, I can clearly see Mack in many of our unit's successes, not least of which is our attitude concerning how discourses on the past function. (Recently, preparing the second edition of *Critics Not Caretakers*, I was rather surprised by the degree to which things that eventually became important drivers of our department's reinvention were already elaborated in more than twenty-five-year-old chapters—chapters that I had not read in many years.)

And so, for those who might not be acquainted with Mack's work on Christian origins—or, I should better say, his work on discourses on origins *as exemplified in* the case of assorted turn-of-the-era Mediterranean social movements that rather later came to be known as Christianity—I invite them to become more familiar with what he accomplished in his long and distinguished career, regardless of the distance from his to their own specifics and examples. For, as with reading Smith, the gain is to be found in looking for the moves that he makes, the questions that he asks, and what he contributes to solving the broad problems that attend studying any group that makes claims about itself and its past. In fact, we may even come to see that *this* is in fact what defines and animates our shared enterprise and thus our scholarly specialty—that is, the work of cross-disciplinary collaboration premised on promiscuous curiosities—rather than having it determined by the details on which we each happen to apply and test our claims. For only in the light of such a shift would it make sense to say, as I certainly can, that my own scholarship is all the better for having read the work of, say, Donald Lopez and Robert Sharf, despite having no credible expertise whatsoever in the study of Buddhism in any of its settings—because I found there, as with many other scholars working far afield from my own interests, larger points of general application that can be profitably translated to my own research. But because making such a shift means cutting across the grain of how many members of our field have long carried out their work and thereby understood, identified, and authenticated themselves as scholars (i.e., seeing their teaching and research as special since their methods and data were presumably so unique), I should close by repeating Mack's caution from the epigraph that opens this final chapter: "the task ahead is for the tough minded, not the tender hearted." For it means being prepared to entertain that, despite the halo that some assume to ring the items that we each examine, what we study is no less mundane than any other moment in human history and culture—utterly commonplace situations and artifacts that gain their significance and utility in scholarship from *our* curiosities about how it is that people do the things that people do. And who knows, if we're successful in demonstrating the larger gains in knowledge that might come from such a reinvented study of religion then perhaps the rest of the academy may start to understand why our field even exists and what others might gain from either taking our classes or reading our articles and books. For, given ongoing changes in higher education that continue to squeeze and even undermine the humanities, it may turn out to be that the future of the field itself, and not just the relevance of each individual's work, is at stake in pushing back against the protectionism, that, as Willi Braun rightly argued, so troubled Mack throughout his career (Braun 2023, 404).

References

Altman, Michael, ed. 2021. *American Examples: New Conversations about Religion*. Vol. 1. Tuscaloosa: University of Alabama Press.

Anderson, Benedict. 1972. *Java in a Time of Revolution: Occupation and Resistance, 1944–1946*. Ithaca, NY: Cornell University Press.

———. (1983) 1991. *Imagined Communities: Reflections on the Origin and Spread of Nationalism*. London: Verso.

Baldwin, Matthew C. 2018. "Mack and Mythic Foundations: A Response to Walsh, Monier, Kugler and Worthington." Unpublished paper presented at the Society of Biblical Literature's Redescribing Early Christianity Seminar (Denver, CO).

Braun, Willi. 1995. *Feasting and Social Rhetoric in Luke 14* (Society for New Testament Studies Monograph Series, Series Number 85). Cambridge: Cambridge University Press.

———. 2020. *Jesus and Addiction to Origins: Toward an Anthropocentric Study of Religion*. Edited by Russell T. McCutcheon. Sheffield: Equinox.

———. 2023. "Burton Mack's Challenge to the Study of Religion." *Method & Theory in the Study of Religion* 35 (5): 401–408.

Braun, Willi, and Russell T. McCutcheon, eds. 2000. *Guide to the Study of Religion*. London: Bloomsbury.

———. 2014. *Introducing Religion: Essays in Honor of Jonathan Z. Smith*. New York: Routledge.

Butler, Judith. 1990. *Gender Trouble: Feminism and the Subversion of Identity*. New York: Routledge.

Choudhury, Samah, Prea Persaud, and Michael J. Altman, eds. 2022. *American Examples: New Conversations about Religion*. Vol. 2. Tuscaloosa: University of Alabama Press.

Cotter, Christopher R., and David G. Robertson, eds. 2016. *After World Religions: Constructing Religious Studies*. New York: Routledge.

Douglas, Mary. 1966. *Purity and Danger: An Analysis of Concepts of Pollution and Taboo*. London: Routledge and Kegan Paul.

Eliade, Mircea. 1990. *1907–1937, Journey East, Journey West*. Vol. 1 of *Autobiography*. Chicago: University of Chicago Press.

Heathorn, Stephen J. 2000. *For Home, Country, and Race: Gender, Class, and Englishness in the Elementary School, 1880–1914*. Toronto: University of Toronto Press.

Hughes, Aaron W., and Russell T. McCutcheon. 2022. *Religion in 50 Words: A Critical Vocabulary*. New York: Routledge.

Kuhn, Thomas S. (1962) 1970. *The Structure of Scientific Revolutions*. 2nd ed. Chicago: University of Chicago Press.

Lease, Gary. 1994. "The History of 'Religious' Consciousness and the Diffusion of Culture: Strategies for Surviving Dissolution." *Historical Reflections/Réflexions Historiques* 20 (3): 453–479.

Lincoln, Bruce. 1986. *Myth, Cosmos, and Society: Indo-European Themes of Creation and Destruction*. Cambridge, MA: Harvard University Press.

———. 1989. *Discourse and the Construction of Society: Comparative Studies of Myth, Ritual, and Classification*. New York: Oxford University Press.

Mack, Burton L. (1988) 2006. *A Myth of Innocence: Mark and Christian Origins*. Minneapolis: Fortress.

———. 2000. “Social Formation.” In *Guide to the Study of Religion*, edited by Willi Braun and Russell T. McCutcheon. London: Bloomsbury.
———. 2001. “Caretakers and Critics: On the Social Role of Scholars Who Study Religion.” *Bulletin of the Council of Societies for the Study of Religion* 30 (2): 32–38.
———. 2003. *The Christian Myth: Origins, Legacy, Logic*. London: Bloomsbury.
———. 2008. “Sacred Persistence?” In *Introducing Religion: Essays in Honor of Jonathan Z. Smith*, edited by Willi Braun and Russell T. McCutcheon. New York: Routledge.
———. 2011. *Christian Mentality: Entanglements of Power, Violence, and Fear*. New York: Routledge.
Masuzawa, Tomoko. 2000. “Origin.” In *Guide to the Study of Religion*, edited by Willi Braun and Russell T. McCutcheon. London: Bloomsbury.
———. 2005. *The Invention of World Religions Or, How European Universalism Was Preserved in the Language of Pluralism*. Chicago: University of Chicago Press.
———. 2014. “Striating Difference: From ‘Ceremonies and Customs’ to World Religions.” *Republic of Letters* 3 (23). https://arcade.stanford.edu/rofl/striating-difference-ceremonies-and-customs-world-religions.
McCutcheon, Russell T. 1998. “Redescribing ‘Religion’ as Social Formation: Toward a Social Theory of Religion.” In *What Is Religion? Origins, Definitions, and Explanations*, edited by Thomas A. Idinopulos and Brian C. Wilson. Numen Book Series, vol. 81. Leiden: Brill.
———. (2001) 2024. *Critics Not Caretakers: Redescribing the Public Study of Religion*. 2nd ed. New York: Routledge.
———. 2003. *The Discipline of Religion: Structure, Meaning, Rhetoric*. New York: Routledge.
———. 2020. “Discourse Analysis as an Anthropology of the Mundane: An Interview.” In *Discourse Research and Religion: Disciplinary Use and Interdisciplinary Dialogues*, edited by Jay Johnston and Kocku von Stuckrad. Berlin: Walter de Gruyter.
———. 2021. *On Making a Shift in the Study of Religion and Other Essays*. Berlin: Walter de Gruyter.
———, ed. 2024. *Religious Studies beyond the Discipline: On the Future of a Humanities Ph.D.* Sheffield: Equinox.
Owen, Suzanne. 2011. “The World Religions Paradigm: Time for a Change.” *Arts and Humanities in Higher Education* 10 (3): 253–268.
Ramey, Steven W., ed. 2015. *Writing Religion: The Case for the Critical Study of Religion*. Tuscaloosa: University of Alabama Press.
Said, Edward. 1978. *Orientalism*. New York: Pantheon Books.

Shekitka, John Patrick. 2022. "School Structures and Curricular Choices: The Social Studies Classroom in Religious and Secular Schools." *Religion & Education* 49 (2): 163–191.

Smith, Jonathan Z. 1982. *Imagining Religion: From Babylon to Jonestown*. Chicago: University of Chicago Press.

———. 1990. *Drudgery Divine: On the Comparison of Early Christianities and the Religions of Late Antiquity*. Chicago: University of Chicago Press.

Tadem, Eduardo Climaco. 2016. "Benedict Anderson, 1936–2015." *Philippine Political Science Journal* 37 (1): 3–5.

Tobolowsky, Andrew. 2023. "Redescribing, but Really, Finally Moving On from Israelite Origins." *Method & Theory in the Study of Religion* 35 (5): 434–444.

Touna, Vaia, and Richard Newton, eds. 2023. *Fieldnotes in the Critical Study of Religion: Revisiting Classical Theorists*. London: Bloomsbury.

Truschke, Audrey. 2023. "Hearing Hindu Stories." *Method & Theory in the Study of Religion* 35 (5): 466–477.

Afterword

It was the day after our department's inaugural lecture in 2012–13's series on the relevance of the humanities and social sciences in the contemporary university (a theme presciently set by my colleague Ted Trost while he was chair of our department) and I was rather troubled by the student feedback that I was hearing. It came from some of our undergraduate majors who attended the event as well as from an assortment of students who were then enrolled in my 100-level introductory course. ("Write me a one-page description of the lecture and you can earn some extra credit in the course"—the professor's old trick to get students who are new to the university to think a few new thoughts, and, as we used to say, expand their horizons by venturing out into campus.) Whether or not it was intended by the speaker—Gregg Lambert, the founding director of Syracuse University's Humanities Center—it was clear that the students heard a message of lamentation for the future of the humanities; it was not a description of how we got here or a renewed defense of our relevance but, instead, a (to their ears at least) dire message from a senior professor concerning the fact that they may be deluded to think that grad school might be for them (since they'll possibly be mired in student debt that will take them decades to repay, making grad school sound like a bit of a scam, to speak frankly); because they were told that they're all apparently just human capital, spewed into the global market from a never-ending pipeline, why continue in their studies? It was a stark message that prompted one first-year student who attended the lecture,

The original version of this afterword was posted on my department blog on September 25, 2012 and October 21, 2012—the former being my first post on the site (the blog was first made by my colleague and now my department chair, Steven Ramey, in the summer of 2012, and initially populated by short posts that he wrote on the wide relevance of the humanities). These two posts are revised and updated here. That the point of both remains directly relevant and thus suits being repurposed as an afterword to a volume produced over a decade later comprises a sufficient indictment of the field for its lethargy in pivoting to meet the challenges that have increasingly been facing higher education for several decades.

sounding both intimidated and incredulous, to say to me: "Declaring a major may be the most important decision of my life?!"

Now, this is not necessarily the lecture that I heard (e.g., the abovementioned pipeline imagery that Lambert used was, in fact, directly contested by our speaker, but the image remained for his listeners nonetheless); but I can understand why certain parts stood out for the students—the shocking often proves the most memorable. "If it bleeds it leads" is the old newspaper adage, after all. And maybe that was our lecturer's intention; perhaps a little cold water was needed to wake us from our privileged slumbers. These sobering words caught some of our students off-guard because we, for all I know, had not hammered home often and loudly enough that higher education is now (whether it always was and we just had the luxury to pretend that it wasn't is a discussion that we ought to have) a part of the cost/benefit economic system as much as anything else. Given the uphill argument that we, in the academic study of religion, feel that we have in helping students (and, more importantly, perhaps, their families or even the wider public) understand that this undergraduate major is as relevant as any other (did you ever wonder why "If you're not going to become a History teacher, then why major in History" never used to be a question for people in that field—but it has certainly become one now?), you would think that our students, perhaps more than anyone else's, had already done some of the hard-nosed decision-making long before declaring their REL major. And given the complex careers that some religious studies faculty have had (yes, I know what it is like to be an instructor and to consider the hard truth that, having earned a Ph.D., I might not have also earned the right to feed and clothe myself by means of those skills), we seem particularly cognizant of these issues and so many of us try to make sure that our students know, too. But because the forces against which we say such things, those that idealize university life and learning, are so numerous and incessant, it needs to be said again and again: structural factors well beyond our control pulled the rug out from under so much of the national and global economy, beginning in earnest in the late 2000s, that it may take decades to recover (if "recovery" is even the right word; we all know what COVID-era budget cuts meant for universities).

But tied to that structural level of analysis there also needs to be one that focuses attention on individual agency—the two presuppose each other, after all—and I wonder if this is what our students also needed to hear during that hard-nosed lecture so many years ago. Now, I'd likely never be accused of erring on the side of the lone and rugged, can-do individual, boldly making meaning in the world, so fear not: I will not close this book with some argument for the self-evident, intangible value of the humanities or presuppose a nostalgia for the noble self. No, not at all. Instead, I'm taking a basic insight from structuralism seriously and noting that while we may emphasize one or the other for analytic purposes, no analysis of a binary pair is sufficient if it normalizes only one half of a pair and thereby neglects the other side of the coin. After all, identifying the ways that the Other-in-our-midst is often silenced or at least minimized (whether it's worth recovering is, of course, another conversation) is a basic building block of the critical theories that have shaped so much of our work in the academy over the last generation or two—from the work of social historians to feminist and post-colonial theorists. So, taking a page from our own playbook—and, as already argued, scholars are often notoriously bad at applying their critical tools to understand their own social worlds—I think that while focusing on structure, we also need to draw attention to the sometimes inventive and effective agents within that structure; for the system did not invent itself (yes, "it" is never homogenous or uniform either, making the pronoun rather misleading) and neither did the agents invent themselves from whole cloth. None of us would be here without the dating and mating rituals that were none of our parents' own making (what the biologists call pair bonding), though they surely tweaked the rules while tweaking each other, to be sure. . . . As we have as well. As our descendants undoubtedly will. And so, around and around it goes: structure made by agents made by structure made by . . . Turtles all the way down, as they say. That's how the critical thinker in me sees it.

And it turns out that this was the part of the message that our students did not hear that day, over a decade ago—that they are operating within a structure not of their making, sure, one that is determined by many factors well beyond their influence, yes indeed, but one in which they are agents nonetheless, social actors who, by their very activity, affect that structure (isn't this the moral of the physicist's classic double slit experiment?); they collaborate and thereby continually remake it, doing so within parameters set by others, to be sure, but given that these parameters are historical artifacts themselves, they are bound to change.

I'm no Pollyanna, of course—despite being called naive by a colleague elsewhere in the country during a recent Zoom meeting where this volume's approach to retooling the field was being discussed and resisted—and anyone who knows me can vouch that I'm certainly no Dr. Pangloss; this is most definitely not the best of all possible versions of higher ed and no one is going to pull themselves up by their own bootstraps, despite how popular the individualist "I made it myself" sentiment has sometimes been. But I would also not like to erase the presence of the actors in these structures, those who help to make the rules, benefit from them, labor under them, but who can and will change them—just how, we have yet to see.

So, this book has not contained some dreamy-eyed message of hope; it's not my style. I'll leave spinning such a tale to political campaigns along with those *seemingly* liberal-minded faculty who remain weirdly convinced that the profoundly privileged "life of the mind" is what academia is actually all about, as if the obviously apparent practical conditions of our institutions were somehow nuisances to them and their very important work. Instead, what I hope readers who are open to thinking critically about their own conditions take away with them, just like what I wished students all those years ago had taken away from that public lecture, is that we all ought to be paying attention to the wider, structural circumstances in which we teach our students and carry out our research, the systems that work on us: all those turtles above us and below, knowing that those social, political, and economic worlds did not spring from the ground like a mushroom overnight, all on their own; instead, people—huge numbers of people, for sure, people who didn't know each other but also people collaborating, competing, and contradicting each other—made them, reinforced them, and even undermined them. Since we're all people, too—good people, salt of the earth people—maybe, just maybe, we can remake it all. If we work together. And if we're self-reflexive, open to complicating simple narratives, intent on doing comparative and redescriptive work that can be applied, etc.

So, I wanted those students to know to be modest but be strategic. Know that your good looks or quick thinking will only get you so far. Know that, at times, you're an almost powerless item exchanged in a network of international capital, but, then again, you knew that as soon as you used a self-check-out lane, faced ever-rising tuition rates, or listened to tenured professors who get to read, write, and talk for a living, despairing over the idea of having to learn how to offer a résumé-writing workshop to their students. (Yes, I've heard that complaint as well—the frequent "but that's not what I was trained to do" is surprising to hear from faculty who supposedly relish the freedom to continually learn new things throughout their career.) But also know that *you have agency* . . . , sure, within structure created by agency exercised within structure, etc., etc., all the way down. And strategically knowing your place within this never-ending system of inventive reciprocal actors in situations-not-of-their-making means that you may have what the ancient Greek called *mêtis* (μῆτις)—cunning intelligence. It's just what is needed at times like this—a time when releasing your grip on your Precious so as to use both hands in seriously retooling the field and your departments, all to meet the demands of the moment, may be more about saving the field along with your own job than selling out.

I didn't start out my career in higher ed thinking all this, to be sure. My undergraduate degree was in what my university (Queen's University in Canada) then called life sciences, or what others might have once called pre-med. Many of us wrote the Medical College Admissions Test (as I did), but not all of us got into medicine (as I didn't, but as my roommate along with many classmates did). In our first year of college, we predictably took courses in chemistry, biology, physics (each of which had its own three-hour lab too, of course), calculus, and psychology—the last being an elective but pretty much everyone enrolled in it in their first year. In other years we took such courses as organic chemistry, genetics, biochemistry, histology, abnormal psych, anatomy, statistics, microbiology, and physiology. I would imagine that many of my classmates who, like the vast majority of us, didn't get into medicine have ended up in one of the many adjacent fields, such as going on to do a master's of science degree in microbiology ("micro" for the initiated), or eventually going into, say, pharmacology, to do research, work for a drug company's marketing division (as one friend did after getting his Ph.D.), or own your own pharmacy (the route taken by another good friend from those days).

As for me, I ended up getting a Ph.D. in religious studies from the University of Toronto and having an entire career in U.S. public universities. What a waste that undergrad degree was, right?

Well . . . looking back now I'd say no, not necessarily.

Maybe my point is obvious; not unlike many students who pursue a degree in the humanities, many who earn an undergraduate degree in any number of other areas also reinvent themselves once they graduate. But—and this is the interesting part—no one seems to see that as a problem in other fields, while it worries us terribly in the humanities. What gives? Enrolling in a BA in religious studies? "What on earth are you going to do with a degree *like that*?" asks Aunt Enid at pretty much every family get-together. But enroll in an engineering degree program, and everyone somehow knows that you're on the right track. That few of my own undergrad engineering friends ever actually did any engineering in their careers—since they all enrolled almost right away in an MBA degree and all became managers who never picked up a protractor again—did not seem to tarnish the luster of their first degree, in which they were immersed in material that eventually proved of little relevance to how they earned their daily bread.

Or . . . was it actually directly relevant, perhaps? Because I always thought, at the time, that my engineering friends, with the insane schedules and workloads that they had (they certainly had it worse than I did in terms of hours per week in class, even though my five classes, each meeting three times per week, plus those three three-hour labs per week made my time pretty hectic), were actually being trained in such things as how to manage their time, how to meet deadlines, and how to juggle multiple balls, how to collaborate and work in teams to solve problems. That is, especially when they all started doing business degrees after graduation, it seemed to me that, despite what their undergraduate classes seem to have been about, they had all actually been taught a host of *skills* and not necessarily *content* in their degree, skills that would be handy to them whatever they should decide to do.

Looking back, with the advantages that come with hindsight, it seems to me that the seemingly practical application of their degrees provided cover for their professors to teach them broad skills that are actually basic to almost any education and useful in almost any career. It turns out that, for many of them, it never really was about the content of those classes, after all.

Well played, engineering professors. Well played.

As for my life sciences training? I didn't do the final year of my bachelor of science degree, which means that I earned a BA instead of a BA Honors (that's how the Canadian system worked). For after three years of petri dishes, fruit flies, and carbon rings, I also moved on to other things, far afield from histology textbooks. But I think that the sort of analytic problem-solving skills that I learned in those early years, the way to break down something overly complex into manageable parts that you can then tackle (i.e., reduction) in reproducible ways, have served me rather well in the place where I happen to have landed—in my research, my teaching, my professional service, and even my years administrative work. It probably also helped to train me to juggle multiple balls without dropping too many (some bounce, thankfully—figuring out which ones is among the keys to effective administrative work while being a productive scholar). And this means to me that my undergraduate degree, seemingly so removed from what I do today, was anything but a waste of my time; for it turned out to be crucial in the formation of the scholar who I am today.

The moral of my story? Not all scientists wear lab coats.

Which brings me back to the unfair nature of our hypothetical Aunt Enid's question, something that is never apparent at the time, when it is asked while you pass her a bowl of mashed potatoes at some family gathering. For she's asking that student to read the leftover coffee grounds in the bottom of a cup that they've not even finished making yet, much less started to drink, making their prediction of the future pretty inadequate. And so, to her "What on earth are you going to do with a degree like that?" question, I would advise a simple reply: "You just watch me!" Students should be inspired to think of themselves as tactical turtles, after all—inventive agents in worlds not of their making, being trained to understand what makes those worlds tick. And just watch out if our curriculums and our work as graduate supervisors finally catch on to this, signaling that we've figured out how to help students with being tactical and nimble from day one of their degrees, always cognizant of the tools that they're learning to use and the many sites where they can be put to good use; for they shouldn't have to do it all on their own. After all, faculty are being paid to train students for the worlds to which those students gain access after graduation and not some nostalgic or even fantasy world that those faculty members themselves wish that they inhabited.

Postscript

"Whereof What's Past Is Prologue": On the Current State of U.S. Higher Ed

When I was invited in late March 2025 to write a short piece for the members of the British Association for the Study of Religion (BASR) describing the current state of American higher education, we were then just a couple of months into the new presidency, but the priorities that this administration had from day one—or even well before any of those initial executive orders were signed, if one believed the news reports during the campaign, let alone the eventually successful candidate's own statements all throughout—were all too plain. But challenges to the humanities, more narrowly understood, or even to the liberal arts as a whole, as seen rather more broadly, had been building in the United States for decades, helping one to understand how some might see the current situation as a change in degree, to be sure, but perhaps not much of a change in kind. Whether that change in degree will be sufficient to present an all new, even more dire situation to those who are working or studying in either public or private colleges and universities in the United States remains to be seen, of course, as will how the ongoing changes specifically impact the public study of religion. What with this book's completed manuscript being delivered to the press back in October 2024, prior even to the election, and given that so much has changed by mid-May 2025, when I am writing this, I feel that there is a need to draw on that BASR report from the trenches so as to insert this postscript just ahead of the book's proofs arriving. My aim is simple: to signal to current and especially future readers not only an awareness of the situation in which we now find ourselves but also a hope that I have concerning the continued relevance of the rationale and the recommendations that I've included in this volume.

Few of us today live in a social media vacuum, so it's probably wise to assume that readers who are contemporary with this volume's publication have, to whatever extent, been paying attention to at least some of the developments in American college life over the past few months. No doubt about it, these changes in policy and priority probably strike many as being so out of the ordinary that it is difficult to look away when the news alert pops up on your phone. The more notable developments that readers might already be aware of may include suspending large sums of federal grants owed to universities like Columbia (which quickly gave in to the administration's demands) along with Cornell and Northwestern (at the time of writing this, Cornell is suing the federal government over its actions) and investigating a large number of campuses across the country for unlawfully tolerating what is being characterized as anti-Semitic harassment (inquiries that are closely linked to how some see last spring's pro-Palestinian protests on a number of university campuses throughout the country). But there are also the ongoing efforts to defund and eventually close the federal Department of Education as well as the drastic cut to the portion of National Institutes of Health federal grants that can go toward a researcher's indirect costs (also known as research overhead—this is now in the courts as well), along with terminating many National Endowment for the Humanities and National Endowment for the Arts grants entirely while, most recently, also freezing current National Science Foundation grants. And just days ago, it was announced in a letter to the Senate's Committee on Appropriations, from Russell T. Vought (the director of the administration's Office of Management and Budget), that among many proposed cuts to discretionary spending the administration will be targeting those Fulbright grants—a mainstay of American higher ed for eighty years—available to foreign students to visit and train in the United States.

The wider context of such current actions is an ongoing series of cuts to universities over the past several decades, thereby shifting the costs largely to families via recurring tuition increases (and the invention of separate fees to fund various aspects of campus life—from the student recreation center to the glassware in a chemistry lab). The result is that students today in American public universities are paying significantly more (even when adjusted for inflation) for their education than members of their families who went to college in, say, the 1970s or 1980s (since their elders did so at a time when taxpayer support, via commitments from state budgets, was significantly more than it is now—California residents did not even pay tuition for their state system until a small, symbolic initial fee was instituted in 1970). In fact, the so-called student loan bubble in the United States, which is now widely reported to total just shy of $1.8 trillion, now outpaces all American credit card debt, while being about one sixth of mortgage loans in the country. If we overlay this with a turn toward professionalizing university programs over the last forty years or so (i.e., in an earlier era one might have gone to a separate nursing college or teacher's college to enter those professions, as opposed to attending a university to earn a bachelor's degree in such areas) coupled with weakened faculty senates and the rise of a professional administrative class on many campuses (i.e., few senior administrators now just serve a term or two and then return to the faculty ranks, as we once might have seen—their salaries often increase by so much in their new position that a return to teaching and research is economically infeasible), not to mention the lasting effects of the worldwide economic collapse of 2008 and then, a decade later, widespread government cuts due to COVID-era funding shortages, then you arrive at the imperfect storm of continually rising education costs, an understandable desire to decrease students' time to degree (and thereby help them to manage their student loans at least somewhat), an equally sensible appetite on the part of students and their families to land decent work after college, and faculty with a considerably lessened voice in how their campuses are run (the faculty member qua employee is pretty much the new norm). So, as should be evident from the title's bow to the phrasing of Antonio in *The Tempest* (Act 2, Sc. 1), it strikes me that one cannot begin to talk about what might seem to be new challenges to higher ed without seriously considering how we got to the point of being so vulnerable in the first place.

To bring it all a little closer to home, many readers might also know that in U.S. higher ed there are a number of disciplines that are poorly represented or completely absent in American high schools and which students therefore encounter at college for the first time. The study of religion is certainly among them, since there are no such things as, say, the United Kingdom's religious education here. While it has been legal to teach courses on religions in the U.S. public school system, doing so in a way that is *about* them as an item of history and culture (I think here of Ninian Smart's onetime phrasing), nonetheless it is still seen by many as so controversial as to be something that most local school boards think it wise to avoid entirely, given that even *describing* how certain others might live their lives can be seen by some as uncritically endorsing them. With the professional units on a campus (sometimes called colleges, schools, or faculties, such as the Business College or the School of Social Work) often playing a significant role in setting campus-wide policies and recruiting many of its incoming students, the main place where such a field as religious studies meets its students is almost always as part of a campus's general education or core curriculum—that specifically American invention meant to, regardless of their specialized focus or major, "liberalize" (Latin: *liberalis*, to be unimpeded, unrestricted, or, simply, free) all students, in the classical sense, thereby presumably helping them to fulfill their duties as informed citizens within a liberal democracy. Accordingly, about a quarter (it used to be a third or maybe up to a half) of a typical student's undergraduate degree here still entails classes that are well outside their specialty, providing students with a broad overview of everything from the natural sciences and mathematics to foreign languages, literature, art, and music—thus the classic notation of the liberal arts with the so-called humanities (usually the home to programs in the study of religion—since we all are thought by some to study the enduring expressions of the so-called human spirit) being but one of its components. This means that the vast majority of students taught in a typical Department of Religious Studies in the United States will never be majors and will, instead, take but one or maybe two courses with us in order to satisfy a school's breadth requirements. Sadly, colleges these days often poorly convey to their students the long-standing rationale for the core, resulting in a feeling among many of them that it is a pointless waste of their precious time—a reasonable enough reaction that colleges then often cite, using curiously circular logic, as a reason to decrease their gen ed requirements even more, so as to satisfy students whom the school has never really educated concerning why they might someday need to know something about art or geography.

At a time when the health of a unit is usually measured by its number of graduates and thus majors (a metric that favors the professional schools, to be sure), as opposed to the overall number of students whom it teaches annually (representative of the total amount of tuition revenue generated, a metric closely linked to a college's bottom line—and one to which, at least in my experience, a humanities unit is just assumed to contribute handsomely, so as to subsidize other, more expensive aspects of campus life), many programs whose classes are all full nonetheless feel rather insecure, inasmuch as they have difficulty persuading career-minded and sometimes deeply indebted students that lucrative futures await them upon graduation. And so, it's not unusual for an average religious studies unit, depending on its faculty number and the size of its campus, to teach a thousand or more undergraduate students per year, though often with just a handful of them declaring it as their major (some units might graduate just one or two students a year—if that). On a campus with several hundred history majors or maybe a thousand business majors, the study of religion is placed at a considerable disadvantage, regardless how much tuition revenue their gen ed classes generate for the administration to spend elsewhere. To put it another way, the days of reporting on so-called waiting lists to enroll in some course (a metric once favored by people in our field, to demonstrate the demand for their classes) are by now well behind us, since, rightly or wrongly, it's the number of majors that matters.

Which brings us back to the current federal administration threatening to revoke Harvard's nonprofit status and Harvard's lawsuit in response to the administration's proposed cuts to its federal grants. But I'm sure you've read on that, too.

My point in all of this? It would probably be wise for one not to see what's now happening in U.S. higher ed in isolation from decades of mounting challenges. The handwriting has been on the wall for years—though it strikes me, as made plain earlier in this book, that too few in our field have taken it seriously. Even those who now claim that universities are dangerous hotbeds of so-called woke, gender ideology (hardly a position that dominates among faculty, to be sure, but one would be misreading the situation to assume that all faculty are on the far left) probably realize that current efforts to weaken colleges (or at least cut sectors within them) did not come from out of the blue. When it comes to combating policies with which they disagree, those on the political right tend to be patient, effectively playing the long game. The manner in which those steady, incremental changes impacted not just humanities units but also programs all throughout the liberal arts, such as closing math and physics departments, was seen most clearly back in the summer and fall of 2023, at West Virginia University (their so-called flagship public institution); it is something worth paying attention to—after all, the reasoning pretty obviously is that one can shift campus resources to the professional schools while still delivering to engineering and business students a sufficient menu of natural science, social science, and humanities courses for the purposes of a (more than likely slimmed down) general education curriculum by relying on contract instructors housed in an interdisciplinary humanities unit instead of tenured professors with benefits who make their homes in departments (itself another time-honored cost-cutting trend in higher ed). After all, the heavy lifting that writing and critical thinking once might have played in a college degree has by now changed pretty dramatically. And I've not even mentioned AI regularly being used by today's students (and often encouraged by the campus leadership who may be using it even more themselves) to such an extent that an instructor may have very little idea concerning how well their students read and write unless they reinstitute old-timey in-class assignments (itself not an easy shift to make, given the move some time ago to more cost-effective large lecture classes). It makes sense, then, that many faculty members, perhaps still also experiencing a post-COVID-era malaise, feel rather dispirited and powerless.

So where does this all leave not just higher ed in general but the study of religion in particular?

With some states now renewing calls, or even already passing laws, to mandate the display of the Ten Commandments in public schools and even to integrate the bible into such schools' routine class exercises, let alone so-called school choice bills in state legislatures to allow more students to opt out of a public education as well as a recent Supreme Court case to allow such publicly supported charter schools explicitly to be faith based (I think here of the unsuccessful *St. Isidore of Seville Catholic Virtual School v. Drummond* as well as its companion case, *Oklahoma Statewide Charter School Board v. Drummond*), the landscape in which the study of religion is practiced in the United States is changing. With that in mind, consider also the Supreme Court's current tendency to favor freedom of expression over a previous era's desire to create a public space that was rather more neutral when it came to religion (case in point, see *Kennedy v. Bremerton* in 2022, in which a high school football coach was allowed to continue praying at center field, since to discourage such action was seen as an unlawful limitation of his First Amendment rights, not to mention *Masterpiece Cakeshop v. Colorado Civil Rights Commission* in 2018, where opting not to serve customers whose lifestyle strikes one as disagreeable for sincerely held reasons was also okayed)—all of this leaves scholars of religion in a position where what for some might have been the field's long taken-for-granted and therefore settled conditions may now be in question. Thus, the wider context in which the North American field arose and matured, just fifty years ago or so, may soon have so changed that programs will have little choice but to change along with it. Case in point: arguments for the ability of the study of religion to make people more tolerant (most recently I think of widespread religious literacy efforts, though this rationale for the field certainly predates such phrasing) can now easily—whether or not accurately, in your opinion—be represented in a rather unflattering light, as can be the field's long-standing effort "to make the strange familiar and the familiar strange," as we've all so often quoted it. (I think here of the current pushback from the federal and state governments on onetime efforts to enhance so-called diversity, equity, and inclusion throughout society, let alone on a campus, not to mention the controversy, given some recent state laws that have been passed, over teaching so-called divisive concepts.) That a number of departments have, in just the past two years, merged, turned into non-degree-granting centers, or just closed—often as part of far wider cuts across an entire college—means that these new challenges come at an inopportune moment for the field, for it is already a time when long-percolating issues are more than bubbling to the top. And with elite colleges now seeming to fall, one by one, in the crosshairs of the new administration, even the onetime presumption that private colleges might somehow skate even if public universities fell through the ice—given how much more tightly the successes of the latter are tied to ever-changing state politics—well, now even that might turn out to be a naïve assumption.

That I happen to think that there are some opportunities here, especially for enterprising units that see what they teach to their students as being more about how culture as a whole works than about how special religion supposedly is, does not mean that a positive attitude, some flashier course titles, and a revamped curriculum will somehow save a unit; even getting *those* to happen is enough of a challenge in most places. (The poor academic job market has, after decades in obvious decline, yet to prompt graduate programs in our field to reinvent the reason for obtaining a Ph.D. in the study of religion, after all—such reinventions are still greeted by many as "watering down" the degree, thus often taking years to persuade faculty members to get on board.) To be sure, the pressures are structural and far larger than any one program's, let alone person's, reply. But this does *not* mean that we give up, of course—although it does suggest that we'd be rather wise to be mindful of the scope of our agency and therefore always to be on the lookout for strategic local sites where our investments might have some effect.

And so, with all this in mind, I'm hopeful that the recommendations of the preceding chapters continue to have some relevance in a world that, admittedly, is changing right under our feet. After all, how to invite a classroom of intro students to study other people when, for all we know, an ever-increasing segment of that incoming class may no longer take for granted that such other people are worth studying? But that this book may someday merely chronicle the naïve optimism of a scholar from a bygone era is a future that I'd rather not imagine right now; instead, it's time to seriously roll up our sleeves and to be willing to toss out cherished old notions (like assuming that humanities scholars toil away alone rather than as part of larger collaborative projects) in favor of some novel ideas that are capable of meeting the novel times that we've now more than entered. And so, until it's proved to be otherwise, I think it wise for us all to assume that we each have agency (happening within discrete and usually limited settings, no doubt about it—but wasn't it always that way?) and that, working in coordination with equally animated colleagues, we can each accomplish something, such as helping to persuade students, parents, colleagues, and administrators to see that studying this thing that some of us happen to call religion—and doing so in a manner different from how the people under study may already be talking about themselves and their own groups—helps us to understand something interesting and useful about people and societies in general.

Appendix

Because there are a variety of works now available that outline practical ways to reorganize the humanities so as to respond to the situation in which we now find ourselves (with regard to graduate education, I admit that I am very much attracted to the proposals included in *The New PhD* [Cassuto and Weisbuch 2021]), this book has not aimed to duplicate them. Instead, it has pressed further a critique that I have long made concerning the ordinary status of that which scholars, let alone the general public alike, often designate *as* religious, holy, sacred, unique, sincere, inexplicable, et cetera. However, as outlined in the opening to the volume, this critique is now connected to our instrumentalized and professionalized moment in higher education, when a variety of measures are being taken that often serve to minimize the role played by the liberal arts and, along with it, our field in particular. But to effectively act to this moment, and thereby to make those abovementioned resources useful to us, scholars of religion must learn to curtail an approach that, or so I have argued in the preceding, while seeming to privilege our field and placate certain of its members' assumptions, has actually isolated us from allies all across the human sciences and made our field difficult to understand and, sometimes, easy for university administrations to live without. This volume, then, has tried to make explicit the linkage between, on the one hand, effectively working in our field today and, on the other, learning to see those things known as religion as mundane—but fascinating, nonetheless.

As should be apparent by this point in the volume, the source of that fascination might reside in some presumed (and nonempirical) essence of inherent, and thereby merely asserted, value; rather than this traditional and, I admit, still deeply entrenched approach, the volume has consistently argued that—as phrased, by of all characters, the most recent incarnation of Dr. Who (played by the actor Ncuti Gatwa), in the last episode of the 2024 season: "we invest things with significance." What better place to land, after opening with a fatalistic reference to Gollum, than another fictional character who is rather more empowering (though also driven by a nostalgia for the once influential British empire, I fully realize). For if we adopt this alternative, anthropocentric approach to the study of religion (as my friend Willi Braun has often put it, with the meaning makers fully in our sights), conceived now as a thoroughly historical, social, cultural exercise focused on the study of items and situations that are susceptible to the methods commonly adopted by our peers from all across the human sciences, then generalizing from our specialized findings, to make evident the wide application and thus direct relevance of our work, will be far more easily done. While it must certainly be left to our students to make this relevance apparent in whatever futures that they aim to establish for themselves, once they find themselves outside our classes—whether our BA alums or graduate students—a field reimagined in this manner will go some distance in assisting them to enter those futures more confidently; for now, right from the very start of their time in our lectures and seminars, they will have had this wider relevance made clear to them, day after day, while the skills that they require to do this work were consistently made explicit to them. As a colleague once said, setting up a LinkedIn account is a curiously challenging exercise in thinking through the specific skills that scholars possess; after all, few outside the university will more than likely be interested in having us write essays but the research, synthesis, and communication skills presupposed in all of our scholarship are very relevant (even sought after) in a wide array of careers. Identifying those skills in an explicit manner, applied widely and, at times, inventively (after all, our students often arrive in our classes also thinking that religion is a special case), is therefore an exercise well worth tackling for faculty aiming to assist their students in seeing a variety of futures for themselves.

I therefore recognize that this volume has had rather modest goals; it has not outlined a revised curriculum or offered a how-to discussion on running a resume-writing workshop (an activity that likely irritates the average humanities professor, who probably hopes that a campus's career center will just step in at that point—a career center that may very well think our major prepares students to be clergy, by the way). Neither has it detailed how to host a movie night (a thought: why limit yourself to films with so-called religious themes?) or argued for the obvious need to make links between current students and your unit's many alums who have gone on to diverse and rewarding careers (does your unit even track its alums?)—but my reasoning all along is that these things come far easier to those who can, as the old saying goes, break the back of still prominent assumptions about our objects of study and the tools by which we study them, let alone the reasons we even engage in those studies, all of which are hampering our effective response to the changing conditions of higher education. But, to close the book, I thought that it would be wise to offer a small number of practical examples that, whether useful or not in classrooms or assignments (whether undergraduate or even graduate), they could at least serve as little thought experiments for readers; perhaps they might inspire those who are open to such a revised field, but who are somewhat new to the idea, by modeling for them specific ways of reconceiving so-called religion as ordinary, as an item comparable to any other human domain—a comparative and redescriptive exercise that prompts us to see, as they used to say, something new in the familiar and something familiar in the strange.

Although this approach also animates the course book that I've written (*Studying Religion: An Introduction*), now in its third edition, I close with two new comparative vignettes (one drawn from the world of motion pictures and one from the world of popular music), to do nothing more than whet the appetite for thinking well outside the box in which scholars of religion have long been stuck; my hope is that they open scholars to seeing the connections between their hard-won specialized work and the far broader futures that the vast majority of our students will be making for themselves. I have confidence that coming to see these as linked can inspire some faculty to be more active agents in helping our students to more strategically tackle the settings in which they have no choice but to work—doing so by refusing to play favorites, by resisting the temptation to simplify the situations that we study, by never forgetting to pay attention to wider structures, by always seeing their own work as an equally curious item, and by always striving to say something new about the world rather than merely paraphrasing how the people we study already talk about themselves and others. After all, as long practiced in my own classes, there's certainly something important to be gained by comparing the U.S. Supreme Court's 1893 decision, in the case of *Nix v. Hedden*, on whether a tomato is a fruit or a vegetable to current debates on which claims get to count as indicative of what are known as "sincerely held beliefs." Adding to this the debates just starting in earnest in the United States, given the Court's decision announced just the other day, over which presidential acts count as official versus private, well, it should make profoundly evident that the skills taught in our classes are relevant well outside those lecture halls.

"There's No Place Like Home"

Nostalgia's Tensions

In the history of American cinema there are likely few lines of dialogue that are more famous than those spoken by the young Kansas farm girl Dorothy Gale (played in the 1939 film by Judy Garland, who was just sixteen years old at the time), repeated as she clicks her ruby-slippered heels together three times, at the instruction of Glinda, the Good Witch of the North. And with that, "There's no place like home. There's no place like home . . ." transports Dorothy from the vibrant world of Oz back to the sepia tones of her room in a farmhouse, where she awakes, as if from a dream, surrounded by concerned family and friends (what with young Dorothy having been separated from everyone else and injured when "a twister" [in the film] or "a whirlwind" [in the novel] swept through the countryside). As is often the case, the novel and the later film have more differences than just that—for example, Glinda on film was an amalgamation of at least two characters in L. Frank Baum's earlier book, *The Wonderful Wizard of Oz*, and, at the close of chapter 23, it's the magical silver shoes that take Dorothy back to Kansas, now with the words "Take me home to Aunt Em!"—but such differences won't detain us here; instead, we'll focus on what's common to both the film and the novel: the longing for, and thus the idealization of, the idea of home. With that specific theme in mind the exchange in chapter 4 of the novel between the Scarecrow and Dorothy, while they are seated by the road for a break, sums it up nicely: "No matter how dreary and gray our homes are," she says, "we people of flesh and blood would rather live there than in any other country, be it ever so beautiful. There is no place like home" (1899, 45).

With the idea of home in mind, we might call upon the common knowledge of many scholars of religion to find an instance to place alongside Dorothy's longing for what the novel describes as a one-room house on the great Kansas prairies (11)—situations in which the discourse around a home, or maybe even an ancestral homeland, whether actual or imagined and whether in the distant past, the present, or the hoped-for future, has played a central role in the lives of the people whom we study. For then we might place these two episodes side-by-side to see if their comparison told us something that we had not seen before. It should not be too difficult to come up with a candidate from within our field, what with the word "home" (which enters English due to Germanic influences, around the mid-sixteenth century, from the Old English "ham," evidenced today in our modern "hamlet") being present within the vocabulary of religion, from an earlier chapter's reference to someone's so-called church home to, at least among some groups, the common phrasing of "going home to the Lord" or "being called/taken home" (with the latter variants placing the agency well outside the deceased person, inasmuch as death is something that generally happens to a person, hence the significant difference from the more agential notion of "going home"), both of which are used as euphemisms for dying (possibly linked to a quotation from the second letter to the Corinthians in the New Testament: "We are confident, I say, and would prefer to be away from the body and at home with the Lord," citing the New International translation). In fact, in earlier English Christian sources, say, those from the mid-seventeenth century, "to come home to the Lord" was even used in the context of evangelization (see Fenner 1657, 20); converting people to the faith was therefore akin to bringing them home.

But the example that might be most useful to compare to Dorothy's nostalgia for going home might be the well-known role played by the imagery of home in many parts of Judaism, that is, the land said to have been promised by God to the descendants of the Hebrew bible's patriarchal character Abraham. While one can see Genesis 12:7 for an example of this, consider just a few chapters later where we read as follows: "[18] On that day the Lord made a covenant with Abram and said, 'To your descendants I give this land, from the Wadi[e] of Egypt to the great river, the Euphrates[19] the land of the Kenites, Kenizzites, Kadmonites,[20] Hittites, Perizzites, Rephaites,[21] Amorites, Canaanites, Girgashites and Jebusites'" (Genesis 15: 18–21, citing the New International translation). While it is certainly debatable what some of these identifiers might have meant when this text was first written (and that itself is open to debate among scholars, let alone among members of a group no less diverse than any other, with some claiming that the text was written by Moses, a figure who is seen in a rather more mythic light by critical scholars of religion), what is clear is that it would have far exceeded the borders of modern-day Israel, formally established as a state on May 14, 1948 (per what was known as the United Nations' Partition Plan for Palestine, passed by the General Assembly on November 29, 1947, and enacted after the British's so-called Mandate for Palestine [devised under the UN's precursor, the League of Nations] to govern the region had ended).

But this difference in territory is also not our present concern (though, for those who cite the bible as providing the precedent for the modern state, these geographic differences might indeed be consequential); instead, we will focus on the nostalgia for home that is evident in both cases. For, on the one hand, there is a desire for a place where the fictional character herself, though stranded in an alien place, once lived while, on the other, it is for a region where, at least prior to the founding of Israel nearly eighty years ago, the majority of citizens had themselves never lived but which was collectively seen by many as the home that was divinely promised to their ancient ancestors. And, although displaced not because of a cyclone, in the latter case a series of no less tumultuous and, at times, far more horrific historical events, said to have spanned thousands of years, resulted in what is often described as the worldwide diaspora (from the Greek, to be scattered) of the Jewish people. Hence the famous lines from Psalms 137 come to mind, part of the Hebrew bible thought by scholars to have been written about 500 years prior to the Common Era: "How can we sing the songs of the Lord while in a foreign land?" it reads. "If I forget you, Jerusalem, may my right hand forget its skill. May my tongue cling to the roof of my mouth if I do not remember you, if I do not consider Jerusalem my highest joy" (citing the New International Version).

Because heated debates around the establishment of the State of Israel in the Middle East more than obviously continue to this day, animating a number public discussions and, yes, even protests as well as violent actions against Israeli citizens or Jews living elsewhere in the world, and because criticism of the Israeli government's policies and practices (which include its military responses in the region) can be represented by some of its defenders as a form of anti-Semitism, some in the field may wish to resist juxtaposing these two examples. However, as a scholar who aims to treat all cultural productions as equally interesting, equally human, and therefore equally open to analysis and understanding, I presume that there is a way in which a comparison between these two instances of a longing for a home can each be treated fairly while trying to arrive at some novel insights concerning how, for instance, identities are created, maintained, and yes, rooted, over time and place. It's for this reason that I include this as one of the comparative examples that closes this book—it amounts to an attempt to model for readers how a scholar of religion committed to a version of the field in which our work is relevant to others can handle potentially controversial or, at the least, impassioned material. And so, we might ask: What can students in our classes make of a claim that there's "no place like home" and the intense desire to return to it?

Keeping in mind what J. Z. Smith told us long ago, no two items are inherently similar or different—but, instead, only *become* comparable with regard to some discrete aspect of importance to the comparativist (i.e., when the observer places them alongside each other in some particular way)—consider the work of the internationally known writer Salman Rushdie to assist us in juxtaposing these two nostalgias (for more on this idea of nostalgia, see McCutcheon 2018). Specifically, I have in mind a May 4, 1992, essay that he wrote for *The New Yorker* magazine on *The Wizard of Oz*, one that is also related to a little book on the film that he later published (Rushdie [2002] 2012). It opens with a recollection of his own (eventually lost) first short story, written at the age of ten and titled "Over the Rainbow"; from what he recalls of it, the story was very much influenced by Dorothy's adventures and, as he looks back on it, probably also his family's own immigrant circumstances, spanning India, England, and Pakistan. After spending some time on two comparisons of his own (first, involving the adventures in Oz as depicted by late-1930s Hollywood as opposed to the fantastical Hindi movies of his own youth, and then detailing a number of variations between Baum's turn-of-the century novel and the film), Rushdie's article settles on the theme of diaspora and the always imagined home for which the one who is on the move longs to return. This leads him to recognize what a depressing place—his words, not mine—Kansas is in both the book and the movie: unlike the whimsical curves and vibrancy of Oz, it is all angles and colorless; the hard life that they live, as Baum narrated in, results in Aunt Em losing the sparkle in her eye and the red in her cheeks; Uncle Henry never laughs, works all day, and is as gray in attitude and complexion as is his wife. Dorothy, an orphan in the book (and so one who is already displaced and homeless), is rather out-of-place in their home; her "merry voice," as Baum put it, shocks Aunt Em whenever she hears it. In fact, as Rushdie reads it, Dorothy (whose own surname is Gale after all) "is the gale blowing through this little corner of nowhere."

All of this presents a problem in his reading of the film, especially its closing line: "And *this* is the home that 'there's no place like'?" Rushdie asks rhetorically, going on: "This is the lost Eden that we are asked to prefer (as Dorothy does) to Oz?" Which brings him to the heart of the 1992 essay; I quote in full:

> Anybody who has swallowed the scriptwriters' notion that this is a film about the superiority of "home" over "away," that the "moral" of "The

> Wizard of Oz" is as sentimental as an embroidered sampler—"East, West, Home's Best"—would do well to listen to the yearning in Judy Garland's voice as her face tilts up toward the skies [when signing the movie's anthem, Harold Arlen and Yip Harburg's song, "Over the Rainbow"]. What she expresses here, what she embodies with the purity of an archetype, is the human dream of leaving—a dream at least as powerful as its countervailing dream of roots. At the heart of "The Wizard of Oz" is a great tension between these two dreams; but, as the music swells and that big, clean voice flies into the anguished longings of the song, can anyone doubt which message is the stronger? In its most potent emotional moment, this is inarguably a film about the joys of going away, of leaving the grayness and entering the color, of making a new life in the "place where you won't get into any trouble." "Over the Rainbow" is, or ought to be, the anthem of all the world's migrants, all those who go in search of the place where "the dreams that you dare to dream really do come true." It is a celebration of Escape, a grand paean to the Uprooted Self, a hymn—the hymn—to Elsewhere.

Accordingly, Rushdie sees the film's addition of that new final line, that "conservative little homily," as he phrases it—"there's no place like home"—as a sentimental and moralizing cop-out. For, in the later volumes in the series that Baum wrote, Oz eventually becomes home for not only Dorothy but Aunt Em and Uncle Henry too. Writing near the end of his long essay, he concludes:

> The imagined world becomes the actual world, as it does for us all, because the truth is that, once we leave our childhood places and start to make up our lives, armed only with what we know and who we are, we come to understand that the real secret of the ruby slippers is not that "there's no place like home" but, rather, that there is no longer any such place as home—except, of course, for the homes we make, or the homes that are made for us, in Oz. Which is anywhere—and everywhere—except the place from which we began.

And so, we return to our original comparison, armed now with Rushdie's comments on the imagined home that so animates the nostalgias of the displaced—whether that displacement happened by choice (understanding a decision to have been made to depart *for* a promised land) or by force (seeing oneself as banished *from* a land of milk and honey, as it were). In both cases, home is imagined, whether from idealized personal memory or from an ancient text still collectively considered to be in effect. But the gap—or, in Rushdie's words, the great tension—between the one doing the imagining and that which is being imagined can sometimes be rather pronounced, making evident that the view that "there's no place like home" can cut in two rather different directions, since a statement of incomparability (i.e., as claimed, no place is akin to home) can also mean that home takes on the status of no place, since we all come to know our worlds, and our places within them, by means of controlled judgments of similarity and difference. After all, this is taller than that, these are heavier than those, and they have less than we do; comparison, whether we like it or not, is a socially formative exercise, what with some posited "we" coming to know themselves as either different from or similar to all others in precisely this or that regard. Thus, a unique or ideal place, which makes it utterly unlike all other places, *cannot be known much less inhabited and its people themselves are therefore unidentifiable.* The great tension of these nostalgias is rather like meeting one's heroes; for, as the old saying goes, one can't help but be disappointed, given that the historical person, in all their situated complexity and ambiguity, can never live up to the idealized anticipation. As I've observed before, it's the same tension that animates the (possibly apocryphal) quotation associated with the once famous American actress Rita Hayworth (1918–1987, whose birth name was Margarita Carmen Cansino), said to have sadly observed how men who thought they were going to bed with the vivacious Gilda, a character whom she once played on screen, inevitably were disappointed to wake up with her.

Perhaps it is just this tension between the real and the imagined ideal that animates continued socially formative desire that accounts for why there is today a movement among some Jews that proposes that their people's exilic status must be retained, given that it has so shaped their collective identity over generations. Contrary to many representations of the diaspora, then (e.g., a Zionist depiction), it is maintained by some that exile should not be seen as a punishment or a limitation to be overcome by finally establishing a homeland (traditionally known as Zion, a name for both the city of Jerusalem and the land known as Israel). I think here of the contemporary scholar of Judaism Shaul Magid, notably his 2023 book, *The Necessity of Exile: Essays from a Distance.*[1] As phrased in the opening to an earlier post on the same topic, Magid (2020) wrote: "The notion that Zionism's success is dependent

[1] See the hour-long book launch and video of the interview with Magid: "'The Necessity of Exile' by Shaul Magid: An Ayin Press Book Launch," Ayinpress.org, November 13, 2023, https://ayinpress.org/the-necessity-of-exile-by-shaul-magid-an-ayin-press-book-launch/, as well as a similar event at the Harvard Divinity School: "Religion, Conflict, and Peace Book Series Spring 2024: The Necessity of Exile: Essays from a Distance & End of Days Ethics, Tradition,

on the idea that Jewish life in the Diaspora is dangerous, either physically or spiritually, is something common both to Zionism's earliest and contemporary formulations. Today, it is no longer much debated. It is theoretically believed, but in practice little discussed in the Diaspora, that Diaspora is an inferior state in which to live." Skipping ahead to his summation of part of his argument, Magid observes how Jewish thinkers from very different parts of the tradition try to resist the settled notion of a home, seeing instead exile as a necessary condition of at least their understanding of Judaism. Case in point, the conservative, Hasidic Yoel Teitelbaum (1887–1979); summing up his position, Magid writes:

> Teitelbaum is suggesting here that "being exiled in every land is necessary in order for there to be Torah and devotion to God in all the lands to purify the air of the world in preparation for the indwelling of the *Shekhina* [the dwelling or presence of God as found in a place]. . . . But this all requires preparing the air of the entire world to be fit to receive the sanctity of the land of Israel. Thus, righteous ones must be spread throughout the world to prepare the air. Due to the sins of our generation our strength has been weakened such that there is no way to accomplish this except by residing in all places."

My point? Despite the prominence for many of the State of Israel's role in finally providing a homeland for the Jewish people—it is, after all, regularly described as a Jewish state, as it was in its 1948 Declaration of Independence—a scholar uncritically adopting such a view silences yet other aspects of the Jewish world, those that would argue that a rather different sort of Judaism results when what is understood as a continual longing for a home is lost. In fact, contrary to the dominant view, the unquenched nostalgia for an always imagined, always distant home is a vital element of Jewish identity, or so some still maintain. While there undoubtedly may be other ways of discovering this aspect to the tradition and this feature of the modern group's identity, it is by means of our comparison to Dorothy's longing, one that was established by Rushdie's observation of the contradictions embedded in its "conservative little homily," that made plain that the idea of a promised land within Judaism is rather more complicated than it may have first appeared to us. And so, regardless of one's own position on all of this—and there are stances that differ markedly along a wide spectrum, to be sure—the

---

and Power in Israel," YouTube, accessed July 2, 2024, https://www.youtube.com/watch?v=5WoasxulH2I.

scholars of religion among us, those aiming to complicate rather than simplify, hoping to treat all human artifacts as equally interesting and no less situated, and intending to redescribe rather than repeat or merely paraphrase dominant discourses, have something of value to contribute by placing novel, unanticipated, or even seemingly unorthodox things beside each other for a while.

References

Baum, L. Frank. 1899. *The Wonderful Wizard of Oz*. Illustrated by W. W. Denslow. Chicago: George M. Hill.

Fenner, William. 1657. *The Works of W. Fenner: A Treatise of the Affections*. London: W. Gilbertson.

Magid, Shaul. 2020. "The Necessity of Exile." *Tablet*, November 9. https://www.tabletmag.com/sections/community/articles/necessity-of-exile-hasidic-leaders-diaspora.

———. 2023. *The Necessity of Exile: Essays from a Distance*. Brooklyn, NY: Ayin.

McCutcheon, Russell T. 2018. "The Magic of the Melancholy: Shifting Gears in the Study of Religion." In *Fabricating Religion: Fanfare for the Common e.g.*, 141–160. Berlin: Walter de Gruyter.

Rushdie, Salman. 1992. "Out of Kansas: Revisiting 'The Wizard of Oz.'" *New Yorker*, May 11. https://www.newyorker.com/magazine/1992/05/11/out-of-kansas.

———. (2002) 2012. *The Wizard of Oz*. BFI Film Classics. 2nd ed. London: British Film Institute.

"Every New Beginning..."

Situating Origins

In the coffee shop where I revised much of this volume and wrote almost all of its original content (including this appendix), they would routinely play the 1998 top 20 hit by the American rock group Semisonic, "Closing Time," just as they were about to close each afternoon. This is a common enough practice in many bars and coffee shops today, quickly signaling to customers that the day is drawing to an end and thereby saving the staff from either shouting or going table to table repeating that it's time to go. After an opening involving a brief guitar solo that is then joined by a simple piano melody, the quiet opening lyrics—no doubt familiar to some readers—start as follows:

> Closing time, open all the doors
> And let you out into the world
> Closing time, turn all of the lights on
> Over every boy and every girl

Then, before the far harder rock of the chorus, the second verse drives home the point rather explicitly, telling the patrons to finish their drinks and exit the premises. Although it's now an older song, that it is still so frequently played to end the day in a variety of businesses means that it is more than likely still rather familiar, even to the younger generation who now populate our classrooms. This means that the closing line of the song will probably resonate with students:

> Closing time, every new beginning
> Comes from some other beginning's end.

I think that this line is worth thinking about if one is trying to revise the goals of a religious studies class, both in terms of its critical approach to the material as well as challenging students to see the relevance of our work for far broader domains—such as studying pop music let alone pretty much any social setting. For the rigorously historicizing tone of that closing lyric has always struck me as more theoretically sophisticated than much scholarship in our field; for it throws down a challenge, as it were, to scholars of religion, challenging them to see what they study as always situated human productions.

For in this lyric we have the acknowledgment that the quest for origins is a pointless exercise—if, that is, it is seen to be a substantive effort, one that is concerned with identifying a first mover or the prime instance of some current practice (consider the quest for the historical Jesus or the historical Paul, pursuits that have preoccupied many New Testament scholars over the years, let alone those common speculative efforts to figure out who the first person was who thought "Hey, I should eat a lobster"). Instead, with a nod to the already mentioned "turtles all the way down" stance, the song that's all about closing itself closes with both wit and insight by informing the listener that every end is really just another start, and so on, and so on. Don't fret the bar closing, since "I know who I want to take me home"—what could be a more hopeful chorus that that? Or, as Dan Wilson (the band member who wrote the song) said in a 1998 interview: "closing time might be the end of bar hours or the end of the concert or the end of, you know, one thing, but the doors open and everyone goes out and that's, like, when the story starts, you know? I'm a late-night person when we're on tour, you know, and I sort of think of closing time as mid-day."[1]

Given that origins are such a common issue in the study of religion (whether it's the topic of those narratives that we commonly call myths or more specifically the subset that we usually designate as cosmogonies [i.e., creation tales] let alone our effort to identify how this or that religion first came about [think of the Indus River Valley tale that we usually tell to start the unit on Hinduism]), it might be of interest to pair this lyric and its view of beginnings as always coming after some prior event with a variety of items already familiar to the scholar of religion. For if we adopt the band's approach to origination—one very much in step with the approach of a more critically minded scholar (and one that's also nicely in step with Edward Said's own sense of the difference between talking about beginnings, which imply a prior setting that caused some later effect, and origins, which presuppose passive novelty [see his 1975 book, *Beginnings: Intention and Method*])—then the very fact of telling an origins tale itself becomes a situated discursive act, one that

[1] The interview is available at YouTube, https://www.youtube.com/watch?v=PRE9h33Z-no&t=2s (accessed June 27, 2024).

raises questions about the social and historical context in which a tale of origination and thus utter novelty was thought to be needed or somehow relevant.

And so, although the longtime Christian doctrine of *creatio ex nihilo* (Latin: creating from out of nothing) might come to mind for some, not to mention the Hebrew bible's well-known opening line, "In the beginning . . . ," consider instead placing the song "Closing Time" and its critical approach to origins alongside a verse in the ancient Sanskrit collection of hymns or ritual chants known as the *Rig Veda*; citing Wendy Doniger's widely available 1981 translation, the opening of hymn (or *sūkta*) 129 of its tenth book (or *mandala*)—a text also known as the *Nāsadīya Sūkta* or simply the Hymn of Creation—reads as follows:

> 1. There was neither non-existence nor existence then;
> There was neither the realm of space, nor the sky which is beyond;
> What stirred? Where? In whose protection?
> Was there water, bottomlessly deep?
> 2. There was neither death nor immortality then.
> There was no distinguishing sign of night nor of day.
> That One breathed, windless, by its own impulse.
> Other than that there was nothing beyond.
> 3. Darkness was hidden by darkness in the beginning;
> With no distinguishing sign all this was water;
> The life force that was covered with emptiness,
> That One arose through the power of heat.

So, on the one hand we have a text that narrates how a rather amorphous situation prior to existence and nonexistence, prior even to extent and presumably also duration, led to the creation of the universe and, as then narrated in hymn 10:90 (the so-called Hymn of Man or *Puruṣa Sūkta*), eventually to the creation of the fourfold (and, importantly, stratified) *varana* system, all from the sacrifice of a cosmic being known as *Puruṣa*. Quoting Doniger's anthology again:

> 11. When they divided the Man, into how many parts did they apportion him? What do they call his mouth, his two arms, and thighs and feet?
> 12. His mouth became the Brahmin; his arms were made into the Warrior; his thighs the People and from his feet the Servants were born.[2]

[2] As examined by Lincoln (1991, 9), the process by which the cosmic being is divided and distributed is narrated in far more detail in the later *Aitereya Upaniṣad* 1.1–2.5; it also appears in the *Manusmṛiti* or Laws of Manu (1.87–1.92).

On the one hand, then, we have an ancient tale of nothingness from which everything arises by means of the central Indian ritual of sacrifice, and, on the other, we have a recent lyric that presupposes the lack of absence and, in its place, posits an endless series of acts and situations that, arising from precursors of their own, inexorably lead to yet more acts and yet other situations.

Now, should both of the texts before us be seen as human productions—a prerequisite, I would say, of scholarship as carried out in the human sciences—then these two artifacts' diametric opposition to each other on the question of origins might strike us as a curious thing, making their juxtaposition possibly productive of some new insights into how discourses on utter absence/complete novelty might function for those who devise and those who are using them. Although he was certainly not animated by a comparison of these two specific exempla, Bruce Lincoln's redescription, as I would call it, of the *Puruṣa Sūkta* as in fact being a sociogony and even a regiogony—a story on the origins of social or regal (i.e., ruling) order (1986, 162)—strikes me as just what might happen if Semisonic's approach to beginnings was applied to the *Rig Veda*'s tale of origins—an application that may seem to some as being quite literally sacrilegious (literally meaning to take, i.e., steal, sacred things), what with the aura of uniqueness that surrounds so-called religious tales and their presumably ontological difference from something so, shall we say, run-of-the-mill or pedestrian as pop music. But, resisting the urge to play favorites means that an interest in such boundary maintenance, so as to rank assorted cultural productions, no longer animates our work; these two items can now instead be treated by scholars as being nothing more or less than thoroughly human products that are inevitably intertwined in the world of identity and power—items on which we can draw to see if there's something new to be said about, at least in this case, creation tales.

If so, then it may not escape us that the *sūkta* did not arise of its own volition but, as a cultural production like any other, was composed and recited by members of what is commonly known as the literate priestly class, or the Brahmins—those who, we must recall, the myth narrates as originating from the mouth of *Puruṣa* (and not its, shall we say, less desirable nether regions, where the servant class supposedly originated). As Lincoln concludes, then, such stories and the ritual institutions around them "provided ideological legitimation for an exploitative and oppressive—and exceedingly stable—social hierarchy (1986, 169). Or, as the late scholar of Asian religions, Graeme MacQueen, once phrased it in an article that's still of importance: "that it is a myth of the *brahamana*, intoned, transmitted, and put forth as a charter of this group—is . . . clear, as is the fact that what is legitimized is not merely 'order' but a particular order, which entails the dominance of this stratum and the graduated subordination of the other three" (1988, 143). As MacQueen then concluded, simply calling this tale "a Hindu creation myth," as we commonly do, fails to complicate the fact that it is a tale of one specific class that justifies their social role, position, and thus authority over others; going further, he made plain how scholars failing to identify the effects of such tales—that is, failing to move from description to redescriptive analysis—inevitably lends support to such claims by normalizing or naturalizing them as if they are ahistorical self-evidencies.[3]

Accordingly, placing these two texts beside one another, in just this particular manner (i.e., with an eye toward their approach to origins: the second one ahistorical and necessary and the first historical and therefore always contingent) makes plain not just two competing ways of talking about origins but, thinking back to Said's use of the term "beginnings" to name the approach adopted by "Closing Time," it demonstrates how one way of talking about origins can become an object of study, that is, a datum, for the other; for adopting the view that history is a continual oscillation between endings and beginnings (a rather dialectical stance that prompts us always to look for preceding causes of later effects that themselves prompt yet more consequences, and so on . . .), makes the disruptive claims of absolute origination a curious assertion that exchanges claims of sheer novelty in the mythic past for inherited authority in the present and continued governance in the future. And so, an ancient Indian tale becomes something other than an idle descriptive interest for scholars of Asian religions; for, in redescribing a cosmogony as a sociogony, the tale can now be seen as indicative of a practical authorizing move that we might also be able to see in many other places, from the still common rhetoric of being a so-called self-made man to the politics animating historical claims of national exceptionalism. That studying those things that are usually set apart as religion can shed such new light on much larger human issues now becomes rather apparent to our students, something that invites them to see their work here as surprisingly relevant over there.

[3] The analysis using Lincoln's and MacQueen's writings is indebted to work published in my earlier book, *Manufacturing Religion* (1997, 46, 120–122).

References

Cassuto, Leonard, and Robert Weisbuch. 2021. *The New PhD: How to Build a Better Graduate Education*. Baltimore: Johns Hopkins University Press.

Doniger, Wendy. (1981) 2005. *The Rig Veda: An Anthology*. Reprint, New York: Penguin.

Lincoln, Bruce. 1986. *Myth, Cosmos, and Society: Indo-European Themes of Creation and Destruction*. Cambridge, MA: Harvard University Press.

———. 1991. *Death, War, and Sacrifice: Studies in Ideology and Practice*. Chicago: University of Chicago Press.

MacQueen, Graeme. 1988. "Whose Sacred History? Reflections on Myth and Dominance." *Studies in Religion/Sciences Religieuses* 17 (2): 143–157.

McCutcheon, Russell T. 1997. *Manufacturing Religion: The Discourse on Sui Generis Religion and the Politics of Nostalgia*. New York: Oxford University Press.

Said, Edward. 1975. *Beginnings: Intention and Method*. New York: Columbia University Press.

Acknowledgments

There are too many people to name and thank when it comes to the long-term exercise to reinvent our own department at the University of Alabama. I've written on this before and so wish only to mention here the colleagues with whom I've had the good fortune to work over the years, those who understand that it was a collective effort from which we all would benefit. I'd like to single out Betty Dickey, who worked as our department's administrative assistant for thirty-two years, about twenty of those with me. She had already planned to retire just as COVID-inspired remote teaching hit our campus for the first time, as we were going into the spring break of 2020. When I arrived back in 2001 her role in the unit was clearly unsung and undervalued; as the new chair I had a host of decisions to make and, at least as I recall it, it occurred to me to say, "I don't know, what do you think?" when she asked me how many seats to open in a certain course. She'd done her job for over a decade by then and more than understood the rhythm of student enrollments, making her a key resource to a newly arrived outside chair who had strong views on the field, sure, but who had never done a job like this before. I benefited from Betty's experience and wisdom all throughout our time working together, making plain to me something that I would now like to think that I already knew from my days as a grad student in Toronto (Muna, then at the Center for Religious Studies, immediately comes to mind) and as a faculty member first in Knoxville (Joan and Debbie) and then in Springfield (Joanne), and, after Betty retired, working first with LeCretia and then Keisha in Tuscaloosa (both for two years, after which we lost each of them to better-paid positions elsewhere at the university), and now Andrea: the staff members on which our units rely are often the most important but unsung members of the team, and that goes double in those settings that are in need of some serious reinvention. So, it's to those staff members that I dedicate this book.

The book has benefited from the eyes and input of friends and colleagues, and I would be remiss not to mention them. So, for looking at some of its earlier parts or the whole of the manuscript, my thanks go to Mike Altman, Matthew Baldwin, Evan Berry, Willi Braun, Emily Crews, Tenzan Eaghll, Sierra Lawson-Etchegaray, Aaron W. Hughes, Craig Martin, Richard Newton, Steven Ramey, Merinda Simmons, and Vaia Touna. I also wish to acknowledge Mark McWilliams for soliciting an earlier version of chapter 1 for the fiftieth the anniversary issue of *Religious Studies Review* and thank the editors of *MTSR* for being interested in the special issue that I proposed and then guest edited for them, devoted to the contributions of the late Burton Mack, of which the last chapter was a part. I also need to acknowledge my coauthors on two of the chapters, Aaron W. Hughes and Andie Alexander, for agreeing to have revised versions of these essays to appear as chapters in this volume. I would also like to mention Carah Naseem, an acquisitions editor for Rutgers University Press, who emailed me out of the blue one day in late September 2023, saying hello and inquiring about any new projects that I might be developing. Having had the good fortune of my work already appearing at a variety of publishers, I welcomed the chance to work with a new team and, perhaps, reach new readers. That she was interested in the idea that I eventually pitched, and that the press's board agreed, was gratifying, and so I'd like to thank Carah for reaching out, thereby prompting the book that you now hold, and also thank the entire production team with which I worked on this book.

Finally, anyone who has visited us in Tuscaloosa or found us on social media likely knows that our department occupies a small, three-story, late nineteenth-century Gothic building, one that was originally a student residence plus a few university offices, including the president's office; a multi-use building made sense at the time, what with its construction happening not too many years after the end of the U.S. Civil War, when, within a week of the war's end, the university's campus had mostly been burned to the ground by Northern troops coming through the city. Upkeep comes with any historic building, of course, and in the summer of 2024 our building was entirely closed to occupants so that the scaffolding could go up and its exterior balconies and staircases (the building has no interior hallways) could be completely refurbished. So, lacking an office for the entire summer—a nice one at one end of the top floor, with wonderfully large windows, into which I had moved just a year before, after stepping down from eighteen years as department chair—I'd like to mention Turbo Coffee in Tuscaloosa, where, five days a week all that summer, I would appear a little after 7:00 each morning, purchase a medium black coffee, and, taking my usual seat at the rear, read, write, or edit until about 11:00 A.M. Periodically meeting students or colleagues there made it all the more enjoyable. Although I had successfully worked from home for a couple years due to COVID protocols (during which Aaron Hughes and I co-wrote two volumes), I admit that I was not looking forward to going back into that lifestyle when our building's work was announced a year before; a little geography between where one eats and sleeps, on the one hand, and where one works, on the other, has always been useful to me as a scholar, with my office being a very productive place in which to work—perhaps because I grew up living in the small gas station where my parents lived and worked. That's why a little coffee shop that welcomed me and my laptop deserves my thanks. It allowed me to leave our two cats, Cora and Bella, to sleep in peace for the morning and then follow me around in order to then sleep even more wherever I was when I was working at home for the afternoons.

Index

About the Author

RUSSELL T. MCCUTCHEON is a widely published scholar of religion who, for eighteen years, also chaired the Department of Religious Studies at the University of Alabama, successfully leading its near complete reinvention and dramatic expansion. An honorary life member of the International Association for the History of Religions (IAHR), he has wide teaching experience and is among those now actively working to reimagine graduate education in the field.